To the three of us

Thanks are owed to many—and they know who they are because I have told them often—but thanks are especially owed to my clear-eyed husband and to my editor, Shannon Ravenel, who has been her usual self—that is to say, incomparable.

My salad days, when I was green in judgment . . .

—*Antony and Cleopatra*

Experience takes dreadfully high wages,
but he teaches like no other.

—Thomas Carlyle

When It Was Our War

PROLOGUE

Some readers of my book, *The Jew Store: A Family Memoir,* which was published a few years ago, have asked me if I planned to write a sequel. Since *The Jew Store* began with my family living in the South in the 1920s and ended with our leaving there in 1933, I took it that these readers wanted to find out what happened to us after we left.

I had written in *The Jew Store* of my family when we were the only Jews in a small Bible-belt Tennessee town where my father was the proprietor of a "Jew store," a low-end dry goods store of the kind that dotted the Southern landscape from the turn of the nineteenth century through the 1930s. *The Jew Store* was basically a tale of eastern European Jewish immigrants struggling to come to terms with equally unworldy Wasp country folk, and as such it gave a personal face to what seemed to me a little-known chapter in the American immigrant experience. It was one I thought needed to be told, and after I told it, I had no plans to write a sequel. I felt that nothing in my family's subsequent story was as rich, as worthy of recounting, as the one I had written in *The Jew Store.*

Still, a kind of a sequel was to be written after all, and I began writing it after the September 11, 2001, terrorist attacks. The attacks had taken us by such surprise that we could only say that we had been innocents living in a fool's paradise. We were as ill prepared psychically and practically as we had been on December 7, 1941, when the Japanese attached Pearl Harbor.

It was then that it came to me that I had another story to tell, for I had lived through those World War II years and felt I had a particular vantage point—that of the wife of a man in the military. And since that story begins almost exactly where *The Jew Store* leaves off, it has many of the elements of a sequel even if in *When It Was Our War* my family recedes somewhat as I take a more prominent place.

The attack on Pearl Harbor thrust us into thinking about ourselves in a new way. Our own soil, whose invasion by a foreign power had been limited to the minor British burning of Washington in the War of 1812, had been deeply violated. And so now we had to go to war, had to put ourselves on a wartime footing, and had to do to others what had been done to us. We had to change and change fast. And what came out in us in those World War II years was sometimes the worst—and in *When It Was Our War* I write of the pervasive bigotry, injustices, and greed—but what came out in us in the middle of our national crisis was often the best. I found myself writing of a thought I often had during those days—that if it weren't for the war, the war would suit me down to the ground.

As the "war" on terrorists morphed into a real war with Iraq, I began to wonder about the "worst" and the "best." Did we learn anything from "our war"?

I begin *When It Was Our War* not at the beginning of the war but in the decade leading up to it. I wanted a picture to emerge of who I was at that time and of the place in which I was living, which happened to be Miami Beach, an American playground, a city exceedingly unsuitable for teaching a young person about life. So as I wrote the book, as it evolved, I came to understand that I was writing about a very naive girl—Southern with all the usual biases in her, and Jewish with all the usual biases against her—who was caught up in a whirlwind and, while she was finding her way in it, did a lot of growing up.

I was nineteen years old when America entered the war, and I was twenty-three when it was over. During those years I traveled with my Army Air Corps husband from air base to air base, both during his cadet training and after he became an officer. It was only when he went overseas that I went home, to stay there for the duration, as we said then, while he flew his combat missions. It was a life I shared with many other American wives of the war years, and even if they came out of altogether different backgrounds from mine and had led altogether different lives, in some ways this is their story, too.

CHAPTER 1

In 1939 we were living in Miami Beach, and on the first weekend in September of that year I was up the road in West Palm Beach at a party my mother had made me go to. It was definitely not anything I wanted to do, especially as I would be the designated date of somebody I didn't give a hoot about. Still, it was not unusual for me and my Miami Beach friends to attend parties in another Florida town. Jewish mothers all over the state were forever looking to our area to fill out their guest lists. All the South Florida cities—Hollywood, Fort Lauderdale, West Palm Beach—had a fair number of Jewish families, but everybody knew that Miami and Miami Beach had the mother lode.

So I was in West Palm Beach as the houseguest of an acquaintance, and even though on the Sunday morning of that weekend in September I had had every intention of sleeping late after the Saturday night party, I found myself awakened by her father, who rushed into our bedroom and shook the morning newspaper at us. It was clear that the paper was carrying news of great import to him, and when I was finally able to see the headline, what it said was that Germany had invaded Poland. Did I jump up and join my hostess's father in agitation? No, I did not. I just said to myself, Oh well, it's only another something about that war in Europe. And I suspect that the same thought ran through his daughter's head.

Actually, I had already had a personal encounter with "that war in Europe," having in the early summer of 1939 observed a ship engaged in decidedly odd maneuverings off Miami Beach. I did not know that in time this ship would become a cause célèbre; all I knew was that the ship was big, and eerie in its way, some days extraordinarily close to shore, some days nowhere to be seen. Then one day I watched it moving out, not knowing that I would never see it again.

Our local paper, the *Miami Herald,* had done a piece on it, the gist of which was that it was called the S.S. *St. Louis* and it had been turned away from its destination of Cuba. The ship, the piece said, was carrying European Jews. Why they were aboard, why they had felt so urgent a need to leave Europe, the *Herald* never spelled out, and it remained unclear to me. Still, I was confident that our government was in some unpublicized way seeing to those Jews. The hint of anti-Semitism was certainly there, but having learned from my parents and from all the other immigrant Jews of my acquaintance that anti-Semitism was ever present in Europe in thought, word, and deed, I thought that perhaps these folks, as others before them, had simply made a decision to emigrate. When I saw no more of the *St. Louis,* I concocted a fantasy in which President Roosevelt had located a welcoming harbor for the refugees.

It would be years before I learned the reality of the incident —that what I had seen was a chapter in the story of a ship denied landing by President Roosevelt and forced to return to Europe, where its passengers were dealt with in the way of all European Jews of that moment in time. The ship's travels eventually came to be called the Voyage of the Damned.

If talk of the *St. Louis* among the Jews of Miami Beach had eventually died out, talk of a 1938 event continued. It was an incident called Kristallnacht, or, as the Jews of Europe more realistically referred to it, the November Pogrom. I had no firsthand knowledge of Kristallnacht, only what I learned from my father. My father usually read the paper for the political news (always with a ringing endorsement of whatever President Roosevelt had done or said) and for whatever surprises it had to offer. Seeing worrisome things, he had no doubt asked me, "So tell me, what do you think of this? You think that *momser* [that "bastard," meaning Hitler] is doing something we got to start getting excited about?" To which my answer would have been that I didn't have time to think about it, that I was getting together with my friends on the beach or at the tennis courts. And with the wisdom of my sixteen years, I might have said, "What makes them do such stupid things over there?"

None of my friends would have said anything different. We were at the age when gratifying our own needs was our topmost priority, and we lived in a place—a resort town—that neatly accommodated this. War, involving Jews or not, was the last thing on our minds. We did not hear distant thunder, nor did we spend time listening for it.

It was this mind-set that had me, on that September morning in 1939, attaching so little personal significance to the German invasion of Poland that the event—one that was to shape the rest of my life—did not prevent me from turning over and going back to sleep. And as if to support my decision, five days later President Roosevelt issued a proclamation declaring America's neutrality.

WHEN I RETREATED into sleep in that bed in West Palm Beach, I would have been glad to sleep away the whole weekend, for the boy I cared about was not there. The boy I cared about was John Parke, and I was suffering mightily from a grieving heart. It was a condition brought about by a promise I had made to my mother when John and I were sophomores —that he and I would sever our relationship on my high school's graduation night. That had been three months earlier.

My mother had felt the need to extract such a promise because John was a Gentile—a *shagetz*—and the chief reason we were in Miami was that my mother did not want me to marry one. In Union City, Tennessee, where I'd been born, my older sister had begun a serious relationship with a Gentile boy, and even though my mother was very fond of the boy and of Union City generally, this relationship had worried her so considerably that she had needled my father—*"nudgered"* him, my father said—until he had agreed to move the family to New York so that we girls, when the time arose, could find appropriate Jewish suitors.

The trouble was that after we arrived in New York, my father couldn't wait to get out of it. Usually a well-disposed man, he found New York hard to take. "What a place," he would say to us over and over. "Everybody looking to get some kind of edge on you." Having lived for twenty-five years in the courtly air of the South, he especially resented the insults constantly flung about. "Like without insults they're not saying anything," he would say.

He longed for the South and its neighborly ways. When challenged on this, when it was pointed out that southerners could possess some exceedingly distasteful views, he would joke, "Aha, but so nice they let you know, it's almost a pleasure." With the southern devotion to politeness, in which making another (white) person uncomfortable was akin to a sin, hostility was almost always veiled in a well-practiced civility.

Of course my father was no fool; he knew about the Ku Klux Klan and its hatred for the "colored races, the Roman Catholics"—always pronounced as one word, so that it was RomanCatholics—"the Jews and other foreigners," as they proclaimed whenever they had the opportunity. My father himself had met with affronts and indignities when he had gone about trying to rent a store in Union City, so not even he would claim that courtly manners prevailed when business matters were on the table. Still, he longed for the South. He missed those "country giants" teasing him about his five foot six. "I swan, Mr. Kaufman," they might say, "you ain't no bigger than a crappie in Reelfoot Lake." His blue eyes would mellow and he would say, "They were my kind of people," which, when you thought about it, wasn't as odd as it might have sounded.

The upshot was that he very soon began looking around for a place where we could relocate, one that would satisfy my mother's need to put her family among Jewish people and his own need to live in the South. To this end he made the mistake of thinking that South Florida was the South, and in 1933 down we came to Miami Beach. To be perfectly fair, in the 1930s much about South Florida *was* southern. Still, there was little that was southern about Miami Beach.

The Miami Beach of the 1930s was a study in light and dark forces, sunshine and shadows. The dark forces—the shadows—were in the domain of the adults. For young people like me, the forces were all light, all sunshine, and we played ever in brightness. Shadows meant no more to us than the annoying chiaroscuro that formed on the tennis court as the sun moved behind a palm frond. My friends and I reacted to only one shadow, that of the lingering Great Depression, but even this required nothing more than accepting that hard times and making do were a part of life, and we went about finding distractions that didn't put too much stress on the family coffers.

The town was small enough that there was only one public elementary school and one combined junior and senior high school—Ida M. Fisher (though a couple of years after our arrival Miami Beach Senior High School was built), and whether we were year-rounders or seasonal, Jew or Gentile, rich or poor, we were one big nest, and every social occasion was come one, come all.

Whether by design or by impulse, we gathered often at the beach, it being both free and near. If it had just been visited by a hurricane, so much the better. The beach of choice was Fourteenth Street, which at night turned into a venue for courting, variously called necking, smooching, petting, or "getting to" first, second, or third base. If home plate was crossed, it was told only to a best friend, of which a girl had perhaps one or two, while the boy had dozens.

Every Saturday night we had a get-together at somebody's house. Since music was what get-togethers were all about, these usually took place at wherever the best "Vic" was located. One house had a record player that went through a stack of twelve records and then nimbly turned them over and played the other sides, so of course it was the house we flocked to most often.

We liked the Andrews Sisters, and if the lyrics to "Hold Tight" were dirty, as some said, we threw caution to the winds and sang on about "fooreeackisacki" and "a tasty bit of fish." We listened mostly to big bands, to whatever vocalists were popular—the Eberle brothers, Bing Crosby, Dick Haymes. But then Frank Sinatra came along and turned our knees to jelly, and we were spoiled for everybody else.

We were passionate about big band music and made it our business to have encyclopedic knowledge of the songs, the bands, and the singers. It was a preoccupation that was very much in evidence during the war years. The war years were full of big band music—songs of exhilaration, of longing, of loss —and they were very much a part of our lives.

We danced all evening, to most any band, and imitated as best we could the god and goddess of dance, Fred Astaire and Ginger Rogers. We had styles—national ones and international ones—to fit just about every tempo. Much of the music demanded the lindy hop, and we danced it to most of Benny

Goodman's tunes, of which "Don't Be That Way" was the hands-down choice. We learned the rumba and samba from expatriate Cuban classmates, and we may have been among the only schoolkids in America to consider the merengue an everyday dance.

Real dates were ten-cent movies and ended at a drive-in restaurant on Fifth Street, the Pig Trail Inn, where we drank five-cent Cokes and ate fifteen-cent hamburgers delivered on trays hooked onto car windows. There was a bit of drinking. Some of us—and we knew who we were—sat in cars and drank rum with Coca-Cola, or Southern Comfort with nothing, a lot of which ended up in a splat on Pig Trail Inn asphalt. Smoking was big. School sports were important and everybody went to the games.

We spelled the small joys of Miami Beach with the big ones in "town"—Miami proper—where we might get to see Gene Raymond or Una Merkel making a personal appearance or we could go to a real department store, Burdine's on Flagler Street. To get to town, we got on a streetcar for a nickel and rattled across Biscayne Bay on the Fifth Street Causeway; or if we had fifteen cents to splurge with, we rode over in a jitney, a kind of raffish taxi with jump seats that carried seven passengers and limited itself to causeway crossings.

In Miami Beach religion did not matter at all. My parents were not exactly religious—my father was most definitely ir-religious—and I knew nobody who was, nobody who consistently went to services; nor did I know anybody who talked about religion, Jew or non-Jew. If you were Jewish, being religious was a lot of trouble, for there was only one synagogue, a very small Orthodox one down on South Beach, and if you felt the need to attend more modern services, you had to go to Miami to the temple there.

Unable in Union City to follow Jewish dietary laws, my mother had gotten used to not "keeping kosher," and in Miami Beach she did not resume the practice. She did, however, go occasionally to the South Beach synagogue, delivered there by my father, who would go by later to pick her up. She was not, as we used to say in Union City, "a fool" for religion, but she felt she should do enough to keep on God's good side, just in case. She did not insist on any of the rest of us going: my brother had been safely Bar Mitzvahed and the girls were in a place where there were plenty of Jewish boys, so she felt that her main job vis-à-vis religion was done.

There were a couple of churches—the most familiar being the little all-denominational Community Church on Lincoln Road—though my boyfriend, John, never went to any, and since we all turned up as a matter of course on the Fourteenth Street beach early every Sunday morning, I assumed none of the other kids did either. I never knew anybody's religious preference, and if somebody's happened to be mentioned, I promptly forgot it.

My own religious feelings were not on firm ground. The small town of Union City, where I'd spent the first decade of my life, had a population of just over five thousand, counting whites and blacks. Since in those days blacks had virtually no power, it could be considered a town of something under two thousand—and we were the only Jews. My family had gone there to open what the locals called a "Jew store," defined as a

Jewish-operated, low-end dry goods store that served the lower economic elements of the town—the farmers, the factory hands, and the Negroes—as African-Americans were then called. "Jew stores" were a convention of the times in many small southern towns in the 1920s and '30s, though their American origins went as far back as the nineteenth century.

Sometimes these stores grew out of peddlers' wagons operated by Jewish immigrants who had left the ghettoes of New York to roam the South and who eventually gave up the nomadic life and settled in some little southern town. But sometimes, like my father's, Jew stores started from scratch. My father *kvelled* (quivered with pride) over the humble origins of that posh department store of legend, Rich's in Atlanta. "Nothing but a little Jew store it was," he would say. "Imagine that."

In Miami Beach, when I told my Jewish friends about the store my father had operated in Union City, I quickly learned to eschew the term "Jew store," for their reaction to it was to look at me as if I had uttered an obscenity. I certainly had come to believe that anyone who employed "Jew" as an adjective, said "Jew lawyer" or "Jew bread," was announcing himself as an anti-Semite, but I was accustomed to "Jew store," for in my town and in most small towns of the South everybody used the term as shorthand. If it was said pejoratively, it was said that way behind closed doors, and I daresay most "Jew store" families never heard it like that. These stores were, after all, in the South, and it is unlikely that the term would have been used as a deliberate, face-to-face affront.

Since in Union City we were the sole representatives of the Jewish religion, any religious yearnings we might have harbored would have gone unrequited, for we had neither a synagogue nor any other Jews to be collegial with, to debate with, to celebrate holidays with. Furthermore, in our corner of northwest Tennessee we had no big city where other Jews and a synagogue might be found. Whenever I was asked to name our nearest big city, I always had to say we *had* no nearest big city.

Another deterrent was that in the South, Jew stores operated just as others stores did—open on Saturdays and closed on Sundays—even though Saturday is the Jewish Sabbath. Jewish-owned stores in the Jewish neighborhoods of the North operated on a reverse schedule, but Saturdays were our big days, and we typically stayed open until two in the morning. Furthermore, since my father was the sine qua non of the store, there was no question of our packing up and going anywhere for any kind of services, even on the High Holidays. If challenged on his lack of effort to get us to religious services, my father would say that Jew-store owners were in these small towns not for religious "entertainment" but to make a living. The result was that until I entered my teen years, I had not set foot in a Jewish house of worship.

My father was oblivious—not to say antagonistic—to the whole idea of religion. He was a nonbeliever, impatient with those who thought that God was looking after them, though willing to admit that he—and "even the science guys"—didn't know "what got the whole shebang started." When, at my mother's insistence, my brother was sent to New York so that he could study for his Bar Mitzvah, my father was so incensed that he stayed mad at my mother for weeks. "Go away from the family?" he would roar at her. "For what? For why? For something nobody knows except they got to do it." And it was true that my mother, like most Jewish women of her generation, knew almost nothing about the religion itself, only that there were certain imperatives: Bar Mizvahs, definitely, and Jewish mates, just as definitely.

So it was that I had lived my early years solely among ardent Protestants. Born in the South, I was a southerner, and I had lived as southerners lived. In their homes I had eaten what they ate and played their games. I had learned what they learned in school, gone on Easter egg hunts with them, run with them to get presents from Santa Claus at a neighbor's house. Yearning for a Christmas tree, I had cut a limb from our backyard pine tree to serve as one, and when I brought it in, my father, trying to talk my mother into it, teased her with, "Well, I'll tell you, Rebecca—it's so small God won't even notice."

Since I never went to a synagogue or temple, I never heard any Jewish prayers, except at what my mother called her "Friday nights." It was then, over lit candles, that my mother, having picked up Hebrew by ear, would mumble some short prayers. In my house we did not say anything resembling grace before everyday dining, as I had grown used to hearing in Tennessee, just as we did not say prayers before going to sleep.

From what I had observed, if Jewish people uttered words that sounded prayerful, the words were in reality quick throwaways. In response to a hopeful remark, one would say, "From your lips to God's ears," or in response to a jokey affront, somebody would offer, "I only pray to God to get you for this." In day-to-day life, I seldom had blessings showered upon me, nor did I hear long, meaningful pleadings, perhaps because Jewish people had learned from some centuries of experience that such addresses to God hadn't done them a whole lot of good.

In the circumstances it is not surprising that I grew up knowing more about my friends' religions than I did about my own. I knew how the Baptists differed from the Methodists in baptism rites—the former dunked, the latter sprinkled. I knew that the Episcopal denomination held the highest social rank and that our one Episcopal family suffered from having to attend a lesser church because we had no Episcopal one. I attended every variety of Sunday school and colored endless pictures of Jesus and Mary. I went to the evangelists' tents, where I listened to Billy Sunday imitators and watched neighbors fall on their knees and declare for Jesus. I looked in the windows of the Holy Roller churches as the Negroes wiggled and writhed and screamed out or, alternatively, muttered in husky voices. I knew all the hymns.

But still. In terms of religion, whatever my participation in Christian practices, however familiar I was with the rites and ceremonies, the thought was always with me that all these churches were theirs, not mine. I knew I was an outsider from the moment I was born, for my mother had known it from the instant the wagon in which she was traveling rolled onto First Street in Union City in 1920, and what my mother felt was never lost on me. The activities that I joined in with my friends at their churches were to me just another way to have fun. It never occurred to me that I was not Jewish. I was not a Baptist, foot-washing or regular; I was not a Methodist; I was not a Presbyterian; I was not a Holy Roller. I was a Jew.

If I had thought that when I got to New York I would at last be comfortable in my own religion, I was disappointed. It was still not my religion; it was now my relatives'. I went to Friday night services in their Orthodox synagogue, but I was not at ease there. It seemed curious to be sitting with the other females in the balcony, separated from the men—"looking down on them," some of the women said, in a wry joke. Though the other girls, like me, could not speak or read Hebrew (Hebrew schools, where these things were learned, being closed to them), unlike me they could sing the songs and could understand some of what the rabbi said because all of them knew Yiddish, which I did not.

Furthermore, my father's derisive words rang in my ears, and Sunday school did not stir my soul. When my mother would protest that I had to go to Sunday school to learn the history of the Jews, my father would say, "Get her a book." At regular school, I felt closer to the Gentile kids than I did to the Jewish ones. And when I got to Miami Beach, all things considered, that I was Jewish I knew, but that it was very hard for me to *feel* Jewish I also knew.

In Miami Beach the other high school—a Catholic one called St. Patrick's, or St. Pat's—was complete with nuns and did, of course, have a religious agenda. Occasionally St. Pat's pupils would join us. Desi Arnaz went to St. Pat's and was always eager—some said bound and determined—to pull out his ever-present guitar and entertain us. The children of the Al Capone crowd (the "crowd" being Al Capone and his followers, who lived on exclusive Palm Island) also went to St. Pat's. Al's son Sonny, a gentle, burly kid who managed to keep a low profile despite having a bodyguard always at his side, often came to our get-togethers with the St. Pat's kids. There was nothing ominous about having gangsters in our midst; to the contrary, we were intoxicated with the idea of them. We felt it put us not only apart but ahead.

We had more rich types in our school than just gangsters' kids, for Miami Beach was a bastion of northern and mid-western (never southern) money. It was a tradition for these rich people to come down when the weather turned cold and put their children in Miami Beach's public schools. Why they were not stowed away in prep schools I can only guess, but I do know that our school had kids from some of the wealthiest families in the country: we had (banking) Chases and Warburgs, (chocolate) Whitmans, (radio network) Paleys, and (among various department store heirs and heiresses) a Bonwit. Then there were the ones who taught us Latin dances, the off-spring of a succession of generalissimos who had flown out of Cuba in the wake of coups and, along with their entourages, had made a soft landing in Miami Beach, where they lived extravagant lives in extravagant houses.

The heading of "the rich" included both Jews and Gentiles. Most of the department store and banking heirs and heiresses were known to be of Jewish heritage, though whether they were still Jewish was open to conjecture.

For the Jewish kids, the presence of Gentiles in school presented no problem. For me, since I had come from a town of all Gentiles, being among them seemed altogether natural. There had, of course, been no Jewish teachers in Union City, so the all-Gentile faculty in Miami Beach also seemed unremarkable.

My friends in Union City—all those non-Jewish friends— would have thought it very odd if I had been shy with Gentiles. "Mercy, what on earth are you thinkin', you crazy thing?" they would have said to me.

John and I were not the only "mixed" couple in school: with Jews and Gentiles intermingling so much, it was inevitable that we had many such couples. And though there was the occasional expression of parental disapproval, most of us paid little attention. But of course I had to: I had made that promise.

If you were a rich kid, you had some extras, like glamorous shopping. You went shopping with your mother on Lincoln Road, in small, posh shops that carried one-of-a-kind garments and charged great amounts. Both the rich Jewish girls and the rich Gentile girls were taken shopping there. Everybody got dressed up when they went to Lincoln Road, and the winters were never too hot for fur. If your mother was Jewish, she'd wear her silver fox jacket over slacks and sky-high wedgies; if she was Gentile, her little Maggy Rouff suit with a small mink cape around her shoulders. The rich kids were driven to school in Packards and Cadillacs and Cords—the girls wearing their Ballantyne cashmere sweater sets from Scotland with a single strand of natural pearls around their necks—and they ate in the best restaurants south of New York. It must be said, however, that those who didn't—couldn't—do these things didn't slink off into dark corners: we were kids, and like kids everywhere, we took things as they came.

Actually, if you were poor, it wasn't so bad either, and there were plenty of poor people on the Beach, both Jews and Gentiles. Miami Beach might have been a haven for the rich, but it also sheltered those who served them (whose children, in fact, were the only other southerners I knew), and in our school being poor was no barrier to mingling with the rich. Indeed, the child of a family who kept a suite in the swank Roney Plaza hotel might very well share the same school clique with the child of the hotel's Gentile doorman or the hotel's Jewish tailor.

This mingling in school of the rich and the poor didn't, however, extend to the residential areas. Economic status definitely determined where you lived, though a case could be made that every area had its special cachet. Even South Beach, which housed the lowest economic groups—working Jews and non-Jews together with Jewish retirees from the New York garment industry—had a kind of mystique, for within its borders was a collection of shanties called Smith Cottages, whose residents had out of all proportion spawned star athletes and girls with looks, who were, of course, among the most popular pupils in school.

In the north part of the Beach—especially in the aptly named Golden Beach—resided the elite non-Jews, though they could also be found on "the islands"—Hibiscus, Palm, and Star—spits of land in Biscayne Bay, exceedingly posh and indistinguishable to those who didn't live there. Plenty of glamour exuded from all these areas, for they were the very model of conspicuous consumption—maids, cooks, and butlers; yachts on the water; mothers who slept all morning and in the afternoons went "to the track" or went jewelry shopping on Lincoln Road. The opportunity to amuse themselves in these "glitzy" ways may explain why the rich non-Jews chose to live in Miami Beach and not Palm Beach, which may have seemed their more natural habitat. Miami Beach was a bit more racy, a bit less judgmental, a bit less bluestocking.

The central section of the Beach was where the middle class lived, and as befitted my family's status as middle-income people, we lived there. It too was an area of some note in that it included Flamingo Park, the town's only real park and the site of the city's recreation department, which offered sports hitherto unknown to me. The recreation department lady, who came to recruit on the first day of school, would cry. "Girls! Get friendly with a ball! Bounce it, spike it, kick it! It's not just for boys!"

With the park so close, almost every afternoon after school I did as she exhorted and got "friendly" with many sports, especially with tennis. A lot of the kids played there as well, and one afternoon there suddenly was a very tall boy I had never seen before. True, he was not blond like my John Parke, nor was he fair-skinned like him—two qualities that had endeared John to me because they had reminded me so much of the boys in Union City—but as I watched him shagging flies before a pickup baseball game, I could see at once that he was a natural athlete. I very much admired athletic boys—I knew deep down that a big part of John Parke's appeal was that he was an all-state basketball player—and I could not take my eyes off this boy who was gracefully loping over to fly balls and surely pocketing them in his glove.

And then as I stood with my friends, a ball all at once headed my way as if it had been pitched at me, and I had only a fraction of a moment to throw up a hand and catch it. But catch it I did, and this boy walked over, gave a big smile, that invited all of us, and, as he took the ball from me, said, "Good catch." He looked at me for a moment and asked, "Want to get in the game?" I laughed and shook my head, and he said, "Maybe some other time," and went back to the other boys. But I had seen blue, blue eyes, and when I put them together with luminous black hair and bronzed skin and with what I estimated as six feet, two inches, I saw someone very "dreamy." A double for Gary Cooper maybe.

When I asked who he was, I learned that he had moved down from New York and was going to the University of Florida. And when one of the girls said, "His name's Jack Suberman," did I hear a drumroll and a blare of trumpets? I confess I did not, but they were surely sounding, for I had had my first sight of my prospective husband, and he was a boy squinting in the summer sun of 1939, playing baseball with his teammates, thinking of the future only in terms of winning or losing the game.

My FATHER, THE ULTIMATE practitioner of boosterism, loved Miami Beach. As he had doted on Union City, so now did he dote on Miami Beach. With the glaring exception of New York, my father found a way to like wherever he was. In Russia, pervasive anti-Semitism notwithstanding, he had liked his little *shtetl*. In the small Jewish-owned dry goods store where he'd worked, he had honed his skills as a salesman—or "sal-es-man," as he always pronounced it. And in Savannah, where he had lived as a young bachelor before marrying and moving to Tennessee, he had been able to find a place for himself in the fabric of the town, even becoming friendly with the

Gentile Savannah girls, some of whom had undertaken to pol-
ish his social skills and to improve his English.

If Miami Beach possessed few of the features my father so
fancied about the South, he found other things to crow about.
He would say, neatly confounding an image, "Just look at the
weather!" adding, "Who's got like this?" He would try to claim
other Miami Beach primacies as well, though they all invariably had the weather as an underpinning.

Being neither idle rich nor working poor, my father was in
the entrepreneur class. He was one of those who, with no family wealth to speak of, went around buying properties with an
eye to opportunities in a growing resort town. To this end, he
owned a strip of stores close by the Roney Plaza, on Twenty-
third Street, which he rented out. In time, however, as in his
bones he felt himself a merchant, he began to feel the call of
proprietorship. "What's a merchant without a store?" he would
ask my mother. "Like you got the mustard but where's the hot
dog, no?"

To address this oversight, he bought a store on Fifth Street,
a busy artery coming off the causeway that connected us to
Miami. Since by now he was heavily caught up in commercial
development ventures and could not devote himself full-time to
the store's operation, he retained the manager; but longing for
the interplay with customers, he would turn up at any odd
moment and without missing a beat get to work. It was as if a
store was where he really belonged.

The store was not a dry goods store, as we had had in Tennessee, but what was called, in a misnomer, a drugstore. The
store had no pharmacy, but it did carry typical drugstore sun-

dries and had a luncheonette and soda fountain. The store had struck my father as promising because it was in the midst of several cut-rate hotels dense with racetrack habitués, and he was quite right: the racetrack men ("touts," I learned they were called, though they would bristle if you said it to their faces), who came to Miami every fall for the Tropical Park and Hialeah racing, were in large part responsible for the store's thriving.

I looked forward to helping out in the store on the weekends, and these men were part of the reason. After a day at the track they would gather there for beer and food and toiletries and medications, though it was clear that their main intent was to pore over racing forms and talk horses. For me the racetrack men were a new breed, and their way of talking, their vernacular, was very new. They called me "kid" and directed a lot of teasing my way. "Hey, kid," they'd say in their big-city accents, "whaja learn in school today? You got a pick in the seventh?" As far as I knew, none of the men had homes other than the hotels. They came and they went, young men and older ones, some Jews but more Gentiles, some seasons the exact same cast of characters, sometimes an old-timer gone and a novice in his place.

My father also enjoyed these men, being a risk taker himself—what better description for an immigrant Russian Jew who had taken his family to a Bible Belt, 100 percent Protestant town in northwest Tennessee in 1920?—and went often with them to the track. Upon his return, he would report in with a "Nice out there today," leaving it up to us to decide whether he was talking about the weather or his luck. My father did something connected with horses every day. On rainy days, he went across the street to the sundry shop, to the bookie installed there, and placed his bets. In a town made for pastimes, my father chose horses.

My mother didn't care that my father had such a pastime. She knew that he would never put betting above business. Having often heard him mention the glories of the Hialeah setting—the luxuriant plantings, the flamingos—she would defend him by saying to the neighbors, "Mr. Kaufman is a man likes what he likes, and it happens he likes fresh air," conveniently forgetting about the visits to the bookie across the street. And then, no doubt mindful of a brother-in-law whose perilous poker playing was a family scandal, she would explain in her inventive way with the English language, "Horses is not cards. They're two different animals."

Though she missed her New York family, Miami Beach suited my mother quite well. We lived in a house with a yard, and her yard (gardening had become a passion for her in Union City) was lush as only Florida yards could be. If in Union City my mother had devoted herself to flowers, here in Florida, because of the heat and the bugs, she went with fruit trees— citrus and mangoes. Still, she did not have the heart to deny Florida wildflowers their moment, and she *kvelled* that the yard was ever scattered with pink, white, and purple periwinkles and tiny wild ur-poinsettias, their dark green leaves splashed with crimson.

Miami Beach suited my mother in another important way: we had Jewish people all around. Still, there was my non-Jewish boyfriend. My mother kept saying she had not come all this way so that one of her daughters could be involved with yet another *shagetz*. "So what's with my children they like only Gentiles?" she would ask, even though my oldest sister, Minna, was now living in the Catskill Mountains with her Jewish husband, just as my brother, Will, was living in New York safely married to a Jewish girl.

My other sister, Ruth, was not thinking of marriage; she was—aberrationally—thinking of a career. Ruth, just fifteen months older than I, was in New York studying interior design at Pratt Institute. Ruth and I were still close (more a question, as I saw it, of her telling me what to do and my doing it), but since Ruth was in a class above me and had her own friends, as I had mine, we were not excessively close, the way we had been in Union City. As little children we had been such a single entity that when Ruth started going to school at the four-room schoolhouse, it was taken for granted that I would go with her and share her little bench and desk, even if I was of an age not yet eligible. It was such an outstanding togetherness that the teachers called both of us RuthStella.

While I was the sports-minded one, Ruth was the artistic one, and she took art classes and spent time roaming Miami Beach looking for especially scenic venues. She several times painted Espanola Way, a street dedicated to looking Spanish by means of arches and ironwork, and I still have some of those paintings. I also still have a pin she made for me in metalworking class, the one incised "StellaRuth."

My name situation was peculiar. Like many southerners, I'd been given a double name—Margaret Stella. And though I was never called Margaret, in school I wasn't called Stella either, but Marcella for the reason that my mother had gotten it into her head that Marcella was a beautiful name and that I should have it. So when she registered me for school in the little four-room schoolhouse, she registered me as Marcella, and in all schools thereafter that was my name. Still, my family—including my mother—paid no attention and continued to call me Stella, as did, with time, all my close friends, and then, with more time, everybody.

In looks Ruth and I were very different. Though we were both dark-haired, she was blue-eyed like my father and I had my mother's dark eyes. Ruth was shorter than I but more bountifully built (in Union City we would have said she had bigger "zooms," shortened from "ba-zooms"), and she was one of the Bathing Beauties drafted by the publicist Steve Hannagan to promote Miami Beach in photography events. These featured girls in identical navy blue, halter-top bathing suits lined up on the beach. Ruth gave the pictures a D for creativity. "We look like we're either in a bread line or a chain gang," she said, bread lines and chain gangs being much in the current news. Ruth was very popular with boys, and my mother did not worry about her, assuming she would find a husband among the hosts of Jewish boys in New York or, when she came home, among those in Dade County.

My mother's stand concerning my relationship with John Parke was one of a kind, for taking stands was not in her nature. She left that to my father. If my mother secretly envied my father's self-confidence, she could not imitate it and was ever reluctant to thrust herself forward. But in the matter of her daughters' marriages, she was quite sure of herself because she was sure of the rightness of her cause.

My mother did not issue a peremptory order concerning my love life. Possibly fearful that a sudden cutoff would in some way upset my smooth progress in school and her pride in it, she instead made me an offer: she would allow me to continue to see John until graduation, but on that night—"on the dot," she said—we would part.

I did not argue with my mother. Being the youngest in a family of four children, I had learned that my views didn't count for much, and perhaps by then I had lost a little confidence in them. "Yes, Mama," I said to her, trying for as much hauteur as I could summon, which wasn't very much. "In two years you can light the candles, I promise." I wondered why my mother didn't know that two years was the same as never.

Truthfully, we both held secret convictions: hers was that the relationship would do a natural fade before the two years were up; mine was that my mother would in the end be unable to resist all the nice things about John and would bless us.

My mother's dictum did not spoil my high school years. I had the southern way of liking people and wanting them to like me in return (though it may have been that I was simply borrowing from my father's personality), so I had plenty of friends, held many school offices (my schoolmates' delight in my southern accent may have played a large part in this), made good grades, and had a popular boyfriend. If my hair turned frizzy in the Florida humidity, if I would never be Carnival Queen or a Steve Hannigan bathing beauty, it didn't bother me all that much. I was as secure as a clam tucked up in its shell.

THOUGH THAT BRIGHT isle of the 1930s was a dreamland for me and my schoolmates, it was also, all things considered, a doubtful training ground for the ways of the world. The dark forces were there and waiting to be grappled with, but so stubbornly did they resist the powerful wattage of Miami Beach's sunlight that we most often simply clung to our right not to bother.

Had I been of a mind to look for those dark forces, those shadows, I would have discovered a whole array. There were, first of all, the discriminatory practices—Gentile versus Jew, rich versus poor, white versus black. Discrimination was the common everyday coin. I was not oblivious to the fact that such practices existed, but it was only after some time—and with input from some important people in my life—that I could see them for what they were.

In school the one glaring discriminatory practice was the barring of blacks. Although we embraced nationalities of all kinds, we did not embrace American Negroes. One could say that it couldn't be helped, that it was the law, that there was a doctrine called "separate but equal" under which all southern schools operated, and that despite their many departures from southern custom, Miami Beach schools could not opt out. But southern or northern, our reaction to the absence of Negroes was identical: we accepted it without a murmur of protest.

As to the section of Miami Beach where the Negroes lived:

there *was* no section where the Negroes lived. No Negroes lived on Miami Beach, unless they lived in the servants' quarters of the families for whom they worked. A very real City Hall curfew saw to this. Under the curfew, temporary Negro workers had to be off the Beach by eight o'clock. Over and above the curfew, Negro performers were not permitted to do their acts on Miami Beach—not at supper clubs, not at hotels, not at South Beach dives. If you wanted to hear black jazz musicians, you went to Miami, to one of the clubs in the black section of town.

Coming from Tennessee as I did, at this point in my life these discriminatory practices and I had no problem with each other. In Union City it was incumbent upon my family to get along with the community, for a living had to be made, and getting along depended on the understanding that we shared the values of the community, especially those that pertained to race. It was, in fact, a tyranny as powerful as the one my parents had fled in Russia. Indeed, for those who espoused racial views opposed to the town's prevailing one, "runnings out of town" awaited.

Having seen many a picture of these "run-outs," I was terribly intimidated by them. Folks in other towns would send us snapshots (as if to prove what good times were being had there) of white families in wagons, their belongings heaped about them, being chased to the nearest county road. "Run-outs" generally had motivations different from lynchings, and lynchings were exclusively meant for Negroes, but "run-outs" were almost as popular.

At any rate, if my parents held racial views different from

our neighbors', I had no clue, for they would not have entrusted me with such pivotal information. I would hazard a guess, however, that their views were actually not very different from those of the town. During the years my parents lived in the South, they had become southerners, and though my father practiced fairness, it was fairness from the point of view of a decent southern white man—humane but guarded.

Furthermore, noble thoughts emanating from philosophical discoursing were not available to my father. Uneducated, ever encumbered by the need to make a living, he was worthy but practical. He could not even look to Brookie Simmons—the most enlightened citizen in Union City, the woman who mentored and protected us—for guidance toward a more commendable view, for though she spoke out loudly against many social ills, she never, as far as I knew, uttered a word against racism.

Still, on one occasion, my father gave evidence that he was tempted to go in another direction when he hired a black man to clerk in our store, something hitherto unheard of. In the end, however, he had to capitulate to Ku Klux Klan pressure and let the man go. The family was well aware of all that was transpiring, and when it was over, I did not reflect on the black man's having to lose the job he had been so proud of. I was just relieved. I could now quit worrying about our family being in one of those "run-out" snapshots.

So it was that I grew up sharing the attitudes of those around me and subscribing to their ways. I certainly never played with any African-American children, and naturally I did not go to school with them. With the exception of those who worked for us, even adult blacks remained at most a vague presence, going about their jobs all over town, doing what was called "nigger work."

In Miami Beach, I held to the Union City maxim "Don't be ugly to darkies, but keep them in their place." I even often voiced this axiom, satisfied that it displayed admirable manners while reflecting appropriate social views. I repeated it whenever race was up for discussion around school, and it was never denounced by any of my classmates—northern, midwestern, or whatever.

Discrimination against Jews was also one of the norms. If you were a Gentile (and also rich), your parents could belong to one of the swank "bath" clubs—swimming, dining, and tennis establishments famous for the practice of "blackballing," in which a single "No" preserved the rarefied air. Jews, rich or not, knew that if they asked to join, they would be summarily blackballed, so they didn't ask. Since this practice was not spelled out and no public announcements were made, it could be considered the southern type of bigotry, in which a patrician civility was laid on.

To their credit, my schoolmates who belonged to bath clubs didn't talk much about any good times on offer there, though there did emanate from them the sense that everybody, even Jews, must reasonably recognize that sometimes the exclusion of Jews was only to be expected. We Jewish kids dealt with this with our only defensive weapon: we took comfort in our numbers.

"Restricted" clubs and golf courses, however, were polite rebuffs compared to some of the other kinds of discrimination, for discrimination could show itself in exceedingly rank ways. Hotels with signs that trumpeted NO JEWS ALLOWED were commonplace, and one hotel advertised with the slogan, AL-WAYS A VIEW, NEVER A JEW.

My parents talked only in vague ways about the restrictions and signs, and actually no one made a fuss. If the hotel owners wanted to lure customers with such ploys, it is possible that there was a kind of acknowledgment among the Jewish community that business was business. Since most of the adult Jews had experienced the central European prejudices, they were possibly shrugging it off with a So what else is new? A case could also be made that because the Depression put the emphasis on economic survival, outmaneuvering a recalcitrant economy took top priority.

Nor did the Jewish residents make a fuss about the curfew. It might have been that to do so would have rocked the boat, and that boat was already balanced precariously on the crest of a pretty big wave. But if, in general, they did not choose to quarrel with the status quo, it was certainly the case that they were Democrats and in the main liberal. It was also the case that a rather sizable group of Miami Beach Jewish boys had joined the Abraham Lincoln Brigade to fight alongside the Loyalists in the Spanish Civil War.

MY MOTHER AND I were both wrong in our respective game plans for John Parke and me: our relationship did not fade, two years was not the eternity I had counted on, and my mother did not soften. Fond of John she might have been, but change her mind she did not. The time that was never supposed to come came. It was suddenly graduation night, and as we took our places in the procession, John and I bid each other a decidedly moist farewell. Then we sat down in the auditorium and listened to speeches about the promising and productive futures in store for us high school graduates. Bright days were ahead, our elders said in the summer of 1939, as bright as all those sun-drenched days of Miami Beach.

AND SO AS I lay in bed at my friend's house in West Palm Beach on that September morning in 1939, there was no thought of peril coming to us from the outside world. The rich who took advantage of our weather, our beaches, our race-tracks, were not concerned with the war in Europe and certainly not with the plight of the Jews; and neither were the service people and the entrepreneurs. The rich were focusing on pleasurable things, the poor were busy supplying them, and the entrepreneurs were concentrating on making money. If it could be said that Miami Beach was a peculiar place to prepare for the ways of the world, it was an even more peculiar place to prepare for the demands of war.

CHAPTER 2

After graduation I spent a summer of missing John. We would see each other at the beach or at get-togethers, and it was painful. Although other couples might have done their best to outwit their parents, John and I strictly honored my mother's wishes. We may have looked at each other longingly, but we never saw each other alone again.

I think if my father had argued with my mother, I would have tried a little deception. But he did not. He had been through this situation in Union City, he had lost, and he clearly did not want to go through it again. And it is not to be discounted that John's mother and father may also have spoken on the subject, thinking perhaps that things had gone far enough, that it was "unseemly" and "a bit awkward" for their son to continue seeing "a little Jewish girl." They would not have said "Jew girl," for they were genteel and they spoke genteelly.

At any rate, John and I stayed apart, and then we went off to college—both of us, as luck would have it, to the University of Miami in Coral Gables. Though at the university we saw each other, we did not make contact. And soon other interests prevailed, other persons beckoned, and in time we could glimpse each other without feeling that stab around the heart.

In those Depression years, after finishing high school, most of the year-round kids went to state universities or to the University of Miami, though the seasonal kids—the "snowbirds" —went where rich kids went in those days: wherever they wanted to.

The University of Miami was just over ten years old and had two nicknames: "Suntan U," for obvious reasons, and "Cardboard College" because its one building was a maze of cardboard-like partitions. At the heart of the building was a large patio, and it was in the patio that I noticed the war, for lined up in the patio were tables bearing petitions. I had never seen petitions before and had definitely never signed any. But here they suddenly were, white boards with big black letters barking out orders: HELP ENGLAND NOW and GIVE TO THE POLES. Or dispensing solemn advice: MR. PRESIDENT, IT'S NOT OUR WAR. Being a new student and not wanting to hurt anybody's feelings (and being ignorant), I signed them all.

At the university I also saw a lot of khaki. Groups of servicemen—army, navy, marine, whatnot—were traveling all over what we called "the campus" (made up of the one building and the patio), but since they did not attend my liberal arts classes —only those in math and engineering—I was scarcely aware of their presence and did not delve very deeply into the reasons for their being there. It was one of those things that didn't seem to be any of my business.

I did know that the servicemen were dating some of the students, but the word got around that they were only interested in "one thing," so the girls who didn't want to gain a "reputation" didn't date them. I was among those girls. As always, I was set on staying in everyone's good regard. Perhaps because in high school I had been keen on holding school offices, "reputation" was a very big thing with me. The word "reputation" had a specific usage among us. When someone was said to have a "reputation," there was no need to put "bad" in front of it: the word by itself meant that he or she was in violation of the moral code.

If the servicemen felt snubbed, they managed to get their own back when, during the elections for Hurricane Queen, they nominated a girl that to a man they had been "dating." They promoted her with the slogan VOTE FOR THE POPULAR FRONT, and of course she won.

The servicemen aside, many university customs were ones I had been familiar with in high school—such as the absence of African-Americans—but now the separation between Jew and Gentile, hitherto in my experience very blurry, was here very distinct. There were two Jewish sororities and two Jewish fraternities among the twenty or so Greek letter organizations, all formed strictly along non-Jewish/Jewish lines. I no longer dated non-Jewish boys, and non-Jewish boys no longer asked to date me, and I joined Alpha Epsilon Phi, a Jewish sorority. There was prejudice at the university that I hadn't seen before—not at my high school, anyway—and I was made aware of this by, of all things, a faculty member. At a campus skit competition, at which my sorority was the hands-down best in the girls' division and a Jewish fraternity the best in the boys', the judge, a professor of mine, gave the award to the boys but not to us. He later "apologized" to me for the injustice by implying that I understood that it would be impossible for him to give both awards to Jewish groups. And at that stage of my life I might very well have said that yes, I understood.

It was also at the university that I first took serious notice of the differences between the not-rich and the rich. It was easy to tell the poor girls from the rich ones: the poor girls lived at home and scrounged around finding odd jobs so they could stay in school; the rich girls were so generously subsidized by their parents that they could eschew the dormitories and dwell in glitzy Miami Beach hotels, where they worked on their tans.

Being neither rich nor poor, I lived at home, but I did not work. I spent my spare hours on the tennis team. The team was coached by the Miami tennis star Gardnar Mulloy, who also coached the men's team. Bobby Riggs played on the team for a couple of months, and when he practiced, I was ever in the stands, trying to learn something from his spins and drops.

At that moment in time I had very definite tennis goals and even went up to Atlanta to compete in the Southern Championships. Though I employed every Riggs strategem I could think of, plus my own pretty good backhand, I didn't do very well and lost in the second round to the future international star Doris Hart, who intimidated me not only by her superior play but also because her mother was on the sidelines cheering her on. This was totally outside of my experience—a mother who knew something about tennis, my own mother unable to tell a tennis ball from a badminton bird. Still, Doris's mother was nice, clucking whenever I double-faulted, at which I was so consistent that a case could be made that while Doris was playing tennis, I was playing some other game entirely.

It was 1940, however, and it was not a time to dwell on my lousy serve. The drumbeat coming from Europe was ever more steady, and even if I tried to tune it out, tried to concentrate on such things as tennis dreams, by June of that year the drumbeat was in my ear and it was very, very loud. In that month, in that year, two momentous events took place: Italy declared war on Britain and France, and Paris—Paris!—fell to the Nazis.

IN JUNE OF 1940, as I was finishing my freshman year at the University of Miami, Jack Suberman was finishing his sophomore year at the University of Florida in Gainesville. I had seen him quite a few times since that first glimpse, and I had a lot of information about him: I knew he lived on the Beach, belonged to what was then Phi Beta Delta but later Pi Lambda Phi, and had won the University of Florida individual intramural sports cup.

After those few words in Flamingo Park, I spoke to him for the first time one night at a summertime party. He was suddenly alongside me when talk of his fraternity's forthcoming hayride came up, and he turned to me and joked that he had heard that I was a country girl—a "hayseed," he said. "Wouldn't a hayseed," he asked me, "feel right at home on a hay wagon?" I laughed at this, and when he asked if I wanted to go with him, I said yes, I wanted to go.

Our date started and ended well, with only a few bumps along the way. I had found in a drawer some overalls that had come with us all the way from Union City (my mother was years ahead of the wartime dictum "Use it up, make it do, wear it out"), and I was wearing them when Jack came to pick me up. He took a long look at me and wanted to know where I'd been. "Has you been out on the farm, Miss Stella?" he asked me, putting on a southern accent. "Has you been out tillin' the soil?"

I told him his accent was terrible, which it was. "Lord have mercy," I joked back, "if you don't sound like a pig jes' been slopped."

In many ways Jack did seem southern to me. He was first of all mannerly: when he came to pick me up, though he didn't employ a "ma'am" when he talked to my mother, he jumped to his feet when she entered the room, and he was careful seeing me through doors, as if concerned that a lady might break with the slightest mishandling. All very nice and southern. Furthermore, as soon as we gathered with the fraternity crowd, it became clear that he liked to be surrounded by talk.

I may have thought Jack looked like Gary Cooper, but he was definitely not the lone stalwart the actor projected. He was very much attuned to people, and whatever the boys at the hayride talked about, they wanted to hear what he had to say. He seemed to be engaged in a multitude of conversations at once, even if most of it was joking and joshing. When we finally got into the wagon, however, he flicked a good-bye wave and told the boys he would see them later. "Right now," he said, "I just want to be alone with my girl."

My girl! He may have said "my girl" in the way he would have said "my date," but it made me catch my breath.

Jack and I settled into the hay, lay back, and the wagon started its clip-clopping. Well-aware that boys liked girls who were sweet, agreeable, and empty-headed, as much like Ruby Keeler as possible, I prepared to contribute my quota of no-content comment. I'm sure I depended on my southern accent to make my vacant remarks seem charming.

Things immediately turned topsy-turvy. Jack did not respond pro forma when I sent forth a typical gambit—"Don't you just love how Bob Eberle and Helen O'Connell get together on 'Green Eyes'?" He didn't answer the question at all, just looked at me and laughed. And when he joked, "Law', you southern girls—y'awl are jes' so triflin'," I had the brains to realize that this boy and I were starting out on a brand-new kind of date. When I found myself teasing back, saying, "We're just trying not to show up all youse Noo Yawkers," it seemed to me a good sign, for in my experience it wasn't worth your time to tease if you didn't plan to be interested.

Jack was majoring in English literature, and we talked a bit about books. On my part, even if I also was considering an English major, I was scarcely reading anything beyond class assignments. I had read the current rage, *Gone with the Wind,* but I didn't mention it: Jack might be dismissive, one of those who said it wasn't in the highest tradition of literature.

Jack, as I was to find out, didn't just read books in the highest tradition of literature. He read everything—from the Depression novels of John Steinbeck and the sociological ones of Sinclair Lewis to the southern tales of Erskine Caldwell to the western ones of Louis L'Amour. And, as I was to find out before the evening was over, to the *Gone with the Wind* of Margaret Mitchell. Tonight he was keen to talk about something by Thomas Wolfe he had just finished reading, an excerpt from a novel called *You Can't Go Home Again,* and he urged me to read it. I had never heard of it, in fact had scarcely heard of Thomas Wolfe, but Jack said I should definitely put him on my list. "He's a writer of such great insights," he said. "And credible ones. About the war."

When I turned to look at him, blankly I suppose, he said, "You know, the war in Europe. The war we're going to be in someday."

Although I paid little attention to Jack's mention of war, I *was* paying attention to the fact that I had never before had a date who had made books a feature of his conversation. I was surprised by the kind of things Jack had on his mind, and I found myself liking it very much, as if, unknown to me, I had been listening out for this kind of talk. And when in the next moment Jack recited some lines from the book, it occurred to me that this was the first time a boy had quoted me lines that were meaningful and not a joke currently making the rounds.

If I had thought that Jack was southern in some ways, I discovered that in other ways he was most definitely *un*-southern. When he disagreed with you, you knew about it instantly. He told you patiently and gently, but he told you.

So when the matter of race crept into our conversation on that night of our first date—no doubt because our driver was a black man and I had referred to him as a "darky"—Jack looked surprised. Thinking to assure him that I'd used the term with the best of intentions, I repeated my axiom about not being ugly to "darkies" but keeping them in their place; and when I did, Jack did not hesitate. "Do you really believe that?" he asked me. "Do you really believe there's a prescribed 'place' for the races?"

Even in the dusk of evening, I could see that Jack's blue eyes had turned dark. Had I made a misstep? Did Jack no longer think of me as just sweetly "triflin'"? The hay I was lying on was suddenly sharp, full of sticks poking at me.

But didn't I believe that whites had their place and "darkies" theirs? Wasn't it Nature's neat little plan? I did believe that, and I tried to say so. "Negroes can't stand beside whites," I said, with what I hoped was conviction. "And they shouldn't expect to."

Jack sat up and tossed a straw in my direction, as if signaling that he was trying to keep the conversation light. Still, he couldn't keep the seriousness out of his voice when he asked me, "Then what do you make of 'All men are born equal'?"

Well, what *did* I make of it? I tried the rational approach and suggested that Negroes were unable to function as equals. I used the usual stereotypical description of the southern Negro I had grown up with, saying that Negroes were "ignorant," and "childlike." I brought in all the rationales of the "considerate" southerner, the notion that it would be "unkind" to Negroes to ask them to meet the standards of whites. But no matter how much I explained, rationalized, defended, Jack was clearly not persuaded. And all at once the word "prejudiced" was in the air.

It scared me, hearing the word. I didn't like it at all, for it had never occurred to me that the word would be applied to me. Had I made an adversary of this boy who had had me from the moment he had said "my girl"? I was losing heart. So I said, timidly, perhaps piteously, maybe even tearfully, "I just can't keep this up any longer. I don't want you to hate me."

Jack suddenly sat straight up. No smile lit his face, and no hay was tossed in my direction. The words flew from him. "Hate you?" he said. "How can you say that?" He reached over and turned my face to his. "It's just me being me," he said. "Ask anybody. They'll tell you. I always go too far." It was as if he couldn't say things fast enough. "Please, please, don't let me make you feel bad. I just didn't think."

It was all right. The hay was comfortable again, and I lay back in it and looked up at the stars. Jack did the same. But, as always after a discussion with Jack, there was a coda. As if he had been meditating on it, he said to me, "It's really not your fault that you feel the way you do. It's not easy to root out prejudice, you know." He reached over for my hand and said, "Especially if, you were born with it as you were."

Even if I didn't feel vindicated, I felt understood. The truth was that I *had* been born with prejudice; it was in my bones, in the very marrow of them, and I could not "root it out" just because someone told me to. More to the point, it was impossible for me at that time in my life to believe what Jack believed —that equality of the races was not to be questioned, that it was a given.

But at that moment I didn't want to talk about it, and I wished sincerely that we had come to the end of the subject. "Can we just not fuss about it anymore?" I asked Jack.

Jack laughed and went back to the teasing and to the terrible southern accent. "Why, Miss Scarlett," he joked, "Ah wouldn't fuss with you for all the world." And adapting a line from Miss Scarlett O'Hara herself, he said, "Let's just say you'll think about it tomorrow, okay?"

That night we didn't talk about it anymore, but later I wondered about "tomorrow." I knew that Jack would be waiting for my "tomorrow," confident that it would come. But was I so sure? Probably not.

On this night in the hay wagon there was another kind of waiting. The truth was that through all the talk, through all the give-and-take, Jack and I had been waiting to be close, to touch, to have our arms around each other. We had been waiting perhaps since the evening began, not inconceivably since we had seen each other in Flamingo Park. So as we settled in for the long ride that would take us out to Greynolds Park, we stopped talking, and in a moment Jack had gathered me in, and we thought to concentrate not on books, not on prejudices, but on us. My own feelings were running deep and strong, more deeply and more strongly than I had ever felt, as if Jack was the exact boy that I had been waiting for, the one I would truly love. I respected him and I wanted his arms around me, and didn't that add up to love?

I believe Jack was seeing in me someone to love as well, even if as yet I was only showing promise. So if it can be said that young people have the ability to detect in one another a reason for loving, you could say that on that very first night we fell in love. On that first night, when Jack held me in his arms and said, "Miss Scarlett, you are just pure perfection," I knew at once that this kind of line from this kind of boy was very definitely going to get him to first base. And though it is certainly true that I had given up first base before, never had I done it more willingly.

As to the Thomas Wolfe book that Jack had mentioned, when I finally read it a year or so later, I realized just how prescient it had been, for I recognized it as a first warning that war was coming to us, that the war had to be fought, and that it was a good war. It spoke of the clouds forming over Europe and, in a substory, of the treatment of Jews. And the line Jack had quoted—"Whereon the pillars of this earth are founded, toward which the spirits of the nations draw, toward which the conscience of the world is tending—a wind is rising, and the rivers flow"—was right on the mark.

IN THE DATES that succeeded the hayride, although Jack stayed away from a discussion of race, it didn't stop him from questioning other of my attitudes. When he did this, when he wanted to know why I took a position he thought untenable, if I answered with "Everybody feels that way" or "It really doesn't matter," he did not yield, only pressed me further.

There were many things for Jack to press me about. He was dumbfounded, for instance, that I was just "not bothering" with the Miami Beach hotel signs. As a relative newcomer to Miami Beach, Jack wanted to know why we long-timers hadn't risen up. "Where are the protests?" Jack asked me. "Why haven't you been taking a stand?"

Protests? Taking a stand? I—and my friends—would never have contemplated such things. "They're just signs," I answered Jack. "Just sticks and stones." The truth was that I had never more than half-examined anything, neither my views nor my attitudes. I was in fact a half-made eighteen-year-old, and a semiserious one at that.

Jack persisted. "Don't you know these signs are calling you a 'dirty Jew'? Don't you know how it is to be called that?"

Well, the fact was I didn't, for I had never had an ethnic slur used against me. I had certainly heard words of anti-Semitism and I had seen anti-Semitism in action. At the very least I had sensed it. But I had never as a young person suffered in any intimate way from being Jewish, never felt any blows to my sense of self, not anywhere, anytime. How do I explain this? That I had just been lucky? Perhaps if I had been involved in a single ugly episode or had had a lone epithet flung my way, it would have made all the difference. To Jack's question, I answered, truthfully, "No, I haven't."

"Well, I have," he told me. In real-world New York, he said, anti-Semitic slurs were "as common as breathing" and he himself had been the direct recipient. I asked when, and he said "definitely" when he had played on his high school's basketball team. "All through the games," he said, "all I heard was 'dirty Jew, dirty Jew.'"

I was incredulous. "Were they talking to *you?*"

"Of course."

It was unthinkable that anybody would call Jack "dirty Jew." My tall, clean-cut, all-American Jack—how could anybody call him that?

I had more to learn. There were the "code words." As a Jew, Jack said to me, it was important for me to get to know "code words."

Code words?

"What do you think non-Jews mean when they call a Jew a New Yorker?" he asked me.

"That they're from New York?"

Jack laughed. "It's code," he answered, "a code for 'loud Jew.' Take my word for it."

JACK WAS THE OLDEST child in his family. His brother, Irwin, had been at Miami Beach Senior a year behind me, and his sister, Sheila, was ten years younger. It may have been the "oldest child" syndrome that made him seem the elder states-man in any peer group. And despite the fact that he was less than two years older than I, the oldest child–youngest child–dynamic may have worked naturally toward my feeling that Jack was a source of superior wisdom.

In New York Jack had gone to Townsend Harris High School, a city-run school installed in a downtown office build-ing. Well-respected CCNY professors moonlighted at Town-send Harris to earn an extra salary, so this was a case of the Depression actually doing somebody some good. The school had a curriculum that graduated students in an accelerated three years and was known as an incubator for CCNY, na-tionally acknowledged in those days for educational excellence. Townsend Harris was where motivated students were sent by perceptive junior high school teachers.

So Jack, the beneficiary of such a teacher, had attended not the usual New York neighborhood high school where the stu-dent body might represent a single racial or ethnic group but a school that drew from all over the city and therefore could provide a grounding in the workings of diversity. The student body president was a black boy from Harlem, Jack's main sidekick on the basketball team was a Dutch-German from Brooklyn, and his chief intellectual adversary—though intellectual adversaries were a common commodity—was an Irish boy from the Van Nest section of the Bronx. Argument was in the air, and no proposition was ever accepted or discarded without every word being held up to the light.

I loved that Jack was from New York, even if among my friends New Yorkers were not held in the highest regard (perhaps because New Yorkers comported themselves as if, being from the Biggest City, they knew better about everything than us small-towners). Indeed many of our Miami Beach stores, as a kind of joke, put up signs saying, WE DON'T CARE HOW YOU DO IT IN NEW YORK.

Ever since Union City, however, despite my father's antagonism, I had clung to the belief that New York *was* superior. Miami's calling itself the "Magic City" notwithstanding, New York had been my magic city ever since my brother, having been sent there for his Bar Mitzvah, had brought back wondrous tales. And it was not lost on me that in Union City when my mother sat at her sewing machine and delivered herself of song, the lyric she offered most feelingly was

> Take me back to New York town, New York
>   town, New York town
> That's where I long to be, with friends so dear to
>   me
> Coney Island down the bay, all the lights of old
>   Broadway

Herald Square, I don't care, anywhere
New York town, boys, take me there.

The mystery of who the "boys" were I couldn't quite penetrate, but that my mother was evoking images of a fabulous place I never doubted.

JACK AND I dated all that year and the next. We called each other "darling" because Jack liked Evelyn Waugh and that's how the couples in Waugh's books addressed each other. When Jack wrote to me, his greeting was "My darling," and every time I read the word, my heart turned over.

When he was home, we danced and went to the movies and I taught him to play tennis. Well, I really didn't teach him. Jack immediately deconstructed tennis as just another "ball" game, and in no time at all he was beating me, which had nothing to do with the prevailing custom of letting a boy win. It had to do with the fact that Jack was a natural-born athlete, all superior instincts and reflexes, and even while I was losing, I had to admire the ease with which he moved around the court.

When I was with Jack, I walked in a mist of love. I loved almost everything about him. I loved that he was long and lean and looked wonderful in his clothes, even if he never seemed to care about clothes at all; I was dazzled, being Depression-trained, that he was the only one of the boys of my acquaintance (including the rich ones) who never knew how much money he had in his pocket and didn't care how much of it he spent; I was smitten by what I perceived to be a handsome face, and if others thought his nose and mouth too generous, to me they were fitting: they reflected his inner spirit.

In more substantive ways, it resonated somewhere deep inside me that he paid attention to things in the world, made some of those things important to himself, and then made them important to others. I was convinced that he was a born teacher, for he was so clearly dedicated to getting others to join him in thinking about matters they would ordinarily pass by. He seemed to know something about everything. He said he got this way from, as a kid, always having had his nose stuck in the *Book of Knowledge,* and if this was true, it reflected what I thought was an admirably inquisitive nature.

We got along very well, though there were some personality conflicts, all of which I attribute to my basically being a southerner and he a northerner. Prepared by my upbringing to believe what people said to me, especially to accept unquestioningly the *nice* things they said to me, I was, Jack thought, too trusting. He liked to believe that he was not for a moment deceived by politicians, religious leaders, or those encountered in the ordinary course of life. We had an obligation, he said, to probe for real intent, possible eventualities, and so forth. "Don't you see how important that is?"

No, I didn't see that. And I didn't want to believe that. I thought Jack was, as I often said to him, a prime example of big-city (and annoying) wariness. What I wanted to believe was that people meant what they said. "Can't you just accept that?" I asked Jack.

"It depends," he answered me. "But I'd sure want to know more before I did."

• • •

BEFORE WE'D STARTED going together, since Gainesville was too far for a quick weekend visit home, Jack had stayed put with other boys who were similarly far from home. When there was no football game or intramural competition, Gainesville was diversionless, and the boys spent the weekends playing Ping-Pong matches that lasted till dawn and drinking a lot of beer—or, as Jack said cheerfully, "We just got drunk in a pile." Weekends passed, I took it, in a beery blur of little white balls.

Things were different after Jack and I started going steady, as we called exclusive dating, for then he came to Miami on most weekends. He hitched rides in whatever vehicle happened to pass by, taking it however far it went, and by whatever route. One ride was with a rural mailman who zigzagged through much of the central part of the state before dropping Jack in Melbourne, on the east coast. "Have you in Melbourne before you know it," the mailman said as he zipped off toward Lakeland, a hundred miles in the other direction.

City born and bred, Jack became familiar with a lot of rural Florida by hitchhiking. He got to know all the orange-grove locales, and the Cross Creek country of Marjorie Kinnan Rawlings, and Ocala horse country, and catfish camp country around Lake Okeechobee. He found himself mostly on country roads, and they were dangerous, chiefly because the Florida legislature had responded to farmers' wishes (and votes) and outlawed fences. Cows—bony, listless Florida cows, not good for much—crossed the roads at will in their endless search for scrub, and they caused accidents. Pigs and chickens also strolled around with impunity, and if you hit any of these—cow, pig, chicken, or the odd goat—a farmer or rancher would appear out of nowhere and announce something like "That'll be twenty-five dollars, mister. Cash." There was a sliding scale, formulated on what you hit and what kind of car you were driving. The saying among Florida drivers was "Watch out for the animal life or you'll be buying the world's most expensive meat."

During the summer Jack was home. Like a lot of the college boys, he worked at construction jobs on the hotels that were forever going up in Miami Beach—Art Deco palaces of aqua and pink and lemon yellow—and we saw each other every night. Jack's parents didn't mind that we were together so much and, in fact, seemed to like me, perhaps because there was really nothing to object to: I was socially presentable, I was going to college, and I had parents who were also presentable. Or maybe they didn't take us seriously, for no Jewish parents expected a son of theirs to marry before he showed promise of being able to afford a wife.

Perhaps they liked me because I so obviously looked up to them as fountains of information about New York. If they themselves were not exactly cultured people, they were aware of culture, and they knew about Broadway and the Metropolitans (the opera house and the art museum), and Jack's father read the *New York Times* every day.

My parents and Jack's had very different lifestyles, due partly to the fact that my father was still active in business and Jack's father was retired. After a series of heart attacks, Mr. Suberman had finally taken the family from New York to South Florida, where he had retreated from the tensions of the business world—he had been a fur wholesaler—to the somewhat lesser tensions of the bridge-playing world at downtown clubs. He was a reserved man, and quiet, as if he always had an ear to his doubtful heart. He sought to keep his emotions in check and tried not to dwell on his losses in the 1929 stock market crash—which he blamed for his deteriorated health—though he would occasionally go over to the buffet drawer where he kept his worthless stock certificates and shuffle them around. "Not even good for stocking the bathroom," he would say. "Too hard and slick."

Jack's mother's personality complemented Jack's father's; while his father was subdued and avoided "making a fuss," his mother was lively and eager for people and parties. She was different in many ways from my own mother, certainly physically, for my mother was plump and short, and Frieda—she insisted that in the contemporary way I call her and Mr. Suberman—Alex—by their first names—was thin and relatively tall. She was blond and blue-eyed, courtesy no doubt of Cossacks, who could always be counted on for a contribution to Russian Jewish families, and had been born in America. Also unlike my mother, whose relationships were limited to kin and neighbors, Frieda had a host of friends, with whom she played a lot of cards, for money. Frieda liked to cook but did not cleave to Jewish cooking, and she made things like prime-rib roasts cooked rare and "tossed salad," a new one to me, for I knew only my mother's tomatoes and cucumbers on a flat plate. My mother paid Frieda her highest compliment: she said Frieda was "modren, modren to a T."

Jack's brother, Irwin, two and a half years younger, was tall like Jack and showed promise of looking like Glenn Ford when he matured. He had just finished high school and was involved with his own crowd, so he and Jack had minimal interaction. Still, like many brothers, during the war years Irwin and Jack were able to find real common ground.

On occasional Sundays Jack and Irwin took turns babysitting their nine-year-old sister, blond and blue-eyed Sheila. If it was Jack's turn, when Jack picked me up, Sheila would already be in the back seat of the car, and Jack would throw a book at her—maybe the latest in the adventures of the Bobbsey twins or Nancy Drew—and make her promises. "If you're a good girl," he would tell her, "untold riches await you at the marble counter of Stella's soda fountain." Then he would find a palm tree near the beach that we could park under and Sheila would settle down with her book while Jack and I noodled around in the front seat. After an hour or so of this, Sheila would let it be known that she was being exceedingly mistreated, and we would mend matters by rushing her to the ice cream sundae of her dreams.

When Jack and I weren't together, we wrote each other every day, mailing our letters by special delivery on Sunday. Did we write of the war? Did we discuss the fact that Japan had joined the German-Italian axis? Or that the British had attacked Italian forces in Egypt? I'd be hard-pressed to claim that our letters contained only items of such import, but whatever we had to tell, somehow it couldn't wait. We sent things that spoke to each other's special delights: I sent Jack books, and he sent me records. I sent him *For Whom the Bell Tolls,* and he sent me a record in which Jack Leonard sang,

> Would you like to be the love of my life for always
> And always watch over me?

To square my blunders and share my dreams
One day with caviar
Next day a chocolate bar?

I don't know if it was the thought of squaring blunders, or sharing dreams, but whatever it was, I signed on.

In 1940 the first indication that the government was taking a serious look at the war in Europe came when it handed down the Selective Service Act—the draft—which called for registration of all men (though we thought of them as boys) between the ages of twenty-one and twenty-six. It was the first draft in my experience, and I found it rather exciting that boys I knew were being called upon. Though many of the Gainesville students qualified, Jack, only twenty, did not quite.

Some men who registered were given "exempt" status. My brother, Will, an engineer living in Rhode Island and working for a company that manufactured war equipment, was one of these. My sister Minna's husband, born and bred in the same town in the Catskill Mountains where they lived, was declared 4F, a classification that meant he was exempt on the basis of disability. We knew Mike had flat feet, but did flat feet really disqualify you? Apparently they did; or maybe Mike had simply been done a favor by old friends on the local draft board, for as the draft took hold, we learned that draft boards were pretty much answerable to no one but themselves.

I for one—still trying for denial—said that it was not our war, so why should there be a draft of American men? Jack, up there in Gainesville, kept telling me to read the paper, all the papers. "Don't depend on the *Herald* for the whole picture," he wrote me. "Try to see the *New York Times* now and then."

I resisted the *Herald* and never saw the *Times*. The big newsstand on Washington Avenue was the only place you could get the *Times,* and it was always two or three days old. I got most of my news from the radio in between musical intervals, or from hearing it from my father, whose practice every morning was to exhaust the paper before leaving the house, and every evening to hunker down in front of the Atwater Kent.

Though the radio and paper brought us a lot of war news, they were relatively silent on the plight of the Jews in Europe. My father often ran into people who had received letters from their families in Germany in which they pleaded with their American kin to act as sponsors so they could get out. My father said that all the letters said the same thing and in the same words. What they said was, "Things are terrible over here." And my father would say, "Where's the *Herald* on this?"

I confess that no war news stayed in my head very long. Still, when my father told me that Germany now occupied Norway and Denmark and had gone on to take over Holland and Belgium, this stayed with me. "Germany's spreading itself all over the map," my father said. "What's next for those *momsers?*"

It looked as if London was next, and when the intense bombing of the city—the Blitz, as it was called—began, I finally started paying attention. Still, I kept asking myself, though with less and less confidence, what did it all have to do with us, with the United States? Weren't we removed, aloof, safe? Didn't we have that "neutrality" thing?

We did have that "neutrality" thing, but it didn't prevent President Roosevelt, after German troops had overrun Greece and Yugoslavia in the spring of 1941, from recommending aid to the Allies, in the form of a "Lend-Lease" program. With this almost hands-on assistance coming from America, even I had to admit that the drumbeat was beginning to sound like thunder.

As this latest news was reaching us, Jack and I had our own personal decision to make. We had begun to think of our geographical distance from each other as a real burden, and we talked about my transferring to a university closer to Gainesville —Florida State College for Women, in Tallahassee. My parents were agreeable to my going. My mother liked Jack very much for himself, but his being Jewish had earned him the ultimate star. If he was Orthodox, Conservative, Reform, or none of the above—as he was—it didn't matter to my mother. She didn't care that he didn't attend a synagogue, hadn't had a Bar Mitzvah. "So what makes him so Jewish?" I teased her. To which her answer was that he had Jewish parents, so he was Jewish "and don't try to tell me no." Also in Jack's favor was his height. Having been surrounded by family and relatives exceedingly short and having produced a family in which my five foot six was called tall, my mother was deeply impressed.

My father liked Jack because Jack was "a sport." Jack would, when asked, take a hand at pinochle, he was fully engaged in college athletics (including, impressively, boxing) and he would "take a drink," and, very important, when he bantered with Jack, Jack bantered right back. Above all, Jack shared his feelings about God. My father tested Jack by stating his own assessment of the concept of God and waiting for Jack's reaction. He said to Jack, "Don't you agree with me that God is just a rumor agreed on by everybody?" and was delighted when Jack laughed and said he did.

I sent my application to FSCW in June 1941. It's possible that it was a more auspicious moment from my point of view than what had just occurred on the world stage: only days before, German forces had invaded the Soviet Union; and as the Germans were capturing Kiev, I arrived in Tallahassee.

IT SEEMED TO ME altogether improbable that Miami Beach and Tallahassee were in the same state. Although Tallahassee was both a state capital and the seat of two well-known colleges, it was in most ways a small southern town. Pickup trucks dominated the streets; speech was not only southern but twangy southern. There appeared to be more blacks than whites, and they lived, as in every southern town, in an all-black ghetto. A church was on every corner, evangelists' tents in outlying fields. Restaurants served vegetables cooked with fatback. I didn't complain, for I still liked southern ways, and I still liked southern cooking.

As to the war, FSCW offered little talk of it and no petitions at all. There was, however, a contingent of servicemen similar to the one at the University of Miami, this one from Camp Blanding at nearby Starke.

I lived in a dormitory at FSCW, sharing a room with a Jewish girl, Myra Rubin, from Daytona Beach, a pairing the housing office had no doubt seen to. Myra, being in her second year at FSCW, was knowledgeable and helpful, and already knew about me. All the Jewish girls at FSCW were fully informed about the Jewish boys at the University of Florida, and Myra was aware that I was Jack's girlfriend.

For the most part, the students at FSCW came from small towns I had scarcely heard of, and many were from no town at all, just straight off the farm. Many were employed at campus jobs, and if there were any girls from rich families, they were outnumbered by the not-so-rich and the downright hard up. It was, however, a fad among Jacksonville debutantes to go to FSCW for their freshman year; then they would leave for schools with higher cachet.

Miamians, especially those from Miami Beach, were exotics. Most exotic of all were the Jewish girls, no matter where we were from—Jacksonville, Tampa, Pahokee—though, just as in Tennessee, there was a bit of bewilderment as to how Gentiles should feel about Jews. Most of the FSCW girls were from homes where the Bible was everyday reading, and the Bible gave them confusing signals: on the one hand it told them that their Lord had been born Jewish; on the other hand it told them that the Jews had killed their Lord. The girls settled this in their minds in various ways, and as a result some of them kept clear of us and some expressed excessive cordiality. Those I knew from the various sports teams were occupied with honing their athletic skills and seemed not to pay much attention.

As at the University of Miami, at FSCW there were no black students. Racial slurs abounded, even among the patrician girls, though they avoided raw locutions. They said "the coloreds" or "Negro," which they pronounced as "Nigra."

Tax money supported Florida Agricultural and Mechanical, a college for African-American boys, just across town from FSCW, but though it had plenty of students, we never saw them, segregated as we were on campus and in town. The only institution for African-American women was Bethune-Cookman College in Daytona Beach, though it received no state support, the Tallahassee tax dispensers no doubt reasoning that black women did not need education to become domestic servants.

FSCW was an established college with good facilities. Since the students were all girls and, as such, assumed to be in college chiefly to capture husbands and not to learn how to earn a living, we were so expendable that the substantially female faculty was free to offer us nontraditional courses, unlike at Gainesville, where the boys were stuck with bare-knuckled career ones. Our off-campus diversions were worlds apart as well: while our Gainesville counterparts might go to Jacksonville to see a Florida-Georgia football game, we might go to Atlanta to see Martha Graham dance.

Some girls did opt for careers, and those who did thought about being teachers and took courses in education. I myself had taken a couple of education courses, which had cured me of any desire I had had in that direction. I had no career of any sort in mind and had never really reflected on what I was going to do with my English major. At Tallahassee I was content to sample this and that—Old French, Art of Mesopotamia—and by now Jack had me reading anything he considered brain nurturing.

We missed the boys and looked forward to their coming on the weekends. At the nightly after-dinner dancing in the recreation room, we were obliged to dance with each other. Benny Goodman's "Sing, Sing, Sing," a top record choice, in my view cried out for the lindy hop, which none of the girls knew but wanted to learn, so I taught them. Some records, like *In the Mood*, were played so much they went off-key and whiny. Frank Sinatra's recording of "I'm Getting Sentimental over You" got so worn out that we finally broke it up into little pieces and parceled it out.

At this point in time some of the girls were getting mighty sentimental over their already drafted boyfriends who were off in boot camp. When letters came in from places like Camp Blanding and Fort Benning in Georgia, the girls brought them to the rec room and read them out loud (excerpts anyway), and we learned all about the horrors of boot camp. The boys apparently took it quite well, no doubt because they believed what they had been told—that they had been drafted for only one year. There was not a letter writer who didn't mention the exact day he would be out. "Just seven months, one week, four days till March 15," a draftee-boyfriend might write. "Can't wait to see you."

Like all FSCW-Florida couples, Jack and I saw each other every weekend, either in Gainesville or in Tallahassee. When I went to Gainesville, I stayed with one of the Jewish families in town and got to know the fraternity house. Like most fraternity houses it had a southern manse exterior, and like most fraternity houses, its interior was bleak, decidedly unclean, and smelled of stale tobacco and old socks.

Jack was now president of the fraternity—the rex, as Phi Beta Delta had it—which was no surprise to me. The boys called me "Queenie," though some, wanting to show they knew their Latin, called me "Regina." I think Jack was astonished to find himself in a fraternity, having so little interest in any group that had a restricted membership and held to blackballing. The one real restriction—and it was a big one—was that you had to be Jewish. The motivation for the restriction was always up for debate—whether it came from the boys' desire to keep themselves to themselves or, since Jewish boys were not welcomed into Gentile fraternities, from an attempt at a quid pro quo. As for blackballing, if the prospective member had nothing to offer academically, socially, or athletically and was not a "legacy," Phi Beta Delta, like other fraternities, said no. Joining any fraternity had one practical plus—and it may have been this that enticed Jack—for if you weren't in a fraternity, weren't "Greek," you were forced to eat at the dreaded campus cafeteria or at one of the typical university-town grease-pit restaurants—which, paradoxically, were almost exclusively owned by families named Aretakis or Thesophides.

When Jack became rex, he made some changes. The requirement that you had to be Jewish remained, as did blackballing, though pleas for tolerance were stepped up. But there was to be no more paddling and hazing, Jack having convinced his brothers that "whamming some guy's butt" was in no way character building, and that it was not a learning experience for a pledge to "puke up his *kishkas*" after slugging a tumbler of moonshine. Still, Jack had no illusions that other fraternities would follow these changes, and they didn't, no doubt feeling honor-bound to uphold tradition.

In Phi Beta Delta the only tradition was making grades. On the campus Jewish boys were seldom respected as campus cutups, only occasionally as student-body politicians (and then usually as the éminence grise), never as athletes, but always as scholars. Jack turned this on its head by being a so-so scholar and an outstanding athlete, and even made the varsity basketball team. When Jack won the intramural cup, it was an achievement widely commented upon. Indeed, one of his professors told him that he "didn't know Jews could handle a ball," adding, "I thought they were just smart." When Jack related this to me, I laughed, but Jack had a different reaction, for the conventional belief that all Jews were smart struck him as just another way to make Jews seem different. "Anyway," he said to me, "don't we both know plenty of dumb Jews and plenty of smart Gentiles?" And I had to agree that we did.

When it came to job prospects, the fraternity boys were floundering, and not only because of the ongoing Depression. Only those who would enter their fathers' businesses were secure, though a diploma was merely a social plus for them and meant nothing to their careers. Most of the others were first-generation college-goers, so only a handful had professional fathers whose firms they could join.

The boys studied hard, but they were studying for careers for which there was no call, and the jobs that *were* available offered rock-bottom salaries. Engineers were earning ten dollars a week, and for Jewish boys there were no openings anyway. (When my brother was searching for an engineer's job, he had flirted with the idea of adding two *f*'s or two *n*'s to Kaufman to make the name seem German rather than Jewish.) For those Jewish boys who wanted to go to medical school, there was another kind of obstacle: a quota system was in effect, by which Jewish boys were admitted in numbers theoretically commensurate with the percentage of Jews in the population.

The ultimate job-hunting frustration was for those interested in the liberal arts—in the visual arts or books or music. In those fields it was not a matter of prejudice or quotas, it was a matter of no jobs at all. And Jack was one of these.

Jack had been given an assistantship in the writing lab, and he liked it very much, though, as he said, it did nothing to guarantee a job. One of his professors, no doubt astonished at having a Jewish boy fresh from New York City sitting in his class, had advised Jack to do himself a favor and learn about country matters, so Jack had taken enough courses in crop propagation and animal husbandry to cobble together a minor. Fun, Jack said, and educational, but no career there either. It was his thought that if you were going into farming, you had to have a family farm. Jack joked about the new house his family had bought in town. "It's got an avocado tree," he said to me. "Do you think that qualifies?"

So it's probably an understatement to say that the future for most of the boys, and Jack especially, was cloudy. Mine was not much better, but as the culture would have it, my future had Jack's to depend on. As far as marriage was concerned, we couldn't and didn't dare think of it. Financial concerns still took priority, and nobody could foresee when—or if—the Depression would end.

THAT JACK HAD not yet been drafted kept me in never-never land, and it was only when I went to watch him take the graduation test for a government-sponsored pilot-training program that I was dragged into reality. The program, which gave college credits, had been offered as preparation for war, but that it would actually be put to such use was not something I cared to think about. I felt that the course itself held dangers enough.

With this in mind, I went to Jack's solo with apprehension

so plain that before Jack took off, he spent some time reassuring me. While we waited for the instructor, Jack stood me by the fence at the little airport and turned my head up to the sky. "Look," he said to me. "There's only beautiful stuff up there — no clouds, no hail, no snow — nothing to harm anybody." The instructor arrived and Jack, ready to go, put his arms around me. "You'll see, darling," he said in my ear. "I'll go up and I'll come down. A simple matter."

There was a moment, however, when Jack's instructor, standing next to me, said, "Uh-oh" and the "down" part became anything but simple. And it was at this point that my heart began doing its own up and down. What was happening, and what the instructor had seen, was that the propeller on Jack's plane, which should have resumed turning when he came out of a planned tailspin, had stayed fixed, and Jack was having to find a way to bring the plane down without it. Of course he did — "Came down dead stick," he announced to his instructor with some attempt at an all-in-a-day's-job demeanor — but what it meant to me was that when you were in a plane, what took place between the "up" and the "down" was risky business.

When the instructor said to Jack, "You learned something today. When you get into action, you'll know what to do," I heard it very clearly.

JACK COULD HITCH for free to Tallahassee — whereas I had to buy a bus ticket to go to Gainesville — so he was in Tallahassee more than I was in Gainesville. He never had any trouble getting a ride: all cars leaving Gainesville heading northwest were going to Tallahassee. When he was there, we went to whatever campus events were on, or to the movies, and then mooned about after dark. If we were completely broke, we ate dining hall food, rumored to be full of saltpeter, a substance thought to discourage sexual arousal. Still, if the saltpeter was in there, it failed, for after dark, in the bushes around the dormitories, plenty of heavy breathing could be heard, and not all of it emanated from Jack and me.

There were a few Jewish people in town—families who ran modest dry goods stores like my father's in Tennessee—and they often invited Jack and me into their homes, as they did all the Jewish students they could find by scanning the enrollment lists. They were all southern Jews, born and raised in some part of the South, some right there in Tallahassee. They laughed that they could never "abide" living amid all that "Yankee talk" in South Florida. "Shoot," they might say to me, "y'all got those New York folks down there," and I wondered if, as Jack had said, this meant "loud Jews" and that perhaps what they were really saying was that they had a problem with Jews from the North. They no doubt preferred southern Jews, those whose social manners and attitudes harmonized with their own, those who spoke softly, showed disagreement subtly, and held attitudes toward blacks—whom they called *shvartzerem*—much like my own.

I felt a wall, however, between these Tallahassee Jewish people and myself. It was as if having lived in South Florida, they felt I had given up my birthright as a true-blue good old southern gal. Tallahassee people—Jews and non-Jews—got a lot of support for this kind of thinking. State legislators, many of whom were from redneck counties, made daily references, according to the *Tallahassee Democrat,* the local newspaper, to "those people down there," meaning Dade Countians, or perhaps meaning Jews specifically, as if we were a species apart.

CHAPTER 3

When the first weekend in December came around, Jack and I spent it together in Tallahassee, but that it was to be different from all other weekends was apparent from the moment Jack stepped out on the road to hitch a ride on Saturday morning. That day, he didn't get a ride; he got a whole car. When he waved his hand, the driver stopped, apologized that he wasn't going to Tallahassee, and offered his Ford Model A rumble-seated roadster. Jack accepted. The guy said, "Fill her up, and she's yours," jumped out, and Jack jumped in.

Although Tallahassee was fiercely cold that weekend, we had a car, so we decided to go the few miles out to Wakulla Springs, a river and wildlife refuge home to strange-looking birds with names like anhinga and osprey, and alligators and turtles that lounged on the river banks. Wakulla was the setting for the Tarzan movies, and in this wild fusion of trees, Tarzan could go, as we would have said in Tennessee (and in Talla-hassee), "a-swingin' and a-hollerin'" to his heart's content.

On Sunday morning we had breakfast with the parents of a fraternity brother of Jack's, who had provided a bed for him. We were invited to breakfast—unusual, in that the normal thing was for the hosts to provide a bed and never be heard from again—no doubt because the father of the house, Mr. Satisky, who owned a downtown shoe store, wanted to talk about the war. The German entry into the Soviet Union was a major event, and a worrisome one. "Next stop Moscow," Mr. Satisky told us. He felt sure that America couldn't stay out of it. Jack agreed that if something triggered it, we'd be in. I tried not to get involved in the conversation. I talked to Mrs. Satisky about the movie we were going to see that afternoon. They were going, too, Mrs. Satisky told me. "Something to do," she said.

It was not until late afternoon that the momentous event—the one that was to dominate that weekend, and many, many weekends to come—presented itself. First Jack and I had lunch at a drugstore counter, fooled around uptown, and then went to the "picture show" to see *How Green Was My Valley*.

How Green Was My Valley was full of passions. Jack and I spent a lot of energy commiserating with Welsh miners, and we decided to reward ourselves with dinner at the Dutch Kitchen, where there were tablecloths and an attempt at professional service. As we walked out of the theater on that cold late afternoon in early December, I had nothing on my mind but the Dutch Kitchen.

We had only just stepped onto the sidewalk when we saw

newsboys hawking newspapers and crowds gathering around them. I had seen movies with hawking newsboys, but the setting was always New York, not Tallahassee, Florida. And wasn't it unusual for the *Tallahassee Democrat* to put out a special edition?

We tried to work through the crowds to get to a boy. We didn't need a paper; all we needed was the headline. And there it was, its big, black letters shouting JAPS ATTACK PEARL HARBOR.

I have to confess that the bare headline meant nothing to me. I had never heard of Pearl Harbor. What was it, where was it, and why did we care if the Japs bombed it? Even after I read through the account, it took me a long moment to grasp what it was telling me. But when I did, I understood that the "trigger" that Jack and Mr. Satisky had talked about had been pulled. The war now included us.

The next morning the news had taken over the campus, and the girls gathered around radios to listen to President Roosevelt's speech. What we heard him say clearly (and perhaps never forgot) was that he was asking Congress to declare that since "the unprovoked and dastardly attack," a state of war existed between the United States and Japan. It was chilling. And yet I, and no doubt the other girls, also felt a frisson of excitement.

That afternoon at a student assembly, President Campbell said that we should remain calm, that we could not do our part if we were in a panic. We nodded and wondered if we could will ourselves to remain calm and what our "part" was. And then Dr. Campbell said something utterly foolish, even though it was a day made for saying utterly foolish things: he said we could do our part best by studying hard for upcoming final exams. Study for final exams? I wanted to say, "Lame, very lame, Dr. Campbell," but it occurred to me that President Campbell had an exceedingly tall order. Could he tell naive Tallahassee Lassies (as we called ourselves) how to react when presented with a life-changing event? When presented with a war? At that moment there was little he could say to help us confront the complications, the disruptions, and the fears that lay ahead. So President Campbell chose to tell us to study hard.

As it turned out, there was another thing they didn't, or couldn't, tell us—neither President Roosevelt nor President Campbell. And that was that at Pearl Harbor the Japanese had just about destroyed the U.S. Pacific fleet.

Whether it was seemly or not, I found myself asking how the newly declared war affected Jack and me. It certainly meant that Jack would have to serve in the military, and like many of the boys, he decided to volunteer immediately. There were several motivations for such speed and enthusiasm. First was the emotional factor: your country needed you. Still, for Jack and many like him, it was not to be discounted that serving in the military meant a meaningful job.

Jack said that if he didn't volunteer and waited for the draft, he would have no assignment choice, and he definitely wanted to keep away from the artillery and the infantry. At Florida, he had put in the required ROTC time with those services, which still operated with World War I equipment and old, tough-mouthed horses, and he wanted no further part. Still, this volunteering notion had me apprehensive, and when Jack came to Tallahassee the following weekend, I wanted to talk about it. "Don't you want to wait and think it over?" I asked him. Jack explained that no, he wanted to volunteer now. "This way I don't have to wait for them to call the shots. I can do what I want." It sounded reasonable. What I didn't know was that this statement had less foresight than any statement Jack would ever make.

His choice was to enter as a cadet in the Army Air Corps, having some confidence that his newly acquired pilot's license, which certified him to operate a one-hundred-horsepower airplane, would be a plus for getting him into the pilot-training program. As for my own feelings about his joining the Air Corps, didn't I remember that "uh-oh" afternoon? Of course I did, but with things moving so fast, any objection I might have would be swept away.

Furthermore, clear sky for Jack meant clear sky for me as well. Jack's being in the service meant a monthly paycheck— seventy-five dollars!—and a monthly paycheck meant that we could choose to get married. Although cadets were supposed to be single, the recruiting officer had told Jack that the rule applied only to enlistment. "You want to get married after, it's okay with the Air Corps," he had said to Jack. "After you're in, you want a ball and chain, the Air Corps says she's your problem."

A lot of his fraternity brothers enlisted at the same time as Jack. Some of them, like Irv Rubin, one of Jack's closest friends, also enlisted in the Air Corps, but Irv and most of the others chose to take the deferment that would keep them out until the end of the school year. Jack asked for nothing beyond the thirty-day leave automatically given upon enlistment. He wanted in, and he wanted to get married.

We made plans based on his leave: we would get married, and when his orders came, I would follow as soon he was settled into a training situation. We then addressed ourselves to taking our final exams—I'm afraid I didn't study very hard; sorry, Dr. Campbell—after which we went home for the Christmas holidays.

This was a very different Christmas break, for we would not be going back to school. The semester that Jack lacked to graduate and the three I lacked would have to wait. Wait till when, we didn't know, but we felt no anxiety about it. Still, consciously or subconsciously we were both aware that school was unfinished business, that we were sidelined only "for the duration," which was a phrase we would find ourselves using over and over as the war wore on.

And when we did return? When I gave myself a moment to look into the future, I saw Jack teaching at a university. It may have been a romantic notion built around tweed jackets and leather elbow patches, or it may have been that I saw university life as a natural match for Jack's personality, but whatever the reasons, my dream was that when the "duration" had run its course, Jack would be a college professor.

For now, however, there were urgent matters to think about, and as if to affirm this, a few days after Jack enlisted, things began moving frighteningly fast. Germany and Italy declared war on the United States, the United States returned the favor, and on Christmas Day the Japanese captured Hong Kong.

On the homefront, Roosevelt was requiring the registration of all aliens, and Japanese-Americans who lived in coastal Pacific areas—aliens or not, and most were American citizens—were being moved into internment camps. We all seemed to think it was a prudent precaution, even if they were forced to give up their land, their homes, and their businesses. Didn't everybody know that the Japanese felt more loyalty to their real homeland than to America? Internment was the right thing to do, wasn't it? After all, right after Pearl Harbor, Japanese troops had captured Manila and had invaded the Dutch East Indies, and who was to say that Japanese-Americans had not provided intelligence? We were caught up in such a panic that there were only a few voices of dissent, and these were accused loudly of being shortsighted. Still, Jack was ambivalent. "They're *citizens*, some of them," he said. "Since when do we deprive *citizens* of their rights?"

Jack's thirty-day leave gave us just enough time to make plans for a wedding, have the ceremony, and go on a honeymoon. The first thing we did was purchase a wedding ring—a gold wedding band with a vine twining round. There was no ring for Jack. Matching rings were seldom seen in those days.

In the circumstances, we decided that a small wedding at home for just the local families was appropriate. My mother and I shopped on Lincoln Road for my wedding ensemble, and we selected not what Union City girls would have worn, war or no war—a white silk gown with Chantilly lace, seed pearls, and covered buttons—but a blue Vera Maxwell suit and a leghorn hat made of fine straw and with a wide, wide brim. "Enough with the boppy socks already," my mother told me, as if she suspected that since I wouldn't be twenty until one week later, I might be planning to wear them. "It's time to be grown-up."

But what I didn't know about being grown-up, my mother was not prepared to tell me. Even if my mother had been racked and pinioned, she would have held to her silence on intimate matters. Such things were not in her province; they were in the province of me and my American friends. So there was not much of a conversation between my mother and me about being "grown-up."

There was yet another way to be grown-up, however, and that was to have a rabbi preside at our wedding. After having had nothing to do with a rabbi for so many years, I felt that for such an important event I ought at last to make a connection. Jack, of course, was opposed. No, he insisted, no rabbi; just a city hall deputy clerk. "Darling," he said, half-joking, half not, "are you asking me to convert?"

Well, he was asking *me* to get a deputy clerk, one of those "city hall hacks," as the locals called them. Could I ask one of these to preside at my wedding? My mother put an oar in by suggesting the rabbi from the little synagogue down on South Beach, whose establishment I had basically ignored all these years. "He won't hold it against you, he's a *mensch*," my mother said, meaning he was a man of character.

The rabbi—no rabbi dustup had us looking at the similarities and the differences in how Jack and I viewed religion. Jack was not only an antideist but an even more determined antireligionist. In all the bull sessions he had been a party to—and bull sessions had been a dominant feature of his life—during the talk about religion, he'd cheerfully proclaimed himself an atheist and wanted to know why we should be obligated to live by ideologies cooked up in primitive times by primitive men. If you pressed him to be open to debating the existence of God, he would laugh and say that he didn't feel an obligation to discuss a proposition that seemed to him to have no valid basis for *being* a proposition.

Jack's progress toward this view was smoothed by a father just as nonbelieving as mine and with even more credibility, as in New York there had been an array of Orthodox, Conservative, and Reform houses of worship that he'd forbade his kids to attend, whereas what with Union City having no synagogue at all, my father's gesture in this direction would have been pretty empty. Furthermore, Jack's father had been successful in prohibiting his sons from having Bar Mitzvahs, while my father had acceded—if profoundly reluctantly—when my mother had sent Will to New York for his, and Will had had a ceremony there, albeit a perfunctory one, with none of his Tennessee family in attendance.

As for the mothers, Jack's mother's lifestyle dictated the way she approached religion. Being social, his mother fell in with the prevailing attitude of her friends that being religious and "keeping kosher" were from "the dark ages," a period of time she and her friends referred to with horror. Despite her husband's antagonism toward synagogues, however, she went to the Reform temple for services during the High Holidays, though more for social reasons than for religious ones—which she readily admitted—and never insisted that her children accompany her.

Still, none of our parents, nonbelievers included, shied away from calling themselves Jews. They loved Jewish music, Jewish humor, Jewish food. They obviously felt a strong bond with Jewishness. Describe it as you will—as a call to ethnicity, to loyalty, to custom; whatever it was, it kept both our families in the fold.

I don't think any of these "calls" satisfied either Jack or me. Jack was familiar with them but refused to be drawn in in any binding way; and I was not even familiar with them. In addition, I was still in a state of unresolved conflict about God. Though I agreed with Jack without question that there was no intervening God, no God putting in time nurturing and protecting, no God to appeal to in moments of stress, I could not characterize myself an atheist. I clung to my father's views in this respect. I felt that a god of creation was something to be considered, and I wished fervently that to avoid the confusion there could be some other name for this kind of god, a name that did not suggest a who so much as a what. Jack had no such wishes. To him it was all accident, all adaptation, all natural selection, all Darwin, all the way.

As for rejecting our Jewishness, it was not unusual for Jews to try to "pass," but neither Jack nor I had any inclination in this direction. In any event, society would not have given us permission to do so, even if society remained unruffled when Protestants changed allegiances. My father always quoted Brookie Simmons, that one educated, enlightened Union City resident, on this maladjusted state of affairs. According to my father, what Brookie Simmons said was, "Protestants can change denominations as if they were samplin' preserves at the county fair, but a Jew could become a Hottentot and take to stammerin' and people would call him a Jew all the same."

Despite my doubts, I felt that there was something, *something*, about being counted as Jewish that was positive and life affirming, though at this moment I did not have time to probe in any serious way for that elusive something. I was busy getting married, and there was an immediate problem: rabbi or justice of the peace?

Just as we seemed to have reached an impasse, a solution appeared in the form of a young rabbi from the Gainesville Hillel Society—a campus Jewish group—who suddenly turned up in town. As he was someone whom Jack liked very much, having fought through many a bull session with him, Jack backed down, and a rabbi, promising to honor Jack's request to keep mention of God to a minimum, presided after all.

That settled, things proceeded. My mother clipped some bougainvillea bracts from her bushes, dethorned them, and made a bouquet for me; the mothers wept, perhaps for the usual "joining of two young people starting out on the road of life" or perhaps because a war was out there waiting for these particular two young people; the rabbi said some words; Jack asked, "Do you mind if I get under this thing with you?," meaning my hat; then he managed to get under it and kiss me; and all at once Jack and I were husband and wife.

Our honeymoon was a week in West Palm Beach. My father rented us a car, and Jack's father arranged for a stay at a nice hotel with a view of Lake Worth. As to the "intimate matters" that my mother was not prepared to discuss with me, they were not exactly a mystery. I had sat in on plenty of discussions about them, how you "did it" and what to expect from doing it, and I had been that "best friend" for girls whose home plates had been crossed. So I was definitely not unaware. Still, it was true that I was not one of those girls.

Of course, Jack and I had talked about it. He'd said over and over that by holding out I was being irrational and conventional, not to say childish. He would say, "It's not as if nobody does it," trying to impress upon me that it was a natural act, indulged in by all creatures. The only plea he didn't offer was the usual "You'd do it if you loved me," for he knew I loved him, and he knew I knew he knew. Still, though my position was implausible even to me, I had been overtaken by a foolish stubbornness that wouldn't let go.

Jack had had the usual teenage/fraternity-boy sexual experiences, and these came in handy on that first night when I was trying to figure out what I was supposed to be doing. Jack tried to tell me what to expect, but of course he had an impossible job. He said it was like climbing a mountain as high as Everest and reaching the top and feeling earth, wind, and fire all at once, and of course it was. But it was more than that.

I was disconcerted for only that briefest first moment with its strange bit of pain. And then I had reached the top, and I remembered what Jack had said, for I was aware of earth, wind, and fire and all at once. But I had another thought. I was convinced that the feelings that coursed through me were not meant for humans but for angels. Had I been able to do that all along and had oh so foolishly resisted?

Since we were young people, and spoke as young people did, Jack asked me—softly, lovingly, as if he already knew the answer—"So, did we climb Everest?"

And I said yes, darling, we did. Not only had we climbed it,

I said, we had planted a flag. And then, as I recall, we planted another. And another.

On the rare occasion when we weren't in our hotel room, we went out to dinner and to the dog races—both of us bearing the genes of fathers who didn't mind a wager or two (though Jack's genes were more demanding than mine). We lost a lot of our honeymoon money and retreated to a cheaper hotel with a view not of Lake Worth's blue waters lapping on the far shore at the mansions of Palm Beach but of the municipal parking lot. It didn't bother us.

In the couple of weeks remaining until Jack's orders would arrive, we stayed with Jack's family in their new home in town. We didn't do much of anything except read the papers and try to keep up with the events that were careening ahead. Tensions grew daily. Jack's father would get the paper early and greet us with a long face. Each morning brought more bad news. Japanese troops had captured Singapore; Japan's naval forces had won the Battle of the Java Sea.

Jack and I went for drives up and down Ocean Drive on Miami Beach, and Jack made his usual acid comments on the signs we saw there, the ones saying NO JEWS ALLOWED or some variation thereof. We tried to do normal things, be with friends, read a book. But few of our friends were around, and I, at least, had no patience for reading. Jack did. While I was busy waiting, he was reading. But I knew he was busy waiting too. Jack was waiting to go to war, and I was waiting to go with him.

Finally Jack's orders came through. He was to report to Maxwell Field in Montgomery, Alabama. Maxwell Field! We knew about Maxwell; everybody knew about Maxwell. What we knew was that it was a distinguished air base where all things military were state of the art, where all matters were carried out with phenomenal efficiency and dispatch. Still, we knew that Maxwell was to be merely a staging center for Jack, a first step before he would be sent out on definite assignment to one of the Army Air Corps flight-training installations. Jack left with high hopes that he would be in and out of Maxwell in jig time and I would be joining him at his training site. Almost too bad, we thought, thinking of all those fabled Maxwell amenities.

Jack's very first letters suggested that we were laboring under a monumental pile of misapprehensions. First of all, when Jack arrived in Montgomery, he found he was not at Maxwell Field at all. The Maxwell Field of lore was on the other side of town, and the prospects of getting in on Maxwell's facilities and diversions were virtually nonexistent. Furthermore, he was not in the trim "quarters" the prewar recruitment posters pictured but in a rough barracks of two-tiered bunks and occasional latrines, all slapped together in a defunct seven-story cotton mill surrounded by a locked fence. As his return address, Jack wrote "Cellblock C, third floor."

The "inmates," as Jack called himself and his fellow cadets, had little to do, and, as befitted inmates, were taken out on "daily exercises," which were nothing more than marching inside the fenced areas. It might seem curious that Jack, whose athletic prowess was never in doubt, could not get the hang of marching, but he wrote me that his drillmaster had suggested that he had an extra foot. I, for one, was not surprised that

Jack could not be taught to march, for doing things in lockstep was not his way. Still, it didn't bother Jack much. "I don't think I'll be marching much after I get into combat," he wrote me, "so what's the problem?" What indeed?

Assignment didn't appear to be in the works. "They don't seem to have heard there's a war on," Jack wrote. "The closest we've gotten to it is wearing uniforms and marching." The housing story got even less attractive: when the mill eventually ran out of space for the endlessly arriving cadets, the earlier "inmates" were sent over to Gunter Field, an airfield that housed a primary pilot-training facility, where they were again superfluous. So they were packed into a collection of tents from which they could watch, no doubt with envy, the flying exercises on the other side of the field.

"Writing from Tent City," Jack now announced. Gunter, like the old mill, provided no activity except marching. Still, there was, finally, a big event. "Big day in Tent City," Jack reported. The cadets had been given baseball bats, though not, as it turned out, for use in the traditional way but for dealing with what Jack called "the Montgomery wildlife"—the rats who had set up a lifestyle in the latrines outside the tents. Since the order also said to wear gloves, and since the cadets possessed only dress whites, they donned these as they went about carrying out their orders. "Our fashionable attire just dazzled them," Jack wrote of the rats' end. "They basically died of humiliation." That was life at Gunter Field, and it was to be Jack's life for almost three months.

MEANWHILE, I MOVED in with my parents and waited. My father suggested that I work in the store again. The draft had taken his store manager, and this loss, together with my father's purchase of another parcel of land (which meant he had to search out draftproof construction workers and cajole them into building his stores), may have meant that he really needed me.

My father said I could work as much or as little as I pleased. "Come," he told me. "You'll be here and you won't be here, whatever you want." And so I went back to being a daughter working in her father's store.

I was usually at the cash register, but I liked working the soda fountain, though my work there—especially with sundaes—was too artistic for my father. All this labor in the name of art took time, and my father would say, "Stella, sweetheart, get a move on. You're not putting up the Empire State Building."

Ours was a famous fountain, chiefly because we were the only one in town to offer mango toppings for sundaes. These came from my mother's two mango trees—a Haden and a Tommy Atkins, both of which were prolific producers. Mangoes being available only in the summer, the winter crowd missed out, but the year-rounders came in droves.

The store's workers were the full-time soda jerks, some part-time high school kids, and the men who did the food. The latter were drawn from the contingent of short-order cooks who journeyed around town from one restaurant kitchen to another. They were usually with us for only a few days. Sometimes they had to be fired—usually for drunkenness—but sometimes they just disappeared, occasionally leaving behind a paycheck. Just as I got to know their names, they weren't there anymore.

As for customers, Tropical and Hialeah were still racing, which meant that the players, though their ranks had been thinned by the draft, were still coming in. The buzzwords were the same: "daily double," "five to two," and "Didja have him?"

I went around a lot with Laura Dunlap, a friend of mine from high school, who was pretty and rich, though not *rich* rich. Like me, Laura had a husband in the service and was living at home with her mother, who, as I understood it, got by on alimony from her ex-husband.

Laura's home was nothing like mine. Our house was the typical Miami Beach concrete-block stucco house, which my mother had furnished with dark things from New York and the occasional wicker piece from Miami; the Dunlap home was a spacious apartment in one of the Beach's signature four-unit buildings. To me the Dunlap residence was a white fantasy out of a Jean Harlow film: white furniture (with gold trim), white rugs, white draperies flanking white venetian blinds. Laura's bedroom was also glamorous—all hers, and the bed was round. Big and round and full of pillows.

Mrs. Dunlap and her friends—which included both men and women—played a lot of bridge, for which the Dunlap men wore Norfolk jackets over Bermuda shorts, and the women wore wide-legged lounging pyjamas (as this kind of sophisticated pajama was spelled, in the British way). They had cocktails before they went out for dinner, a concept new to me. The only drinks at my home were ceremonial wine and the occasional schnapps that my father drank when his appetite was low or when we had company. Most Jewish people I knew drank this way. It was said that the Jewish country clubs in

Palm Beach were forced to ask huge entrance fees because the bars simply didn't pull their weight.

Laura had been at college when Bobby Quigley, the boy she had gone steady with in high school, had been drafted. Just as the romance was petering out, Laura had quit school and rushed back to marry him. Bobby's family lived in Smith Cottages, and he was older than we were, having had a couple of setbacks in school—which, since he was a football star, we made part of his legend.

Bobby had not gone to college. It was the practice of banks then to hire popular hometown boys to act as the bank's personal face, and Bobby had gotten hired by First National as their greeter, the one who stood at the lobby door and smiled. Now, however, Bobby was a private in the infantry, in Camp Blanding.

JACK AND I WERE still writing each other daily, and after I read each letter to myself once, twice, and then to my folks and Laura, I carefully put it on the growing stack in my drawer. The Montgomery–Miami Beach letters that flowed between Jack and me were the first of the hundreds of letters we would write to each other, to our families, and to our friends during the war years. Letter writing was what we all did then. The country was in a constant state of flux: sons (and daughters), fathers, and husbands were stationed here, then there, and then only at mysterious APO addresses. Civilians traveled around the country, and sometimes overseas, to conduct war business. Letters were the glue that held all of us together.

My family had had a head start on the practice of intensive letter writing, for when we were living in Tennessee, all alone, our kith and kin far away in New York, letters had gone back and forth until it seemed they could find their way by themselves. My mother wrote to her parents every week, and to her brothers and sisters often; we children took turns writing to the cousins. When my brother went to New York, the letter-writing pace picked up considerably. And when we left Union City, we wrote regularly to the friends we had left behind.

In my family there was no question of throwing any letter away. My father was so proud of his children's ability to "write a good letter," as he would say, that when we were away from home every letter went into a shoe box, then into a dress box, then into a chest of drawers (or "chifforobe," as we said in Union City). Our family knew to save letters.

Everybody knew to save war letters. Instinct said that you would someday want to read and reread them, those you got and those you sent. And it was true that letters were considered so important that if any were found in the effects of those killed in action, they were carefully gathered and sent home to the family.

The letters I saved from Jack's Montgomery assignment were only the beginning of my stash. The fact was, I wrote more than anybody else in the family, and for understandable reasons: I was either away from home, traveling around with a husband in the military, or I was at home and he was away, in the States or overseas. I was somewhat surprised to learn that no matter the situation, no matter the conditions, Jack was able, as I found out, to keep my letters as well.

In the after years, as I have read through my letters—not just to Jack but to my parents, to my sisters and brother—it seems to me I must have by heritage or by osmosis acquired the southern love of storytelling, for I have been astonished at how much I wrote and in what detail. I found one letter to Jack in which I devoted two pages to our soda jerk Stan and the lady who sat in her Auburn night after night waiting for him. In the letter I quoted Stan often, especially his endless double entendres, like "Hope she's keeping her motor running." In answer, Jack wrote, "Hope you're keeping your motor running, too."

FOLLOWING OUR ENTRY into the war, Miami Beach entrepreneurs were exceedingly gloomy about the town's immediate future. Think about it, they said; this is a resort, and who's coming to a resort during a war? When you looked around, however, it didn't look as if the tourist industry of Miami Beach was doing a whole lot of suffering. You saw as many tourists as ever. Lincoln Road was jammed with Packards, Lincolns, and Cadillacs; hotel lobbies were all a-chatter; the bath clubs were bustling. Bath club members were often quoted in the *Herald*'s society column, proclaiming they were in Miami Beach for the winter because it was patriotic to stay fit. "Why do they need to stay fit?" my father would ask. "To talk to their investment brokers?" My father's sunny disposition, which turned cloudy only when he thought an injustice had been done, turned very dark indeed when he thought he had spotted a slacker.

There came the day, however, when business as usual was turned on its head. All at once the rich tourists in bathing attire and tuxedos had metamorphosed into men in khaki, and they were swarming all over the Beach. The Army had turned Miami Beach into a training ground for the U.S. Army Air Corps Officer Candidate School—or OCS, as it was referred to forevermore. It was a three-month course, and the OCS students were called "ninety-day wonders."

When we recovered from the shock, it seemed logical, for here in Miami Beach were all these hotels, and hotels meant housing. The only surprise was that the Army—which I, at least, had come to believe didn't always do things in the straightest line—had also thought it a logical solution and, more to the point, had acted on it.

So it was that in short order the hotels were taken over (with generous compensation, to be sure) by the Army, and men in government-issue khaki took up residence in these posh hotels—those "portholed" and "eyelidded" Art Deco palaces originally intended for the custom-made-suit set. And soon the town was alive with military movement and sounds.

Truly the whole town was a drill field. There was not a moment in the day when I could not hear men marching through the streets shouting "sound off" repetitions. The drill sergeants would sing out a line like "I left my girl in Singapore" and troops would echo; then the sergeants would sing out, "She left me at the kitchen door," with the men again echoing, until the routine was completed with "Sound off, one two *three four*." Platoons marched to and from classes, and from some street or another "I've got sixpence, jolly, jolly sixpence" would fill the air. It was exciting—no, thrilling, more like a movie; in fact, exactly like a movie. And it was happening in my Miami Beach.

If the celebrities no longer performed in the hotels and night-clubs, it didn't mean an end to the celebrities. We had them as soldiers. I often spotted Tony Martin dining out with local girls, and since he wore an enlisted man's uniform, I assumed he was not a "wonder" but was doing some kind of office work. Sports stars turned up. Miami Beach Jews *kvelled* over the presence of Hank Greenberg, and if he didn't make it to dinner in every Jewish home on the Beach, it didn't mean he hadn't been invited. Some hosts, clearly not dedicated baseball fans, never got it straight and called his team the "Detroit Yankees," but no matter.

Then there was the day when Miami Beach welcomed the celebrity of all celebrities—the brightest star in the firmament, as Louella Parsons would say. Clark Gable arrived for OCS training. Clark Gable! We not only adored him as a movie star, we now sympathized with him, for he was a grieving husband. His wife had been the actress Carole Lombard, and she had been killed in a plane crash after a bond rally. The movie magazines—at my father's store I read every one of them—had it that Clark was so distraught that he had enlisted.

It was not enough for Clark Gable to be glimpsed; he was to be stalked, and one day Laura and I stationed ourselves in what an educated guess told us would be his line of passage. We waited, and then suddenly there he was, marching along, singing as lustily as everyone else. He was shorter than I had imagined, not short but not tall either. Still, the shoulders were there and the strong face. We staked him out a couple of times, watched Clark Gable coming, watched Clark Gable going. And we finally had to say he seemed just a soldier in among fellow soldiers, another officer candidate going to class, striving for his officer's bars.

It was interesting to see how Miami Beach responded when the trappings of war descended. Miami Beach was a special case, we thought, a resort town that could not be expected to play a serious wartime role except to house soldiers, though we did take the step of changing the name of the causeway—hitherto just the Fifth Street Causeway—to MacArthur Causeway.

Townspeople were now making a practice of inviting the OCS boys into their homes. It may have been that Gentile families invited only Gentile servicemen, but Jewish families definitely made an effort on behalf of Jewish servicemen, feeling they would like to have Jewish food and perhaps talk in the *mamalushen,* the old tongue. My parents had servicemen over almost every weekend, and the boys seemed to thoroughly enjoy my mother's kasha *varnishkes.* I liked having servicemen in the house: in their company I could try out my new role of Army wife. But that was about it for the "war effort" until the day a tanker was hit by a German submarine up the coast.

It was that disaster that finally shook the community. When another tanker was hit soon after, we felt something ominous closing in on us. This one involved a neutral Mexican ship carrying crude oil that had been torpedoed by a German submarine. Thirteen Mexicans had been killed. As the ship burned offshore, we stood on the beach, rooted to it, unable to tear ourselves away from what we were seeing.

It was then that blackouts were ordered, and we drew our shades after dark, though since dim car lights were permitted, it seemed more a "dimout" than a "blackout." Still, the idea of trying to stay safe, of thwarting the enemy wherever we could, had taken hold.

The torpedoings of the tankers were only the beginning. Before it was all over, 165 tankers and freighters would be sunk in the shipping lanes off our shore. Down at the beach, I had to pick my way around tar and oil stains, tattletale signs of submarine-sunk ships. It seemed inconceivable that there were submarines off the coast of my Miami Beach, my land of frivolities, but I could not deny the evidence.

"Contributing to the war effort" was now everybody's goal. My father had already stuck flags in various places around the store—in the windows, behind the counters, hanging out from the patent-medicine shelves—but he sought a way to do more, so he joined a group of older men who took turns patrolling the beach looking for submarines. And like everyone else, he bought war bonds with great enthusiasm. Now, as he would say, he could put his money where his mouth was. "We don't win this war, what good's my money anyway?" he'd ask my mother and me.

The *Herald* had been reporting that England was in a bad way for consumer goods, and my mother joined in with a group of neighborhood women to cobble together care packages. The women filled the packages routinely with sugar and oils and canned fish—and cigarettes, cigarettes, cigarettes—but on the list of suggested items in the *Herald*, canned hams (hams!) were right at the top. What to do? In the end, even those who kept a kosher home went out and bought canned hams, and when after a while canned hams got scarce, the women substituted cans of Spam, which never seemed to be less than plentiful.

As for me, I became an occasional nursing assistant, hospital nurses having been recruited for the services. Our biggest hospital—Jackson Memorial, in town—seemed to be the one most in need, so I drove over in the family Buick a couple of afternoons a week and, after an emergency course, learned how to check pulses and take temperatures. The nursing staff insisted that I have a graduation ceremony, and they presented me with a cafeteria cake with a big 98.6° on it.

But it was at the old rambling pier down on South Beach that I put in most of my war-effort time. Somebody had decided that all these soldiers marching around town needed recreation, so the pier—a fishing pier hitherto known simply as Municipal Pier and whose claim to fame was that down at the end of it was Minsky's Burlesque theater—was renamed Servicemen's Pier and reinvented as a recreation venue.

Recreation meant dancing, and when a call went out for partners, Laura and I took ourselves down to the pier and answered the call, along with a lot of other girls—married and single, tall and short, fat and slim, Jewish and Gentile. Whatever our motivation—answering the call that our country needed us, hoping to meet guys, or just wanting to dance—we turned up. No black girls came, for surely no recruitment plea ever went out to them.

When we went to the pier, we got dressed up. We wore our Lincoln Road dresses and hats—little ones with feathers or flowers that wouldn't get in anybody's way. We wore high heels and stockings, never bobby socks. It was hot in the hall, and we perspired so profusely that dresses shrank while we were wearing them. One night the long sleeves of my fuschia crepe climbed to my elbows and the medium hemline to the tops of my knees, and at that point I went home.

We didn't just dance, however; we also listened. The servicemen clearly needed somebody to talk to, and they talked and they talked: of their hometowns, of their old sports teams, of the girls they'd left behind. They were also not beyond casting a line that might catch a replacement for the girl they left behind, and sometimes a pier girl allowed herself to be reeled in.

The men liked to complain—"gripe" was the current word—about the difference between the picture they had had of military service in Miami Beach and the reality. They had pictured sunbathing on the beach and instead got rigorous beach calisthenics. They had envisioned luxury hotel rooms and they'd gotten them, though it was a case of being careful of what you wish for, since, as one soldier told me, his room had venetian blinds that had to be dusted every day, "on *both* sides." And how were they supposed to make hospital corners on eight-inch mattresses with "skinny" army cot sheets?

When I wrote Jack about their gripes, he wrote back that "those guys at Fort Miami Beach" brought tears to his eyes. "Having to endure that seventy-eight degree weather must be murder," he wrote. "And all that sun and surf. What a nightmare."

The servicemen did appreciate the weather, but they felt that "Fort Miami Beach" was like any camp, except that in this particular fort the rifle range was on the edge of the ocean. We watched it often—troops on one side of the street firing at targets on the sands on the other side. And we had to wonder again at the thought processes of the army that put officer candidates in hotels so close to the sea. German submarines were in that sea, and why wouldn't they just fire away late at night and eliminate all future Air Corps administrators?

At the pier, we had servicemen from all the services, and we had foreign servicemen, some from installations where they were taking pilot training, some just passing through. We had Poles, Brits, Chinese, nationals from all countries except the Axis ones. We did "hands, knees, and boompsa daisy" with the British; we did the polka with the Poles. The Chinese were very hard to follow, but we did our best. The most dazzling were the South Americans. They more than just rumba'd and samba'd and mamboed; they tangoed. I was never truly able to conquer the tango; all those impetuous, imperious leg twists and head thrusts defeated me. We knew to watch ourselves with the South Americans. They seemed to us the embodiment of Spanish "bloods," those dashing young men we had read about so often in romance novels. They spoke lovely words and flashed beautiful smiles, and their moves were very, very sensual.

The only servicemen not represented at the pier were black servicemen. I took it that there were no black servicemen in the OCS program, and we did not draw any from the larger area. I had never seen any using the beach, though it was true that even before the soldiers came, local blacks never swam in "our" ocean. If they wanted to swim, they went to the all-black beach on Virginia Key.

Although there wasn't much drinking at the pier, there was an intense amount of smoking. I, for one, smoked all I could—there was no possible way that I could work more smoking into my day. And as I had only to grab a pack off a shelf in my father's store, cigarettes cost me nothing. I had always smoked Lucky Strikes, which came in a green package, but all at once the package was white, and the slogan was "Lucky Strike Green Has Gone to War." The word was that green pigment was needed in the war effort. It was the kind of explanation that nobody ever questioned: the words "war effort" were enough.

We danced with everybody. No one was ever slighted, no matter what he looked like, no matter if he was a "dreamboat" or a "drip," no matter if he danced as if he had forgotten to take off his army boots. Cutting in was an accepted practice. All the girls were popular, though Laura was perhaps the most popular of all. With her tanned skin and sun-streaked hair, these unworldly boys found her glamorous and sophisticated, the very manifestation of the Miami Beach girl.

We lindied (the lindy was now danced with a lot of bouncing and capering and was called jitterbugging) to fast swing music, like "Stomping at the Savoy" and "Goody Goody." But with the slower stuff—"I'm in the Mood for Love" or "All the Things You Are"—the atmosphere went quiet and a little dangerous. That's when the boys held the girls close, and the girls' heads slipped to the boys' shoulders. And nobody cut in. I had a passing thought that somebody was going to get into trouble.

There were plenty of "good-time girls," married girls or single ones who dated boys whose marital status was iffy. Since men did not routinely wear wedding rings, it was a guessing game. The modus operandi for these girls was to exclusively date somebody in the present class, say good-bye, and then date somebody in the new class. It was like going steady for a few months at a time, and if the girls were married, you figured that after the war, they'd just scurry back to their husbands. These girls talked among themselves about the men, discussed who they thought was married and who not, compared notes on the best places to go for privacy. It was a game a lot of the girls played—the "other" girls, certainly not Laura or me, I thought.

In the early winter of 1942, though the war was not going at all well, spirits at the pier were high. Patriotic banners and exhortative posters—REMEMBER PEARL HARBOR! and OUR BOYS CAN DO IT—hung from the walls and ceiling. Every once in a while the place broke into song, and we often sang "Over There." We knew it was from World War I, but we sang it anyway, for singing about the Yanks being on their way felt very, very good.

JACK AND I HAD been writing each other for weeks, planning a time for me to come to Montgomery, and the weekend finally arrived. I had thought Laura would go see Bobby at the same time, but she said Bobby had written that there was nothing to do in Starke. I didn't anticipate that there would be much to do in Montgomery either, but Montgomery was not the reason I was going. Two months had passed since Jack and I had been together, and though letters were fine and said a lot, they didn't take the place of my being with Jack. I wanted to love him and not with words and not from a distance.

I was to stay in a downtown Montgomery hotel, and I took a taxi from the train station. All the way in, I was in a state of near breathlessness. At the hotel, as I stood at the reception desk, I was thinking that I was early and would have to wait before Jack would come knocking at my door. As I took the pen to sign the register, there was a movement at my back and someone was whispering in my ear, someone trying to do a southern accent and failing badly. "Ah'm jes' so pleased to see you, Miss Scarlett" was what I made out, and when I turned around, there was Jack.

The man was Jack, and yet not Jack. At least he was not like any Jack I had been envisioning, because this Jack was wearing an olive drab cadet's uniform, and he had taken on the appearance of a military man, even if he was a military man whose arms I wanted to throw myself into. Uniforms and long-legged men seemed to go together very nicely.

Never mind how he looked. He had smiled that smile, the one that radiated over everything around him, and when he took me in his arms, I thought my heart would jump right into his. If I had been almost out of breath coming to the hotel in the taxi, there was at this moment no breath left in me at all.

We held each other all the way up in the elevator. And when we got to the room, we could not let go. Unpacking could wait, talking could wait, dinner could wait. Only one thing couldn't: us, in each other's arms, in the bed.

Afterward, when we started out for dinner, I put on one of Jack's favorite dresses—an apricot-colored silk dress with a very swirly skirt—and Jack said that I looked "a-bloom."

Well, I *was* a-bloom. I was with Jack and I was a-bloom with love.

Jack had brought another uniform, which was exactly like the first one, and had changed into it. If I was not surprised that Jack was wearing uniforms beautifully, I was surprised that he hadn't carped about it, as in the past he would have, and loudly. I came to understand this to be a reflection of his attitude toward the war. He seemed not just to have accepted but to have strongly embraced the idea that this was a war that had to be fought, and he seemed glad to be a part of the team that was going to fight it—even if it meant wearing a uniform. As he later wrote to me, "The uniform symbolizes what an army is—a vast mechanism with a single mission. And in this case the mission is a good and noble one." It was Jack writing in his literary mode, but he was telling me what I needed to hear.

Still, in downtown Montgomery the next day, where there were, of course, multitudes of uniforms, when I saw him saluting officers, everything again seemed preposterous. Jack in uniform and saluting? Where were we? In the Army? And what were we? Grown-ups?

I was in Montgomery for two nights, and Jack was allowed out of Gunter until noon on Monday. He brought me out there, just long enough for me to confirm the tents and the latrines, if not the rats, and he took pains to have me meet his commander, Lieutenant Abercorn. Lieutenant Abercorn was so fresh out of ROTC that he still wore his ROTC-isssued calvary boots and, being a southerner, was nice and polite. We engaged in a little conversation, though Jack was not interested in a little conversation; he was interested in my hearing Lieutenant

Abercorn say "hep." Lieutenant Abercorn obliged almost immediately, right after the how-do-you-do's. "Your visit will be a mighty big hep to Jack's morale," he said to me.

Since Jack had also gotten a special pass to visit Maxwell, we spent an afternoon at this installation that was so huge and at the same time so precise it seemed its greenery might have been tended with nail clippers. Jack's cadet pass did not extend to any of the real splendors—the officers' club, the dining room, the gymnasium—so after taking a panoramic look, Jack joked, "Just think, someday all this will be ours."

What he wanted to know, I knew, was when "someday" would be. He was clearly frustrated that there was still, at Gunter, no promise of the flight training that would lead to his becoming a pilot and an officer. Jack said he'd never thought he would be itching to get into a war. "The war's just running away from me," he had written to me.

A war "running away" would have been okay if, in the running, some military successes could have been scored. But at this point in time there were few triumphs. A lot had indeed been happening, but most of it was bad. Especially awful news had just come in. Allied naval forces—American, British, Dutch, and Australian—had taken severe losses in a Java Sea battle with a Japanese invasion convoy, and Japanese forces had overrun the Netherlands Indies.

At Gunter Jack was not alone in feeling frustrated. It was a combination of things—the war going badly, no assignment for flight training, and, not to be overlooked, unrelieved boredom. The days apparently consisted of going to class to learn about the history and the exploits of the Air Corps, reading

This Is Your Air Corps manuals, and marching. As for the man who said he was there to "hep" them, his "hep" was minimal. His only real role was as an ear for listening to gripes, though, as I knew from my experiences with the servicemen on the pier, it was a help not to be underestimated.

At any rate, after seeing Maxwell, Jack and I had dinner downtown, along with other servicemen and their dates, at a restaurant with a pianist pro who knew all the songs. Dancing with Jack was the next best thing to a real embrace. He may not have been the most adventurous of dancers (though on this night he twirled me a lot, so that my swirly skirt could swirl), but when he held me close, close, close, I wouldn't have exchanged the moment for all the Argentine tangos in the Southern Hemisphere.

When it got late, the pianist stayed with the softer songs, and played them with a kind of sweet melancholy. As we danced, as we sighed, we may not have been precisely what Dinah Shore sang about in "A Boy in Khaki, a Girl in Lace," but we would do.

The next morning, Jack got me to the train station, I went back to Miami Beach, and Jack went back to his tent.

AFTER I GOT BACK from Montgomery, I continued my duties at Jackson Memorial and at the pier. And then one night things at the pier seemed not to be proceeding as usual. Laura was not doing her typical changing of partners but was, in fact, dancing with just one guy. I knew him: he was Don Nager, from Detroit, a lieutenant stationed at the Opa-Locka Naval Air Station. This warranted taking a better look, for the song they were dancing to, "Fools Rush In," was one in which caution had to be exercised. When I took another look, I saw that Don's lips were on Laura's cheek, and I knew instantly that when Mrs. Dunlap was out, Don was in that Dunlap apartment, in Laura's round bed.

It wasn't long before Laura told me that she and Don were in love. "We have what you and Jack have," she said to me. "We talk." I didn't mention something that perhaps I should have: that Jack and I had talked for a long time, and she and Don had talked for two weeks.

How to explain the reasons for Laura's defection? Was it simply the "moon over Miami" effect? Was it more serious— that like a lot of servicemen's wives who had married in haste, Laura was now full of regrets? Or was it the "anything goes" state of mind that we were going to see a lot of?

When I wrote Jack about what was happening, he wrote back, "Sorry about Laura and Bobby. Guess Bobby's in line for a 'Dear John.'" So it was because of poor Bobby that I was introduced to the term "Dear John," the servicemen's name for those dreaded letters in which a serviceman was informed by his girlfriend or wife that she was going to be his *former* girlfriend or wife. It wouldn't be the last time I would hear it, either; there would be many "Dear John" letters in the days ahead. Furthermore, in the days ahead there would be moments— moments of triumph and moments of trial—that would put Laura's dilemma into the category of the inconsequential.

CHAPTER 4

Icould not dwell on Laura: there was hard war news to be thought about. Everybody knew the war was going badly, especially the war we considered "our" war, the war in the Pacific. The papers carried no good news, only reports of defeats, one after another. The Japanese were not, as we had all predicted with such certainty, lying down and playing dead. They were proving surprisingly aggressive. Yet at this point we were still thinking of losses as minor setbacks.

And then in early April, after a long and bloody battle, American and Philippine forces surrendered to the Japanese at Bataan. Even if we had yet to learn the details of that battle and of the horrific march to the prisoner-of-war camp that had followed—an episode that came to be known as the Bataan death march—we understood that losing Bataan was a body blow.

Bataan was the true wake-up call. Until that loss, we had

never entertained the notion that we would not win any battle in which we were seriously engaged. It was as if the other losses were throwaways, perhaps even part of a strategic plan. The feeling had been that once we were definitely in, had definitely declared ourselves, our know-how and power would be invincible. But now, incredibly, we had fought a battle we had meant to win, and we had lost.

It was in that same month that Jack's orders finally came through. He was to leave for Victorville, California, for bombardier training. As there were apparently no spaces for prospective pilots but plenty for prospective bombardiers and navigators, pilot training was out for those Gunter cadets who wanted to go to war *now*. So, in spite of promises and aptitude tests, in spite of—as in Jack's case—flying qualifications, half the class went into bombardier training, the other half into navigator training. Once more the army had worked in its mysterious way.

On balance Jack was more elated than disappointed. He was out of Gunter. "Out! Dislodged! Extracted!" he exulted on the phone. As soon as he got to Victorville, he would find a place for us to live, so I was to get ready to leave home immediately. In order not to blight Jack's euphoria, when I talked to him I stayed clear of the feelings at home about the war. I certainly didn't mention Bataan. And neither did Jack.

Victorville, California. I knew nothing about Victorville, had never even heard of it. It didn't matter. I didn't care if Victorville was a teeming metropolis or a one-filling-station town at a crossroads. All I cared about was that I would at last be joining Jack.

My mother and father were of different minds about my going. This went right along with their opposing natures. As far as my father was concerned, when Opportunity knocked, you opened the door wide; my mother said "Just a minute" until Opportunity lost patience and went away. So while my mother cautioned that there was danger in my going—as if joining a husband in military service put you right smack in the middle of combat—my father thought that my traveling across the country should be thought of as an adventure, a way for me to see a few things, to learn a few things.

I agreed with my father. Even if my main goal was to be with Jack, I very much wanted to see what was out there, to see who was out there. The only hitch in this enlightened plan of my father's and mine was that these things would come my way because of a war.

I packed with no understanding at all of what I would need in the days or months ahead. All I knew for certain was that the trip meant an overnight to Chicago, three hours waiting for a connection, and then two overnights to Los Angeles. No sleeping car would be available. So I packed, and dressed, accordingly.

For Victorville, and wherever else after that, I packed two large suitcases. For the train, I filled an overnight case with the necessities for graceful train living, which meant toiletries and several changes of underwear. It was already very hot in Miami, and with no thinking at all of the consequences, I decided to get on board in light clothes—my new linen jacket with the big Joan Crawford–style shoulder pads, my new spectator pumps, my white gloves. I made a single gesture to practicality by including a hat that was semicrushable.

My mother issued one last advisory: did she have to remind me that it was cold in Chicago in April and that my blood had gotten thinner from living in Florida? "Do I have to tell you this?" she asked me. She didn't have to tell me this, for we all believed it—that South Floridians felt cold more intensely because the constant heat had thinned our blood. My mother, still on it, said, "Not even a sweater you're taking? Sweetheart, do Mama a favor—take your new angora." So as a concession to being a South Floridian and exquisitely sensitive to cold, I put my new angora in my overnight case.

Two days later, complete with luggage, I was down at the little pink Miami train station. It was a curious setting in which to find the war, but there it was. Servicemen were everywhere, and the station was dotted with posters. Some urged the purchase of war bonds: INVEST IN YOUR FREEDOM; some cautioned against unnecessary travel: DON'T GO IF YOU CAN STAY. I said good-bye to my parents and boarded a train. From the farthermost southeast corner of the country, I was starting my climb up the long peninsula of Florida and into America.

The three-hour wait in Chicago had sounded fine. Chicago had been a fantasy destination for many Union Citians, and I'd pictured leaving the station and seeing a bit of the town. I was already planning a letter to a friend in Union City to tell her that I had been in Chicago and had done some Chicago things. As it turned out, the Chicago things I would get into were not the kind of Chicago things I would care to write her about.

There were no niceties on the train. All amenities had disappeared. In the need for seats, only the rest room remained as it had been. Some of the cars were exclusively for servicemen:

white servicemen in some, black servicemen in others. In my car, there was only one other civilian, a girl who sat next to me. She was going to Memphis to meet up with her serviceman husband, whose existence she had not known of until a week before the ceremony and whose face she couldn't exactly remember. She recalled only that he was short and had wavy hair, and she was having severe doubts. "What if I see some short somebody with wavy hair and throw myself into his arms, and Tommy's looking?" she wailed at me.

The car was full of talk. If conversations started out as one-on-one, as the day wore on they morphed into one big one, and the topic was the war. Bataan was on everybody's mind. At the first mention of it, the servicemen, who clearly felt themselves to be spokesmen for the military, expressed gloomy thoughts about the whole Pacific war. I heard somebody say that his brother was on Corregidor, and somebody else said that Corregidor would be next.

Talk shifted to Europe. Of course I was not among the most informed of those on the train, but I knew that events in that particular "theater of war"—a strange term, I always felt, for an arena where actual life-and-death struggles took place—were not going well either. We all shared a soft spot for England and expressed sympathy for the terrific pounding London was now taking, and someone mentioned the African campaign and said the British weren't doing "so hot" there either. Even so, there was a feeling among those on the train—though there was no crowing as there had been back at the pier—that when the United States got its full forces into Europe, England would be able to breathe again.

There were no kind words for France, and the vaunted Maginot Line—that system of mostly underground fortifications built by the French along the German frontier—came in for jeers and hoots. Chiefly because of my father's unrestrained disgust, even I knew that the infallibility of the Maginot Line had been a myth. Like most people, my father had at first been taken in by the high praise for it, but when the line had proved to be fatally ineffective, he'd railed on about it. "How could they have been so *meshugeh* to think they could shoot down bombers if they're hiding under the ground?" he'd ask of anybody who would listen. How indeed could they have been so crazy?

The servicemen agreed that this was not going to be a trench war and would not in any way be like the last one. It was air power, they said. Air power was going to make the difference. Hearing this, I finally sat up and took real notice. What did "air power" mean? Did it mean fighters or did it mean bombers? Of course it meant both, but bombardiers were in bombers.

It goes without saying that the man everyone loved to hate was Adolf Hitler, his status as a demon now definitely incised on our brains. Epithets flew. He was a "nut," a "loony," a "maniac who's out to conquer the world." There was no talk of Hitler's involvement with the atrocities. At this point, because there had been no meaningful reporting, we were scarcely aware of them.

As we pulled into Memphis and my seatmate got up to leave, she gave me a troubled glance and said, "Wish me luck." The train continued on to Chicago. I sat up all night, sometimes dozing, more often awake. The night got cold, and I put on my sweater—thank you, Mama. In the morning I took my overnight case, went into the ladies' room, performed my ablutions, and changed my underwear and blouse. My jacket was now badly wrinkled, my shoes hardly white any longer, and I was forced to admit that these were not the best ideas I had ever had. I sat back down, ready for another long day.

The trip was enlivened by the military police patrolling all the cars, whether they had been taken over by the military or not. What they were checking for, I have no clue, but they came through regularly and by the second day were like old friends. One of them stopped by my seat each time he walked the aisle. After all, a young women traveling alone, even one wearing a wedding band, must have been an agreeable sight to a soldier. I was friendly to him, offered him my snacks and cigarettes, and did my best to laugh at his jokes.

I may have overdone it. Just before we reached Chicago, our MP asked me to meet him during the three-hour layover. "I can arrange to be off duty," he said, "and maybe we can socialize." I certainly didn't want to offend him, so I struggled to find a way to say no. After all, he was a serviceman, and by now servicemen—whether they had volunteered or had been dragooned—were icons. I finally fished out an excuse and said that I was meeting friends, rattling on and on about their being Union City friends, et cetera, et cetera—after which the MP turned very cool, perhaps disappointed at having to let go of the nice fantasy he'd been having of being holed up in Chicago with a pickup.

The train station in Chicago was big and it was crowded.

Soldiers, sailors, marines, all manner of servicemen and civilians thronged through, heading this way and that. As in the Miami station, there were posters advising against unnecessary travel. SAVE A SEAT FOR THE BOYS, they said, and DON'T GET IN THE WAY.

At first I looked for the "white" waiting room, until I remembered that this was Chicago and waiting rooms were for everyone. To avoid the MP with the hopes of "socializing," I dragged my suitcases to as private a corner as I could find, sank onto a bench, and lay low, though in that dense mob my own mother would have had a hard time finding me. It was hot in the station, and I took off my sweater and put it back in my overnight case.

What had I been thinking? Knowing nothing about lockers, I had luggage to look after, so there was no opportunity to get out and see Chicago. It seemed that Chicago was going to be just the station, the travelers, and the posters. My home poster —the one on the wall behind my bench—showed children playing games under the shadow of a swastika, with the caption DON'T LET THAT SHADOW FALL OVER THEM: BUY WAR BONDS. The one across from me encouraged children to buy and fill out books of war stamps, the little brother of war bonds; it showed schoolchildren plastering bits of paper on the faces of German soldiers, with the caption STAMP 'EM OUT.

Buying war bonds and stamps was something else we all did. It encouraged us to feel that we had both an emotional and a financial stake in the war. When a gift was in order, we gave war bonds, and it achieved multiple goals: someone bought the bond, someone received it, and both felt they had made a contribution. All celebratory events—a Bar Mitzvah, a Confirmation, a birthday, a wedding—were marked with the giving of bonds. Even if buying bonds and stamps was a minimal (some said negligible) contribution to the costs of the war, as a public relations stratagem, it did its job brilliantly.

In the Chicago station, with nothing much to do I took a pad out of my handbag and decided to write home about my trip thus far. I described the station I was in, wrote of the servicemen and what they had said, and told my father, "Everybody agrees with you about the Maginot Line. All the boys said it was a joke." I put the letter back in my handbag until I could find a place to mail it.

I waited for the announcement of my train. I waited some more. Finally it came. Redcaps being either nonexistent or nowhere in sight, I dragged, shoved, and kicked my suitcases over to the platform. I handed my ticket to the conductor. He handed it back. "Your train's been requisitioned," he told me. "Military orders." My train was now a troop train.

I dragged, shoved, and kicked my suitcases to the information window. I told the man in the window of my situation and asked him what I was supposed to do now. "Get another train," he said unhelpfully, glancing around for something more important to look at than me. I steeled myself in the face of his lack of interest to ask when another train might be coming through and whether that one might not be "requisitioned" as well. He finally looked at me—though it was a look that said I was ink spilled on his papers—and asked the question that in the upcoming months we would all come to know very well: "Don't you know there's a war on?"

I persevered. I asked again when he thought a train might be available, and he finally offered that there might be a train going my way later in the evening. Or, he said in an afterthought, maybe in the morning. Morning? I lugged my suitcases over to the Western Union counter and sent a telegram to Jack, to the Victorville Air Base, saying that I would be a day late. I did this with little confidence that the telegram would get to him, but, as I found out, it did.

I plunked myself down on yet another bench. I drew my suitcases close to me on the floor, held my handbag in my lap, and waited. While I waited, I smoked, adding my cigarette butts to the profusion on the floor around me. Butts, cigarettes, smoke, smokers; lighting up, crushing out. The cavernous train station was the world, and the world was smoky gray.

I heard no announcement of trains going to Los Angeles. At midnight I had still heard no announcement. When I could fight sleep no longer, I put my gloves and hat in my handbag, put my handbag under my head, stretched out on the bench, and slept. I awoke to a firm rapping on the soles of my shoes. The rapping turned out to be from a policeman's nightstick, and hovering over me was the policeman in whose grip it was. I sat up.

The policeman looked at me with no discernible fondness and asked what I was doing there. I glanced at my watch. Three o'clock it said, and it meant three o'clock in the morning. I explained that I was waiting for a train.

The policeman looked around. "In that case," he said, "shouldn't you have some suitcases?"

What? I looked to the side of my bench, where my suitcases

should have been. All I saw were cigarette butts. I got up and searched around the bench. I searched under it. My suitcases were nowhere to be seen. I tried to tell the policeman that someone had taken them. "I'm on my way to be with my husband," I rattled away to the policeman. "He was in Montgomery, and now he's in California." I said, "He's a cadet." He's waiting for me." In my nervousness, I was all fits and starts.

The policeman said, "Uh-huh."

Only once before—when I was a very little girl and was being what my mother called a "pestnik"—had anybody grabbed me by the arm and pulled me along, but the policeman did it now. As he did, he said, "You girls waiting for our boys, making a few bucks for a few minutes." And he hustled me out the door of the station, saying, "Well, you ain't going to do it on my shift."

I may have still have been a person-in-progress, but I was not so naive that I didn't know what he thought I would be doing on his shift, though I seemed to have no way to convince him that I had no plans for doing it. The only thing I could think to do was to put on my hat and gloves.

The policeman talked in a steady stream about how "girls like you" were not worried about the war, how it made no difference to "you girls" who won. He said, "Come to that, you'd do it with Nazis or Japs, don't make no difference." He seemed to have startled himself, and offered the thought that it made him sick to think of "doing it with Japs."

Whatever I said to the policeman, he told me to tell it to the sergeant. But at the station house I couldn't tell it to the sergeant, for the sergeant was not going to listen. By now I was definitely scared. I wanted Jack, I wanted my father. In my head I heard myself crying out for them.

The sergeant rummaged through my handbag and pulled out my train ticket. He turned it over a few times and asked me if it was mine. When I said yes, he said, "How do I know you didn't steal it, steal the handbag with the ticket in it?" He then took time to express his job philosophy, how the police had to watch out for more things than ever these days, what with the war looking so bad. "They"—and I took this to mean people like me—"are doing everything in the book." He sighed. "We never had nothing like this before." I guess he had forgotten the time when Chicago was gangland headquarters.

I nodded my head. I could scarcely take in what he was saying, but I wanted to be nice, to be polite, and, mainly, to be forgiven. For what, I didn't quite know.

That his words hadn't fallen on deaf ears seemed to mean something to him. At any rate, he was looking at the ticket again and asking where I had bought it.

"Miami," I said, hoping he didn't have anything against Miami.

He seemed gloomily satisfied and told the policeman to take me back to the station. "I don't think she'll be any more trouble," he said.

Any *more* trouble? More than what? If I expected apologies or a plea for my understanding, there was certainly none of that. Just a turning over of my handbag. All in a day's work.

On the way back to the station, my policeman escort kept up a steady line of talk. The police had to be careful, he said, since girls were hanging out at the station at all hours and sometimes even getting on the trains. "If you ask me," he said, "those trains are just rolling cathouses."

I finally broke into his monologue to ask if there was any way for me to get my luggage back. But if he heard my question, he gave no sign.

So I had had my experiences with "Chicago things." Considering the MP who had plans for "socializing" in Chicago and the Chicago police who were johnny-on-the-spot for prostitutes, did "toddlin' town" mean that Chicago was wide open to racy adventures? This may have been true, but there was another explanation for what had happened to me, and a more mature head would have known it. Surely what I had experienced were signs that a war mentality had already taken over the country.

Still, as my father would have advised, I didn't take what had happened to me "personal." Not taking things "personal" was something my father had had a lot of experience with in Union City. Only on very few occasions had he had to take things personally, for the customers liked him. But he didn't "take it personal" on the occasions when some customer came in complaining about "you high and mighty storekeepers" who had no shoes that could "ease a body's bunions." My father would say that the man wasn't mad at him, Morris Kaufman, but at the entire dry goods establishment that hadn't found a way to make his bunions comfortable. And I was willing to say that because of the particular circumstances, my bedevilers were not suspicious of me, Stella Suberman; they were suspicious of every woman in the station who was traveling alone without baggage. I had simply fit the profile of the Chicago train station prostitute.

At eight A.M. I was back in the station, but now I was traveling light. I went into the little station drugstore and replaced my toothbrush and toothpaste, immediately put them to use in the ladies' room, and came out feeling better. But I still had no train, and already burdened with my share of rejections, I had no inclination to go to the information window to inquire about one.

I sat down on an empty bench, and in time a black serviceman sat down next to me. In what I told myself was a subtle move—following my dictum that I ought not to be "ugly" to "darkies"—I slid to the end of the bench. Whether the serviceman read my motives, I cannot say, but I would guess that the odds were that he did. I held to the idea, however, that my action could have been seen as a considerate one to allow the serviceman more room, though what I knew was that I simply did not want to sit next to him.

On the bench I pulled out my pad and wrote up my Chicago experience. This letter, with all the details faithfully told, would go not to my parents in Miami Beach but to my sister Ruth in New York, with the instruction that she keep everything to herself.

An appropriate train finally came. I handed the conductor my ticket, and this time he did not hand it back. Still, I was to have one last rejection before I could leave Chicago. It came from the train porter, and it was about my lack of luggage. I thought I should explain that it had been stolen, but if I had hoped for a sympathetic hearing, I was disappointed. All I got was a look that said, Yeah, sure, whatever you say.

I finally found a seat, and I sat down to assess my situation. I had only the clothes I was wearing, and I was to spend two more nights on the train. The loss of my baggage together with the depressing war news promised a bleak trip. What sustained me was that Jack was at the end of it, and I had the profound wish that by the time we got together, the war news would have taken a turn for the better. It would have been wonderful to greet Jack in an aura of nothing but joy.

I settled in and inventoried my losses. Topping the list were my new alligator shoes and matching handbag. Well, I thought, trying to make a joke, I had my comb and lipstick, which were the really important things. In fact, I did have the important things—my ticket and my money.

As I was rejoicing over this bit of good luck, an awful thought struck: my overnight case was gone and with it my sweater and underwear. What was I going to do without a sweater? And worse, without changes of underwear? I couldn't borrow. The only one I had spoken to on the train was my seatmate, a serviceman who had gotten on with me in Chicago, and nice as he was, he was not going to be very helpful in the way of underwear. There was only one thing to do: wash the items I was wearing and dry them on my body. Which meant I was going to sit in my seat for long periods of time, sweaterless, alternately wet and dry, awaiting pneumonia.

As on my trip up, everybody talked to everybody, and it was always about the war. The tone was dark. Somebody said that we needed good news and needed it fast, and we all agreed. We wanted to hear of a victory, somewhere, sometime. We were sick of reading that "we've had our clocks cleaned," as one of my trainmates put it. When were we going to read that the Japanese had been vanquished, that America had raised its flag? We talked about the fact that U.S. forces had surrendered in the Phillipines, that Japanese troops had taken not just Singapore but the whole of the Malay Peninsula, and more. Those places whose very names—Bali! Bangkok! Rangoon!—had spoken of romance, all of them were gone. And with their long-standing treaty with Thailand, the Japanese controlled the strategic railroad center at Bangkok. Where was some good news? What we did not know at that moment was that it was out there, waiting to get on the train.

As night fell, I tried for sleep, but sleep did not come. I was cold. My seatmate had lent me his army-issue overcoat, but it was a thing so heavy and so stiff I would not have been surprised if it had gotten up and walked around all by itself. It certainly defied cozying up in. Still, not to hurt my seatmate's feelings, I continued to try, and I finally used it as a sort of tent. No help. I still couldn't sleep.

I finally faced the real reason for my sleeplessness: I couldn't keep the depressing war news out of my head. Even those unpleasant policemen—in Union City we would have described them as "just so ungallant"—had been sensitive enough to be dejected by the progress of the war.

When I looked over at my seatmate, I saw he wasn't sleeping either. He too had been thinking about the war, and he had begun to wonder whether we were being told everything. I began to wonder as well. Maybe we had had more losses, more casualties than they were telling us? More "sure things" that had turned into disasters?

That night, perhaps at that moment, I at last had a release from the grip of denial, for I found myself looking at the war as never before. It seemed that for the first time I was able to see things realistically, to acknowledge that the war was not a diversion designed to make our lives interesting: it was real and it was dangerous, and many lives were in the line of fire, including my Jack's.

And then into my head crept the unthinkable: what if our forces did not prevail, what if the impossible was possible? What would be the consequences then? Could I be realistic about *that?* No, I had gone as far as I could go: the consequences were more than I could contemplate; they defied thinking about.

As the night went on, what settled over the car seemed not sleep but gloom. People played cards, but quietly, and no jokey insults were exchanged. If they fell asleep, they awoke to carry on troubled conversations.

I turned from one side to the other. I threw off the army coat. I put on my jacket, now looking as if it had not only been worn on a train but run over by one, and then I took the jacket off. I got up and washed my underwear. I sat back down and gazed out into the blackness of the night. Yes, in my wet underwear. What had I done? Now I was not only cold, I was *wet* and cold.

My seatmate had a deck of cards and invited me to play. We tried gin rummy, but concentration deserted me after a few hands. He tried to teach me a Chicago game called Schnapsen, but it was so complicated that I fell into obtuseness. It required close attention, and my attention span was zero. I was caught between anticipation and anxiety: the promise of seeing Jack on the one hand, the war news on the other.

I turned off the light over my head, looked out the window, and saw we had pulled into a station. As I glanced at the platform, I was thinking, Good news, we have to have some good news.

The good news came the same way the bad news had come in Tallahassee—by way of a hawking newsboy. This one burst into the train and started moving swiftly down the aisle, shoving newspapers at passengers, money changing hands quickly. He was shouting something, but I couldn't quite make it out. It sounded like "Doolittle dood it." Had I heard him right? If I had, it was nonsense, a joke. I waited for the newsboy to come to our seats. When he finally did, my seatmate dropped a coin in his hand, grabbed two papers, and handed one to me. I looked at the headline. It said, DOOLITTLE RAIDERS BOMB TOKYO.

Unlike my bafflement at the Pearl Harbor headline, this I understood. I knew what "raiders" meant, and I knew what "Tokyo" meant. Only "Doolittle" remained a mystery. As I read further, I came to understand that sixteen B-25s under Lieutenant Colonel Jimmy Doolittle had taken off from an aircraft carrier—the *Hornet*—and had proceeded to drop their bombs on Tokyo.

It was only a matter of seconds before the train erupted, before passengers were jumping from their seats and running toward each other. "Didn't I tell you?" they were saying, and "Didn't I say it was just a matter of time?" Nobody remembered that just a few hours earlier, we had been talking only gloom and doom.

Doolittle's raiders changed all that. Doolittle had indeed "dood" it. His boys, we yelled at each other, had the "guts and gumption" to reach Tokyo, had "the balls," someone said (sharing the general feeling that this was not the time for decorous speech), to bring the war to the enemy, to "bomb the hell" out of the place. And how about that all the guys had volunteered for the mission? Was that the American way or what? We exulted, we crowed. Just think, we said, just think of the ingenuity that went into planning such a raid. "Took off from an aircraft carrier," someone said. "If that don't take the cake!"

Oh, it was magnificent, that moment of hearing of the Doolittle raid. It was the news we had needed, had longed for. The raid lifted our spirits, buoyed us, renewed our faith in our country's ability to fight a war. And, of course, we on the train were not alone in these feelings: as we found out, with that single bit of news, the entire country had floated into an ecstasy.

As talk of the dazzling event died down, singing started up. Stirred as we were with patriotic fervor, we wanted to sing songs that expressed this. Curiously, as at the pier, the songs we went to were those written not for this war but for the last one. And so we sang "Over There" and then all the George M. Cohan songs. Whether they pertained to the war or not, they seemed American and country-loving and just what we wanted to sing.

What we were beginning to realize was that no new war songs equaled the old ones. There were none like the ones that had sent World War I soldiers to battle and inspired the homefront. We of this war found it impossible to be roused by the likes of songs that seemed more appropriate for sending boys off to play football than as exhortations to battle. "Remember Pearl Harbor" recorded by Sammy Kaye? Remembering Pearl Harbor as we did the Alamo? Were they equal on the scale of cataclysms? Yes, we had songs to dance to or to yearn by, but aside from the Air Corps song telling of our boys thundering off into the wild blue yonder, we had nothing to stir our soul. We had no song like "Over There."

The good feelings—the euphoria—lasted all through the day and into the next night. The singing too popped out on and off. And as the train came into Los Angeles the following morning, we were singing "Give My Regards to Broadway," and if the song made no contextual sense, it didn't matter; it just felt right.

Much, much later we learned the true facts of the raid over Tokyo—that it had been almost without strategic benefit, that the damage to the intended targets was modest, that none of the planes had landed as planned at Chinese airfields, and, most sorrowful of all, that eight airmen had been captured by the Japanese and three of them executed—but it could not take away our memory of how sweet it had been. No matter that little strategic damage had been done, it was the kind of brash, audacious action that at that point in time we needed so desperately. Later, when Doolittle himself was asked about the raid, he said, "It was only a pinprick, but it pierced their heart."

I KNEW NOT TO count on anyone meeting me at the Los Angeles train station, and no one did. So I fell back on Plan B, which was to take a bus from Los Angeles to Victorville. I took a taxi over to the bus station, my bus came along in an hour or two, and with no baggage to worry about, I climbed on.

The bus left Los Angeles on an interstate highway and almost immediately began a gentle climb toward San Bernardino. At San Bernardino we were at the bus station just long enough to board a few passengers, among whom I took to be a couple of cadets, and I wondered if perhaps they were Jack's fellow bombardiers-in-training. For a couple of reasons, I didn't ask: if they were friends of Jack's, I didn't want them to see his wife looking like what we used to call "Mister Baggypant's sister, Miss Droopydrawers"; furthermore, I didn't feel the need to talk to anyone. I was too busy looking out the bus window at California.

Once the bus left San Bernardino the gentle incline turned precipitous. My first real climb, I thought to myself. Though on the train I had climbed the granddaddy of all mountain ranges—the Rockies—the passage had been mostly at the night and the climb gradual. Here we were going up, up, up at an angle so alarming it seemed the front end of the bus might at any moment jackknife over on the back.

The bus in which I was traveling was not a sightseeing one, but the country through which I was passing was certainly worth taking a good look at, especially as we got into the Big Bear area of mountains and forests east of San Bernardino. It was here that I began to challenge what my father always said about Miami Beach. "So beautiful," he would say, "it makes a big nothing out of anyplace else." Well, Dad, this place was equally beautiful, if very different. The road ascended and dropped, the air was cool (cold, I called it, in my sweaterless state), the trees were thick and green, and the views were both up and down, very unlike the long views—from the top floors of hotels—that in Miami Beach were so sought after. In the mood I was in, in that post–Doolittle raid mood, I did a silent gasp of delight as each twist of the road brought a new spectacle. Though I tried to remain loyal to Florida, I had to acknowledge that this landscape was not my father's "nothing."

Just as suddenly as the bus had begun its steep climb, it began to descend. The green trees began disappearing, and ahead lay the Mojave Desert. Before we plunged into the heart of it, a few little structures appeared, the first after San Bernardino. I had to wonder at these sheds and cabins sitting so isolated out in the desert.

It was when the bus pulled up to one of them—a squat concrete-block building surrounded by a few cactus plants that seemed not to be growing out of the sand so much as stuck into it—that I realized they were not just odd edifices; they were Victorville. And the squat building was the bus station.

I had expected to be met, for I'd suspected that if Jack couldn't meet me, he would find someone who could. With this thought in mind, before exiting the bus and before meeting this someone, I took a moment to try to make myself presentable. I had, of course, lost most means of doing so, and I fell back on one of the few things I could do, which was to comb my hair. This led to my first hint of what to expect from my new home in the desert, for when I combed, I was stunned to find that here in the dry air, my hair, heretofore maddeningly curly, had gone totally straight, straight as the desert-loving agave stalks.

There was no Jack, but walking toward me with purpose, if not enthusiasm, was a heavy-set woman enveloped in an air of doing her duty. The woman turned out to be Mrs. Gillis.

I was to stay with Mrs. Gillis, who had an extra bedroom that she rented out to air-base men. She made no comment on my lack of baggage, nor on the fact that I was shivering with cold. Her car was waiting, we got in, and we drove the short distance to her house. It was gray, made of stuccoless concrete block, and was very small, with a tiny sand front yard and a cactus here and there. No steps led into the house. You came right off the walk, went through the front door, and found yourself in the living room. It was like something in a western movie set in pioneer days.

The house had no furnishings to speak of, and my bedroom was spare to the point of skeletal. I was still cold, and the room was no help. Nor was Mrs. Gillis. The only cheering moment came when she told me that Jack had been calling to check on me and would probably call again that night.

Talk of the telephone reminded me that I needed to call my parents, and I was able to do so only after I had assured Mrs. Gillis that I was calling collect. I kept the call short and said I would write a long letter in the morning. Mrs. Gillis stood close by, perhaps ready to pounce in case I tried to follow up the collect call with a noncollect one.

Early in the evening Jack telephoned. I tried to express my joy at hearing his voice—and perhaps to suggest that my accommodations were not all one could wish for—but Mrs. Gillis was hovering, so all that I could muster was Yes, I'm fine. He said he was coming in this weekend. This weekend? Three days away! I did manage, with Mrs. Gillis hearing every word, to say "I love you."

I slept that night in a cold bed, in a cold room, next to the bedroom of what I was beginning to understand was a cold lady. At breakfast, she came to the point, the point being "what kind of name" Suberman was. Even if Jack thought I was ignorant about codes, I was familiar with this one. Decoded, Mrs. Gillis's words meant "Are you Jewish?"

I was suddenly alert to the possibility of Jewish "difficulties," and I knew in my bones that an insult was on its way, that at this moment Mrs. Gillis was going to involve me in my first ugly episode, that I was going to receive the epithet that had never before been addressed to me. I knew with a terrible certainty that I had arrived at the end of my innocence.

I was not wrong. Mrs. Gillis said she had thought Suberman might be a Jewish name but had been hoping that it wasn't. She said these things openly, as if, even if I did turn out to be Jewish, what she was saying couldn't possibly be disagreed with. "I never have liked Jews," she said. "They're always out to gyp you."

I sank back in my chair, unable to speak. Mrs. Gillis began talking about a lump—a lump on the back of Jewish necks. It was, she said, as if she had been researching the topic, a characteristic of Jews, and when she saw that I didn't have one, she figured—hoped—that she had been mistaken about my being Jewish. "You better believe I took a good look," she said to me, "and I praised God when I didn't see any lump."

A lump on the back of Jewish necks? This was a new one to me, and I suspect it would have been to most Jews. In Union

City many townsfolk thought Jews had horns—a well-traveled myth known to all Jews—and my father had reported another one, the time when a man came into the store and said, "With all respect, Mr. Kaufman, the only trouble with Jews is that they're RomanCatholic"—but I daresay no Jew had ever heard about a lump.

I was at a loss. It was hard for me to blurt it out, to say to this intimidating woman, Yes, I'm Jewish. Shouldn't I try to make her like me, to let her know I was different from what she might think of as "Jewish"? As I looked into those staring, ice-blue eyes, I steeled myself to answer. "Yes, Suberman is a Jewish name," I said to Mrs. Gillis. "But it's derived from the German." I was aware immediately of what I had done: it was as if I had attempted to soften an awful truth.

Mrs. Gillis shook her head. "It looks like I've got a Jew on my hands," she said glumly. "Well, all I can do is make the best of it." As my mother would say, she pinned a rose on herself.

How did I handle my first personal encounter with the ugliness of anti-Semitism? Not very well, I'm afraid. I had had no experience with exchanging insults, with fighting back, and my first essay into this kind of combat was one in which I take no pride. I had allowed Mrs. Gillis to put me on the defensive. Worst of all, I had tried to placate her. I could not, as I had done in Chicago when I had had the encounter with the police, tell myself not to "take it personal." This was profoundly personal. Mrs. Gillis didn't like Stella Suberman, for the reason that she didn't like something that was a part of me.

Comfort was out there, though I didn't know it at the moment. After breakfast I left the house and walked into town. I found a little ten-cent store that carried a variety of stuff, and I bought some underwear and a sweater. Though food was the last thing on my mind, I went over to the café across from the bus station, the Green Spot, took a booth in the corner, and ordered a sandwich.

I lingered over the sandwich, not wanting to leave, not wanting to return to the house of Mrs. Gillis. I sat through the lunch hour, I sat until the crowd thinned out. I would have liked to sit there until Jack came in on Friday night. I was still sitting when the cashier lady walked over, slid into the booth, and looked at me.

She was Midge Folsom, and she wanted to know who I was and where I was staying. She had seen me get off the bus, and "it didn't take a whole lot in the brains department," she said, to figure out that I was an air-base wife, especially when she had seen Mrs. Gillis pick me up. "You getting along okay?" she asked me.

Getting along okay? I wanted to tell her that no, I was not getting along okay, that I had been horribly insulted, that I was feeling like a piece of seaweed washed up on the beach. I wanted to cry out for Jack. I wanted to tell somebody about the absurdity of the "lump." Could I tell this woman? I was three thousand miles away from home, in California, and maybe in this mythic state Mrs. Gillis was standard. Still, I had no choice, and I made up my mind to bet on Midge Folsom.

I won the bet. Midge listened. And afterward, Midge Folsom said the words I wanted to hear. "There are all kinds of goons in the world," she said, "and you've just met one."

Midge was the very model of the "can do" person. In a split

second she had decided that I would leave Mrs. Gillis and stay with her. Since I had left nothing of importance at the Gillis house, I would just not return there. Midge would call. "I'll tell the old bag that she'll get her week's rent anyway," she said.

Midge lived not too far away. She and her husband, Wesley, had two bedrooms and no children, so the second bedroom was available, their former renter having just graduated and left for the wild blue yonder. Wesley, Midge explained as we got into her car, was a "long-haul" truck driver and was at this moment on a "haul" to Arizona.

Midge told me not to worry about clothes. She said that tomorrow she'd take me shopping, and no matter what, she said, Jack was going to be very glad to see me. My heart fluttered at the way she said "Jack," as if she already knew him, already knew us.

It was a short ride from the bus station to the Folsom house. This house was also very small and built of concrete block, but unlike Mrs. Gillis's house, it had a stucco finish, so it was white, and it had steps leading up to it. There was a living room, a kitchen, and two bedrooms and a bathroom down a short hall. There was no dining room, just a table in the kitchen.

The white plastered living room was full of stuff—flat-armed wood-and-cushioned sofa and chairs, and a lot of what my mother would call *tchotchkes,* little adornments. They were mostly western style—tooled leather lamp shades, rope-trimmed picture frames, an Indian blanket on a wall. What was to be Jack's and my bedroom had a double bed covered by a chenille bedspread, with another Indian blanket on top.

When I asked if I could call Jack and let him know I had

moved, Midge said the boys weren't allowed to get calls but she'd spread it around at the Green Spot. According to Midge, the base was pretty strict in general about things. "Lord," she said, "they've really got the boys' balls under lock and key."

I did take notice of Midge's language, but the horse players at the store had talked like this when they thought I wasn't listening, so I wasn't put off. How could I be put off by anything that came from my rescuer, this lovely Midge person?

When I finally had had a "good soak," as Midge put it, she gave me one of her robes—a pink one and, like the bedspread, chenille—and I joined her in the little living room. Out came a couple of bottles of beer. If I had always before declined beer— not on moral grounds but because it tasted really, really bad— this day, sitting in this living room with this very nice lady and knowing that Jack's weekend was coming up, I was overcome with a feeling of such well-being that I drank several, while I laughed at Midge's language and her jokes and her stories.

Midge was the kind of woman who had heard it all and told it all. This was almost literally true. As a cashier at the Green Spot Café, she welcomed the men from the air base who came in—and all of them came in sooner or later—and they talked to her endlessly. Some flirted with her—"They're all horny as toads," she said of them—but she would have none of it. "They're just kids," she told me, "so I just tell them to go back to their barracks and write to their mamas."

Midge and Wes were both on their second marriages. She was from Indiana, he from Idaho, both places hitherto mysterious to me. All I really knew about Indiana was that it grew a lot of corn, had spawned John Dillinger, and had once provided an environment where the Ku Klux Klan could thrive, although there was a counterclaim from some Tennesseans that the Klan had had its real beginning in Pulaski, a little Tennessee town, and Tennesseans were variously proud or ashamed of this. Still, it was conventional wisdom that the Klan had reached its zenith in Indiana.

Midge was not at all what I would have expected an Indianan to be, for I would have expected a blond, soft type in a pinafore, not a dark, wiry woman in dungarees and embroidered western shirts.

Midge had met Wes down the road in Barstow, when Wes had come into the Route 66 truck stop where she had been working. Midge was younger than Wes—thirty-six to his fifty-eight—but she assured me that I didn't have to worry about the age difference. "Wes has all the essentials, plus a few luxuries," she said. I would be able to meet Wes in a few days, when he came back from his "long haul."

We talked on, about Jack, about Victorville, about Wes, and we talked easily. It was when Midge said that Wes was going to have the "red hots" over meeting us that I began to feel uncomfortable. Was Wes going to have the "red hots" over the fact that we were Jewish? Over having a couple of exotics in his home to joke about with his long-haul buddies? Still, at the moment, I was having a good time with Midge, and I put it out of my mind. I laughed when she excused herself to go to the "can," saying, "You don't buy beer, you just rent it." It was my first exposure to this expression, but it was certainly not going to be my last.

Midge not only spoke plainly, she had a language locution

all her own. When I asked her if she didn't occasionally want to go out on the road with Wes, she said, "Hell, no. When Wes mentions it, I just nip the idea in the butt." I told Jack later about these "Midgisms," and we agreed that they were a blending of malaprop and metaphor, so we portmanteaued the two into "malaphor." When I told Midge this, she laughed and said it was because she never read anything. " 'Andy Gump' and 'Gasoline Alley,' and that's it," she said.

If at first glance the Folsom house had seemed to me unremarkable, in the late afternoon, when I saw the sunset, I certainly changed my mind. The sunset I watched from the Folsom back porch would make "nothing" out of all other sunsets. I had seen sunsets in the Keys—red suns over blue waters; and when the sun sank into the sea, I had been one of the lucky ones to spot the elusive "green flash"—but I had never seen a sunset like this one. Between the house and the bluffs the sun had turned the sands into yellows and oranges and reds, and on the bluffs themselves the sun had done the Keys one better and shot them through with a glittering show of reds and blues and greens.

"Ain't it a beaut?" Midge said. Then, remembering where I was from, she said I must have had plenty of views in Miami. "Right?"

And I had to say, Yes, we had plenty of views. And I remembered the hotel slogan that proclaimed, ALWAYS A VIEW, NEVER A JEW.

I hoped that the wonderful sunset signaled that Victorville was going to be wonderful as well; and in some ways it was, and in some ways it wasn't. The fact was that even if I could put the painful moment with Mrs. Gillis behind me, there was to be another one, an even more emotionally draining one, waiting for me.

In the morning after Midge had gone to work, I sat down to write a letter to my parents. I wrote eight pages. And then I wrote six pages to my sister Ruth, with a lot of Midge in them, including the "butt" malaphor and another one—how Midge was in a quandary about a way to keep Mrs. Gillis off the housing list and how she had "wrecked" her brain trying to come up with an answer.

Midge came back at noon to take me shopping, but first she showed me the town, which didn't take long, as Victorville's population was a mere thousand or so. Most Victorvillians lived in the small houses clustered around the highway. The highway had the town's only real stretch of pavement except for a short length coming off the highway onto a couple of streets. There was not a curb in sight, and a mile or so out, what pavement there was turned into gravel and sand.

As Midge and I drove these roads, I was for the first time in my life on rugged terrain inside town limits. Union City and Tallahassee had a few hills, but gentle ones, and Miami was flat as a flounder. And New York? Well, I would be hard-pressed to say what New York was. But here, in the foothills of the Sierra Nevadas, as it were, I was acutely aware of going constantly up and down, curving right and curving left, climbing up steep grades, riding precipitously down them.

The moneyed town people lived on the outskirts, on ranches —or "spreads," as they were called. Some of these, the ones owned by hobbyists, were elaborate and done out with architect-designed houses and swimming pools and riding stables; but some were working ranches owned by families in the cattle business. Since the land around Victorville produced only sparse grass, in order to be able to graze horses and cattle, the working ranches had to have vast holdings that were measured not in acres but in miles.

When I had first heard that Victorville was on the edge of the Mojave Desert, the desert that had come to mind was the only one I had seen pictures of, which was of course the Sahara: empty, undulating sands and romantic oases. The Mojave was very different. It grew things. Not only was it studded with yucca, cactus, and Joshua trees, it was strewn with wildflowers (since this was April, their month for coming out). But in its own way, it was romantic, for it was a land of cattle and cowboys. And on this, my very first day in the West, out of nowhere came a cowboy, and then another, and then many— horse-riding cowboys, with chaps on their legs and horns on their saddles. They seemed so much as I knew them from the movies, I could believe they were extras adding color to a Gene Autry film. But they weren't movie cowboys: they were real cowboys doing what real cowboys did—riding the range and working their chores.

Before we left the countryside, we drove a few miles out to the air base. Victorville Air Base seemed mostly runways holding small twin-engine trainer planes, plus a few long hangars and a small collection of two-story wooden buildings. The buildings had obviously once been white, but because the unremitting desert sun had peeled the white paint off, they were now an uncertain gray. Somewhere inside those identical buildings—barracks or administration offices or classrooms—was Jack, and it was a curious feeling to know he was in one of them and yet have no way to get to him. Of course I wouldn't have tried, for as Midge said, we didn't have a pass and it would be bad form to ask the guards to go against orders. Even so, the men at the gate waved at us and called out, "Hi, Midge," and Midge waved back and said, "Hi, guys," adding that she would see them later, which of course she would.

Downtown Victorville was a short spate of shops lining the highway. In addition to the bus station and the Green Spot Café and the ten-cent store, there were a movie theater, a grocery store, a snack shop, a bowling alley, and a tack shop, all of them, except for the tack shop, having no doubt sprung up in the wake of the air base. I saw no churches and no synagogue.

Midge took me to the post office in the rear of the snack shop, and I mailed all my letters, including the ones I had written in the Chicago train station. Then we went to find me some clothes. The tack shop and the ten-cent store both had offerings, but since I wasn't anticipating much in the way of saddling up, we focused on the ten-cent store, which was a ten-cent store in name only, stocking as it did everything from thumbtacks to blankets. I found items to tide me over—a couple of everyday cotton dresses, or "wash dresses," as we would have called them in Tennessee; tennis shoes and socks; and a few other necessities. Anything for "puttin' on the dog," Midge told me, would have to be looked for in San Bernardino, which she called "San Berdoo." I couldn't imagine that I would have occasion to "put on the dog," but I wanted to shop in San

Berdoo, for I didn't want to have to dive under a table at the Green Spot Café should one of the cadets come in.

It seemed Friday night would never arrive, but then it was Friday night and here Jack came. He had gained a couple of pounds—which on his rangy frame looked very good—and he had a desert tan. My new vision of Jack was a Jack in a uniform, so his uniform didn't startle me. He was at the door, and then he was in the house, and then I was in his arms and my heart was jumping into his again.

Though they were expected later, neither Wes nor Midge was at home. With the house to ourselves, there was nothing to be careful about, and we went charging down the hall and into what was "our" bedroom. Without so much as a look around, Jack stripped off the Indian blanket and the chenille bedspread, and as soon as they were on the floor, we were in the bed. The couple of pounds Jack had gained seemed to me all muscle, and when his arms went around me, the misadventures I had had—the thing with the police in Chicago, the loss of my clothes, even the awfulness with Mrs. Gillis—went right out of my head.

Afterward, we wanted to take a shower together, the way we had done in our honeymoon hotel in West Palm, but there was no shower in the Folsom bathroom. We had to make do with the bathtub, and though it may have been a close fit, we were determined and we did it. Jack joked that since Victorville was always short of water, we were doing the right thing. "Just being good citizens," he said.

Back in our bedroom there were things to talk about, and of course Mrs. Gillis was right at the top. I told Jack all about it, detail upon detail. When I got to the business with the "lump," I felt myself choking up. But I was with Jack, and the tears could come. I thought Jack would understand that I was asking for, needing, sympathy.

Surprisingly, sympathy did not come immediately. Indeed Jack was at first offhand, as if the incident was one to be analyzed in a scholarly way, and he offered that Mrs. Gillis's use of "lump" may have come from mishearing "hump." Then he carefully—maddeningly—explained that "hump" came from the image of a Jewish person walking bent over and humped. "To suggest the obsequiousness of Jews, I suppose," he said.

I didn't want to hear this. I didn't want to hear theories. I wanted Jack to put his arms around me, tell me he was so, so sorry that I had had such a terrible experience, and then to let me know what to do if it happened again.

No doubt in his frustration with Mrs. Gillis and all the Mrs. Gillises of the world, to my astonishment Jack grew angry with me. "How could you let her get away with it?" he scolded me. Why couldn't you at least *say* something?"

I tried to defend myself. "How can you not understand?" I wailed at him. "Don't you know I was in an awful position?" Could I tell Jack the truth—that I had been hoping that by some miracle Mrs. Gillis would rethink her position and end up liking me? No, I could not say this, not to Jack. Even I didn't want to hear it. So I said, still hoping for indulgence, "Don't you know I've never been talked to that way?"

Jack didn't give an inch. "Well, now you know how it is to be talked to that way," he said. It was as if we had reached that moment when my abiding modus vivendi, in which I liked everybody and everybody liked me, was finally on trial. "You've learned something," he said.

Yes, I had learned something. I had learned that I was not a special case, that I was just as vulnerable to slurs as any of my brothers and sisters, no matter who they were, no matter where they were from. At that moment I clearly understood that I was now in the shoes of others.

But I wanted more. I wanted a method for handling such matters. I wanted to know how those people whose shoes I now inhabited dealt with slurs. Did they try to teach? Did they argue? "So what do you do in a situation like that?" I asked Jack, and I waited to hear the formula.

No formula was forthcoming. There apparently was no tried-and-true way for dealing with a Mrs. Gillis. No matter that Jack had been so adamant earlier, he just took me—finally! —into his arms and hugged me close. He had no answers, he said, only a hope. He told me that nothing I would have said would have made a difference, that Mrs. Gillis and the people like her were lost causes. "It's too late for Mrs. Gillis," Jack said. "No light could penetrate the dark density of that brain. But don't worry. We'll get her kids, and if not her kids, her grandkids. It'll just take a little time." And I wanted fervently to believe that, for I wanted to know that there would come a time when nobody would feel that humiliated, that helpless, again.

So I tried my best to forgive my craven behavior, and in the end we let it go. Now so glad to be together, we were able to turn it into a joke, and Jack said, "I wonder what your Mrs. Gillis thought might be in that lump. Jewish gold? Chicken fat?

A matzo ball?" And then he came up with the perfect idea for what I should have done. What I should have done, he said, was "pop her one."

Later, we came out into the living room, and I went into the kitchen and brought out a bottle of beer for Jack and a Coke for me, and I sat on his lap while we drank them. I told him about my visit to the Chicago police station, and since laughter now came easily, Jack took a long look at me and joked, "Come to think of it, you probably did look like a hooker."

"What? In my hat and gloves?" I protested.

About the Doolittle raid, Jack said the men at the air base were as exhilarated by it as we had been on the train. Still, he acknowledged that they had finally decided that in reality it was a stunt—a brilliant stunt, but a stunt. "It was a showpiece," Jack said, "and we're going to need more than that."

Jack told me a bit about what the training was like at the air base. What he had been doing was learning how to bomb. "That's what bombardiers do, you know," he joked. The main tool for doing this was apparently a "bombsight," which, as I understood it, was a calculator kind of thing into which the bombardier put the figures for the altitude, air speed, and so forth. The bombsight would make adjustment for these factors and then the bombardier would look through the eyepiece and line up the crosshairs to hold on the intended target. Working with a bombsight was a surprising direction for Jack. "I keep wondering what a word guy like me is doing with all this math," he said.

Using the bombsight, the boys practiced bombing in hangar

mock-ups or by actually dropping bombs in the desert from AT-11 twin-engine trainers. They'd fly over the desert at five or ten thousand feet and drop their bombs at bull's-eyes in the centers of football-field-sized targets painted on the desert sand. They'd go north and east of Victorville, up around Sidewinder Mountain.

I was astonished at what Jack was telling me. Bombing the desert? He told me no, they were not bombing the desert, and furthermore the bombs didn't do any damage because the bombs were "ersatz." "Ersatz," meaning fake or imitation, was a German word, a hangover from the First World War when, after the war, it was learned that the Germans were making ersatz bread out of sawdust.

In one way or the other, the cadets practiced ersatz bombing every day. When they flew out over the desert to practice bombing, was it dangerous? Not the bomb, Jack said; the bomb was full of harmless black powder and when it landed it simply sent out a puff of smoke so that hits could be assessed. And the planes? Were *they* dangerous? "Well," Jack said, "planes are planes, with a lot of complicated stuff in them." Meaning, I took it, that a lot of things could go wrong.

Jack told me he had heard from Irv Rubin, his old college buddy, who'd said that he was now in pilot training. The timing had apparently worked out right for Irv. When he had graduated and his deferment had ended, the jam for pilot-training spaces had cleared, and he had gotten one of the slots. I could tell that Jack was a little disconcerted by this. Being the pilot—the captain of the ship—was of course attractive to any airman, and Jack was no exception. When I asked him about it, he said, "Well, the whole mission—the preparation, the training—is geared toward getting me over the target, and that feels good enough."

In one letter Irv had written that his two brothers—Jack (yes, yet another Jack) and Harold—were also now in the service, Jack a G.I. in the infantry and Harold an officer in the artillery. His parents, Irv said, felt that they were being sorely tested. "They don't know which one of the three of us to worry about the most," he wrote Jack, "though it probably should either be Jack or Harold. It's possible I'll be in the CBI [the China-Burma-India theater of war], but they're very likely to be fighting Germans, and on the ground."

What that meant, of course, was that in case of capture, Jack's and Harold's dogtags would have an *H* for Hebrew, and by this time we knew a bit more about what the Germans were doing to the Jews. When I'd first heard about this dogtag letter *H*, I'd had a doubtful moment, but Jack said that it wasn't for discrimination purposes but to designate the kind of burial service required. "So I'll be going to my reward as a religious man, like it or not," Jack joked.

Dogtags carried three different letters denoting religious affiliation: *C* for Catholic, *P* for Protestant, and *H* for Hebrew (which I guess was thought to be less crude than *J* for Jewish). And if you died as a Muslim or Buddhist or one of the variety of religions not *C*, *P*, or *H*? For these irregulars, no doubt a generic burial awaited.

After we had talked, Jack and I went back down the hall to our bedroom. Well, to our bed. When we finally got up, we dressed and came out again. Midge was home. Wes was home as well, in the back of the house getting dressed.

Wes emerged all scrubbed and fresh, smelling of aftershave, and his verve, as if it had finally broken free of the truck cab, leaped about him like lightning strikes. He was medium height and spare, with close-cropped gray hair and very blue eyes. Though he was open and engaging like Midge, he was very unlike her in how he chose to express this, for his words were softly uttered, and circumspect. But like Midge he was full of energy. Indeed, after a long haul, when most truck drivers might have opted for bed, Wes Folsom, after a bath and a change of clothes, was ready to welcome us to dinner. He stood before us, offering drinks. "Who's having what?" he asked, as an encouragement announcing that he himself was having an "Old Lady." "It's just a straight shot of Ancient Age," he explained to us. "In trucker language."

If Jack was waiting to hear Midge's way with the language, if he was waiting for a Midgism, he was rewarded almost immediately. She had only just greeted him and asked how he was doing at the air base when she said, "What with the air base getting so big, there's an awful lot of riff-rats moving in."

Wes more than anything wanted to talk about books. Midge had told me that Wes was what she had called "a bear for books," and I had thought it something to write home about that we were to be in the home of a truck-driving bibliophile. Though Wes was exceedingly down to earth—as down to earth as a cow flop, we would have said in Tennessee—he had a very lofty hero in Mortimer Adler. He had just finished reading Adler's latest work, *How to Read a Book,* and he was awash in ideas. Had Jack read much of Adler's work? What did he think?

As it turned out, Wes's "red hots" that Midge had predicted derived not, as I had feared, from our being Jewish but from Jack's being a reader. Since Wes was one as well, the "red hots" were about being able to talk about books.

Wes actually was delighted that we were Jewish. Our being Jewish like Adler made us seem like family. Wes was one of those who thought Jews had a lock on intellectualism, and he had even added his own little wrinkle. "Jews are born that way," he said to us. "It's inherited." Jack tried to refute this with historical reasoning, in which motivation was invoked instead of gene theory, but if he impressed Wes with these thoughts or not, it didn't matter: the fact remained that Wes Folsom was clearly pleased to be among Jews.

In the living room, at the little card table specially set up for guests, the meal went on and on, pleasantly, with Jack and Wes talking books, agreeing, disagreeing, and drinking a respectable number of Old Ladys. But pretty soon Jack looked at me, and I looked at him. Jack put down his drink, I said I was really tired, and we walked back to our bedroom. Well, yes, I *was* tired, but it was a long time before we disengaged and went to sleep.

CHAPTER 5

The next day, with Jack's seventy-five-dollar allot-
ment check in my pocket—courtesy of the U.S. government—
we borrowed Midge's car and went to San Berdoo to buy me
some clothes. I found that there would be an occasion for
"puttin' on the dog" after all—Jack's graduation, a couple of
months away—so we bought me a dress-up dress, and I tried
to describe for Jack the dresses that had been stolen away from
me in Chicago. Jack put his hand to his forehead and pre-
tended to "see" them. "Ah, the pink silk," he joked. "I see it at
a gangster gala draped around some moll."

When we got back from San Berdoo, we went to the movies
and saw George Montgomery in *Riders of the Purple Sage*.
One would have thought that Victorvillians, even temporary
ones, would have had enough of the "purple sage" state of
mind, but no, townspeople and cowboys and military people

filled the theater to overflowing. The next day, Sunday, we went bowling in the afternoon, and then Jack returned to the base. And I went back to Midge's to wait another week for those precious hours with Jack.

Waiting for the weekends was chiefly what my stay in Victorville was all about. During the week I had a lot of time for letter writing, so I wrote to my parents every other day, to Jack's parents (Jack wrote to them whenever he felt like it, which was not as often as I thought it should be), to my sisters, to my brother, to friends. I wrote to Laura a couple of times but received no answer. My sister Minna wrote me that she was pregnant, so I bought some yarn and a crochet needle at the ten-cent store. Despite not really knowing how to crochet, I managed to work the needle in and out, and pretty soon I had made something the size of Rhode Island with less form. "I don't quite know what it is," I wrote to Minna, "but maybe you can use it for a nursery rug?"

I had my first letter from my father. When he wrote a whole letter, not just a postscript to my mother's, I knew it was important. This letter told of a battle between a German submarine and a tanker that had taken place just up the coast at Pompano Beach. My father was still patrolling, and after the incident at Pompano, he was taking his job even more seriously. "We know U-boats are out there," he wrote. He had gotten fond of footnotes, and he'd put a big star after "U-boat," explaining at the bottom of the page that "U-boat" (just coming into our vocabulary) was short for *Unterseeboot,* German for "submarine," a fact he had no doubt picked up from a German-born acquaintance.

For the purpose of spotting U-boats, he had bought the most powerful, most expensive binoculars available. They were Bausch & Lomb, which meant they were German made, and he wrote, "It would be a nice joke if I spotted a German submarine with my new German-made glasses." Still, the binoculars "weren't the ticket." There was apparently nothing wrong with the glasses, but he had a morning shift and had to look into the sun. "You imagine you're seeing subs and everybody gets excited," he wrote, "and then what is it—a stingray."

I walked into town every day, usually right after breakfast, when the desert air had not yet warmed and was so crystalline that if you looked up, you felt you could see directly into some other world. On the skin the air was cool and crisp, a bit standoffish, I thought, very unlike the hot, moist, intimate breath of Florida. My routine was to have lunch at the snack shop—named the Scuttlebutt, no doubt for the servicemen's word for military gossip—come home for a bit, and then have dinner at the Green Spot Café.

The Green Spot was a mecca for disparate groups—townspeople, air-base personnel, bus passengers, Mexican laborers from the spreads. Appropriate to its name, it was a study in green. The walls were green, the floor green linoleum. Green leatherette sheathed the booth benches, the barstools, the chair bottoms.

Spelling the green were endless streams of shiny chrome. It was everywhere shiny chrome could be: bar rail, bar mirror and seat-back edges, salt and pepper caddies. Being lately from Florida, I found such lavish use of chrome—or any metal, for that matter—downright unnatural. In South Florida, and especially in Miami Beach, metal was employed sparingly, for in the salt breezes metal rusted even as you looked at it. My father complained about the problem, particularly as it concerned his much-loved Buick. "One day you got a shiny black fender," he'd grumble, as if it were all a plot conceived by General Motors, "and then you get a little nick and all of a sudden you got a red something you don't know what." My father had learned to drive only after we'd moved to Florida—having in Tennessee depended on my brother and, after my brother left, on a local black man—and as a result was an imperfect, if serene driver who got more than his share of "little nicks." At any rate, out here in the dry desert air, my father's fenders would have remained pristine.

The jukebox at the Green Spot, at the far end of the room, was festooned in chrome, and never quiet. Some of its songs unmistakably spoke of war, some didn't, though even those that didn't were interpreted that way. Novelty songs usually related, like "They're Either Too Young or Too Old," about having to date the pickings left from the draft. Among the big bands, Glenn Miller and Benny Goodman reigned on, though Charlie Barnet and Woody Herman and Harry James were definitely in the running.

Lack of space meant the Green Spot was not good for dancing, though one tiny place next to the bar stayed clear, and every once in a while a couple, overcome, would get up and dance there. The nation was now completely won over by jitterbugging, and if you sat in the vicinity of the dancers, your chances of being hit by a flying arm or leg were pretty good. But the jukebox sent out slow music as well, and on one occasion Jack pulled me up to dance when Helen Forrest sang "I Don't Want to Walk Without You." No jitterbuggers joined us, and we danced on alone, not speaking, just holding each other closely, listening to the words.

For serious dancing, we went to the Scuttlebutt, a barn of a place where cadets and enlisted men took their visiting girl-friends or the few town girls. Though it had a jukebox, the Scuttlebutt could not be called a "jook joint," since it served no alcohol at all, not even beer. It was done up in light-colored wood with a coat of shellac and was furnished only as neces-sary—jukebox, fountain with stools, a few booths, a couple of tables and chairs—so you could jitterbug without danger of maiming.

The few town girls were dated up into infinity. When they happened to come into the Scuttlebutt on their own, they had only to walk in the door to be "hubba hubba"-ed by dateless servicemen. "Hubba hubba" was a military expression, a wolf whistle in words, that had sprung up and taken hold, and when-ever girls came into the vicinity of servicemen, the call was sure to be heard. By use of voice inflections, some servicemen were able to communicate a whole range of messages. They were vir-tuosos of the "hubba hubba," and much respect was paid.

In the back of the Scuttlebutt a windowed cubbyhole served as the post office, and behind a partition the women of the town gathered in a program called Bundles for Britain, whose purpose was to collect useful items, pack them in boxes, and send them over. Jocelyn, the young woman who owned the Scuttlebutt, took me back there and introduced me, and on my second day in town I sat in.

The group collected clothes, cleaned them, packed them, and sent them off. If the clothes needed repair, they were repaired. I started with buttons, graduated to rips, and realized that my mother's interest in sewing had taken hold in me. From the ranches we got cowboy garb—everyday dungarees and embroidered dress shirts. Somebody donated some chaps, but we didn't send them. We couldn't quite see how chaps could be put to use by the average Englishman.

Like my mother's group at home, we packed cans of food, cartons of cigarettes, and enough candy to trigger a cavity epidemic in the British juvenile population. We rolled and packed bandages as well. We did whatever we thought the people of Britain needed, felt deprived of, or were nostalgic for. To bind the friendship we sent peanut butter and chewing gum, which we had heard they knew nothing of.

On the walls of the little workshop, we pasted newspaper pictures of bombed-out London sites and of children being sent on trains to strangers in the countryside. We felt very close to the British and smiled at what we thought we knew about them—their stiff upper lips, their reserved demeanors, and especially their courage—though since none of us had ever been to England, we had no way of knowing whether these qualities actually prevailed. Still, we liked the idea of them.

When finally the British bombed Cologne—the first really big attack on a German city—we stuck up a picture of Churchill giving his V-for-Victory sign at some air force base, threw ourselves a party, and sang all the British songs we knew. We sang the last war's "It's a Long Way to Tipperary" and "Roses of Picardy," as well as this one's "White Cliffs of Dover." All very sentimental to be sure, and if I cried, so did everybody else. During moments like this, I would be saying to myself that if it weren't for the war, the war would suit me right down to the ground.

At Bundles for Britain I got to know some of the other cadet wives. One stood out—Violet Fay Cousins, who was living very differently from me on a ranch owned by a hobbyist couple from Los Angeles. Violet Fay was from Texas, not very pretty but very proper. She was tall and blondish, always perfectly groomed in a mid-calf dress, high heels, and gloves. She spoke in a Texas drawl and talked a lot about "the way we do it in Texas," as if "the way we do it in Texas" was written in stone for all others to heed. What I had heard in Miami Beach— "the way we do it in New York"—did not come close to the certainty of "the way we do it in Texas."

Violet Fay spoke often of her mother and father, whom she called "Mama and Daddy," and of her grandparents, whom she called "Big Mama and Big Daddy," all apparently customary Texas terminology. The family, Violet Fay told us, was in the oil business, and Big Mama and Big Daddy lived in the "big house," with Mama, Daddy, and Violet Fay and her siblings living on the land in another house, presumably the not-so-big house.

Violet Fay had a mammy. "Really a member of the family," she said. This was a note I was very familiar with, how a particular servant was "a member of the family." But even I, unquestioning as I had been, knew that when you took real notice, there was the servant serving and the family being served. It was true that at a funeral for a family member the servant sat with the family, her presence in their pew being noted by all, and at the house after the church services a fuss would be made over her and she would be sat down and served, but when you saw her on Monday, there she was in her familiar role, fixing the biscuits, making the beds.

I too had had a mammy in Tennessee, but I didn't mention this to Violet Fay. My part-time mammy simply didn't measure up to Violet Fay's Texas mammy, who, according to Violet Fay, would have "given her soul" for her mistress. My Lizzie Maud had clearly been fond of me, but would she have "given her soul" for me? No, and it's my opinion that Violet Fay's mammy would not have either.

I guess I was learning to be a bit doubtful, because these stories of Violet Fay's in which she starred as southern belle were definitely suspect to me. I wrote my sister Ruth about my suspicions, and she wrote back, "I think Mammy has pulled Miss Violet Fay's corset too tight." Still, the rather plain Violet Fay had snagged the very handsome Gordon, who had left his Texas hometown and gone on to be a male model, so she might have been the oil heiress she claimed to be. I had no difficulty in believing that Gordon had been a model, for he was indeed extremely good-looking. I was somewhat disappointed to learn that he had not been the Arrow Collar Man but one of the smiling blond men in the Sears Roebuck catalog.

Other cadets' wives turned up at the Scuttlebutt and, occasionally, a cadet sweetheart. Priscilla Lane, one of the Lane sisters of the movies, tiny with long blond hair and the sweetheart of one of the upperclassmen, sat in once. She was in the middle of making a movie and had to go back to Hollywood. Surprised by her reason for leaving, I had to remind myself that ordinary life was going on out in the country, something that while I was living in Victorville, California, was sometimes hard to remember. Later, when I was living hither and yon and the war was making its presence known minute-to-minute, it was just about impossible. As it turned out, Priscilla Lane was going to war in her own way: she was making a movie called *The Saboteur,* which had a wartime setting and was about sabotage in an aircraft factory.

Violet Fay's mention of her mammy made me notice that I had seen no blacks in the whole of Victorville. I certainly never saw any around town or at the Scuttlebutt, and when I mentioned this to Jocelyn's boyfriend, Lamar, who was a sergeant at the air base, he said there weren't any out there either.

Raised as I had been in a place where blacks outnumbered whites, I found this circumstance exceedingly strange. Could it be true—that Victorville was a town exclusively white? Once I was convinced that Victorville was such a town, I wondered if it followed that there were no race problems, such as were always on the front burner in the South. If there was an absence of blacks, was there therefore a problem-free environment? No, I was to discover that other problems in the West took the place of that familiar southern one. There was indeed one particular and puzzling issue that I never would have guessed at had I not gotten to know one of Jack's fellow cadets.

Aside from whatever else I did at the Scuttlebutt, as a soda-fountain veteran, I often sought out Jocelyn for some professional talk. Currently she was feuding with Coca-Cola because she carried the less expensive Pepsi-Cola syrup for her fountain drinks, and when customers asked for a "coke," the Coca-Cola people said that meant Coca-Cola and not Pepsi. It was not exactly a pivotal moment in history, but Jocelyn, who was doing what was normally considered man's work—owning and operating a business enterprise—felt she was being singled out. She would get so disgusted that she would point to the Rosie the Riveter posters around the store and say that if Coca-Cola didn't leave her alone, she'd just go into factory work. "Anyway," she told me, "it's more of a contribution to the war effort than just having a place for rowdy boys to hang out."

There was a lot of "Rosie the Riveter" talk going around, and we saw many a Lockheed Aircraft poster of a young woman, riveting gun in hand, riveting away. After the Norman Rockwell cover on the *Saturday Evening Post* came out, Rosie was always shown wearing her helmet and, under it, her trademark snood, a kind of mesh bag for holding back the hair. In the country there were Rosie the Riveters by the thousands. Indeed, it was due to all the Rosies that America was able to produce a hundred thousand airplanes in four years, rather than the measly fifty thousand that President Roosevelt had promised.

If Jocelyn or any young woman wanted to make an official contribution to the war, there was the Women's Army Auxiliary Corps, which was based on army regulations and, furthermore, promised smart Philip Mangone–designed uniforms. We soon called it the WAAC, which gave those unimpressed with the idea of women as soldiers the opportunity to refer to them as Waacos. Jocelyn said often that she was sorely tempted, but in the end she decided to stay with her rowdy boys and her boyfriend, Lamar.

Lamar was what was called "permanent party," which meant that he was part of the infrastructure and therefore not as subject to transfer as the cadets. I very much looked forward to Lamar coming over and sharing my booth, for he was privy to all the scuttlebutt and would tell me everything. In the case of accidents, I always heard of them first from Lamar, after which I would rush over to Midge to find out what she knew that Lamar didn't, which, in many cases, was the rest of the story. Most times she was able to tell me not to worry, that she had already checked and found out that there had been no fatalities. As I would come running into the Green Spot, even before I had a chance to ask, she would call out, "Don't worry, honey, he's okay."

As to her problems with Coca-Cola, Jocelyn finally beat them. When customers asked for a "coke," she had worked out that if she responded with "Did you order a 'cola'?" it got her off the hook. It was a great solution, I thought, one worthy of my father, the Solomon of the retail business. When I wrote him about it, he wrote back that Jocelyn must have a *"yiddisher kop."* A Jewish head.

My mother wrote to me often in Victorville with all the news—local, family, and war. After the German U-boat attacks in the Atlantic, she wrote that gasoline rationing had come to the East, under which my father had been given a Class A stamp (to be displayed on the windshield), which limited him and his Buick to three gallons a week. Their routine had been to grocery shop at the Piggly Wiggly in town once a week; now, my mother wrote, "One trip to the Piggly Wiggly, and the car goes back in the garage." As my father had never really liked to drive and my mother had never really trusted him when he did it, for them a Class A stamp was actually something of a blessing in disguise.

There were also stamps that allowed more gas: Class B stamps went to those, such as traveling salesmen, who needed them for work, and Class C ones to doctors and law enforcement people. There had initially been a Class X for such VIPs as members of Congress, but people got mad about it, and it was withdrawn.

My sister Ruth was back home, and my mother wrote that they were sewing together. Never mind that Ruth was now qualified as an interior designer; my mother was impressed by her sewing skills. She wrote me, "You wouldn't believe what a maven Ruth is at making faced buttonholes," faced buttonholes being to my mother the ultimate in sewing achievement. In one of Ruth's letters, she said she had met an OCS guy at Servicemen's Pier. "I like him a lot," Ruth wrote. "And the folks like him too. He's from New York and Mama's thrilled that he speaks such good Yiddish."

When my mother wrote that she had planted a Victory Garden, I was not surprised. I had always known that at the first suggestion that homefronters might want to think about growing their own food, my mother would do it. "So hot out there you could faint from it," she wrote to me, "and mosquitoes on you like a blanket." Nevertheless she went out daily to tend her tomatoes and her squashes, and, using the Tennessee expression for canning, she sometimes wrote that she had spent the morning "putting them up."

In the West, rationing was yet to happen. California gave

you the feeling that you were sort of living in another country, or at least not in the same country on the same day, that you were always one day behind. But when President Roosevelt called for a nationwide "scrap drive," we knew he was talking to us as well. The drives were mostly for rubber because, after the Japanese invasion of Malaysia and the Dutch East Indies, rubber had become exceedingly scarce. So old tires were turned in at the collection point—the local filling station—as were even minor items like raincoats, garden hoses, bathing caps, and gloves. Some women from the Bundles for Britain group took on the obligation of going door-to-door collecting, though I made sure that someone else knocked on the door of a certain Mrs. Gillis. Still, even though the country's participation in "drives" was enthusiastic, it did not forestall rationing.

My father did the writing whenever he had learned a bit about the Jewish situation in Germany. In one of his letters he cited an item by a *New York Times* correspondent (with a big star by his name, and when I looked at the note below, I learned that the man had been trapped in Germany when the United States entered the war). In the item the correspondent had reported that the Germans had massacred half a million Jews in the Baltic States, Poland, and western Russia. "It's awful," my father wrote in that letter, "but at least somebody's paying attention. Could be we'll begin to know some things."

This was the first serious consideration, the first in-depth reporting of what was happening to the Jews of Europe. There had, of course, been dribs and drabs of information before this, coming to us by way of evacuees who had made their way out of Germany and into New York, coming to us third- and fourth-hand, coming to us through the air. My father said that these early emigrants had gotten to America "by the seat of their pants," meaning that they had been forced to improvise with maneuvering, deception, and *shmeering* (bribing). But the stories they told, carried by word of mouth from one part of the country to the other, were all we had. The newspapers and the news organizations were silent.

There was no debating whether the papers had known all along about the Nazi designs for the Jews: they had known about it since Hitler's declaration in October 1939, in which he'd proclaimed that the Jews would henceforth be "isolated." They had known about it in 1939, 1941, and 1942, when in three speeches Hitler had said that he would exterminate the Jews. They had known about it in September 1939, when the publisher Julius Streicher wrote in the Nazi organ *Der Sturmer* that "the Jewish people ought to be exterminated root and branch. Then the plague of pests would have disappeared . . . at one stroke."

Why we were learning so little and why the papers did not carry reports commensurate to the enormity of the events was intensely discussed among Jews. Opinions varied widely. My brother, like many others, was of the opinion that the *New York Times* was to blame because in its role as the national newspaper, it was in a position to influence other papers to treat the story in a bigger way. "It could lead the way," he wrote to me. "Instead it says nothing." Those who held this view maintained that since the *Times* was owned by Jews, it took pains to avoid presenting the appearance of a Jewish organ agitating on Jews' behalf.

Some few blamed Roosevelt and said he had asked the papers to go easy on the Nazi horrors. They said he was "playing footsie" with Hitler, just as Chamberlain had done; and they criticized him for his reluctance to permit Jewish refugees to enter the country. These Roosevelt blamers were in the minority, and my father was not one of them, for like most of the other immigrant Jews, my father considered Roosevelt his hero, and he could not bring himself to fault him. If Roosevelt appeared indifferent, my father and these others argued, this consummate politician was simply biding his time, waiting for the right moment to bring America into the war—the moment when psychology, preparedness, and emotion came together. The contention here was that Roosevelt was well aware of the virulent anti-Semitism in the United States and felt it quite conceivable that some citizens secretly applauded (and others not so secretly) the slaughtering of Jews. At any rate, this position argued, if Roosevelt decided too early to go out on a limb for the Jews, he would risk losing the big victory in order to gain the small one.

Not being privy to the byzantine political issues, not having any more inside information than anyone else, I did not know then and I do not know now the reasons we were kept in relative ignorance of what was happening to the Jews of Europe. The only thing I know for sure is that we were made fully aware of the Nazi crimes against Jews only when Allied troops entered the concentration camps at the end of the war in Europe.

It was then that we also heard about the reports that had been repressed. We heard, for instance, that as early as August

1942, while Jack and I were still in Victorville, a cable had been sent by a Jewish-German intimate of a particular German industrialist to the State Department and to the British Foreign Office with information about Nazi plans as regarded Jews. The Nazis, this cable confirmed, were making plans to exterminate four million of them "at one blow," the cable said, and even gave the particulars: the method of extermination was to be prussic acid. As we discovered, the cable had been passed around—and around—to ambassadors, to vice consuls, to the British parliament, to the legendary rabbi Stephen Wise, until it was finally acknowledged.

My father had clearly been looking everywhere for information, and the next week he enclosed a clipping from the *Times*, a summary of the report of the Jewish Labor Bund of Poland verifying Nazi massacres of Jews. My father said to take a good look at the clipping. "Notice," he wrote, "that it comes from an inside page of the *Times* and it's a big two inches long."

My mother added a postscript to this letter. "Have you cooked a meal for your husband yet?" she asked, and she enclosed her recipe for noodle pudding.

CHAPTER 6

It was true that I had been married for almost half a year and had yet to fix a meal for my husband. Acting on my mother's nudge, I decided to do it. Nothing to it, I told myself: get a cookbook, follow the recipes, and—presto!—turn out a wonderful dinner.

I was confident. Invite some people, I told Jack; let's have a dinner party. So Jack, mistaking confidence for competence, invited Clayton Harms and Jerry Bulla, two fellow cadets. There would just be the four of us. Wes was on the road, and Midge was working.

I decided on an all-American dinner: steak, french fries, peas, avocado salad, apple pie, iced tea. Except for the avocado salad, there was almost nothing on my menu that I had ever seen my mother do: she never made steak or french fries, and though she did bake apple pies, I had never watched her do it, as I was not what you would call the kind of daughter who trailed her mother around the kitchen. Never mind. I could read; I could follow directions, couldn't I? And I knew how to fix iced tea, didn't I? Open a can of peas? Of course. I saw the dinner ending in glasses of iced tea lifted in a toast to my skills.

Clayton and Jerry had been to the house often. Clayton, tall, fair, and thin, was from Alabama, and we talked a lot. We did as all southerners do in alien territory and used as many southernisms as we could, like "dassent" and "no-count" and "Miz." We said we had a "yearnin'" for southern cooking, and I agreed with Clayton that "chittlin's"—pig's intestines—were delicious, even though I was thoroughly repelled by them. But I was truthful when I said I missed banana sandwiches—bananas squashed with mayonnaise on white bread—and Clayton said, "We'll have to fix us some sometime." We did some southern "trash talkin'," about the scarlet ladies in our towns and how in Clayton's town their scarlet lady had taken on the whole high school football team; and Clayton told the story of how he himself had consumed "about a gallon" of the South's favorite party punch, Purple Jesus (white lightning, or moonshine, mixed with grape juice), and had spent the night in a defunct outhouse.

Clayton had gone to Auburn University, which meant that he and Jack had a special bond: Auburn and Florida were in the same football conference and shared the frustration of knowing that no matter how successfully the Auburn team or the Florida team performed during the season, in the end the conference championship would be won by the University of Alabama.

But I especially liked Jerry. Jerry—short, dark, and cherubic

—was Mutt to Clayton's Jeff. Jerry was a whole new breed to me, having been, as he said, "hatched" in Hawaii. And as if longing for his homeland, he kept a Hawaiian shirt at Midge's house, a gaudy green affair replete with parrots and hibiscus blossoms. Whenever he came over, he put it on.

Thank goodness Jerry was there for my first dinner. Without him it would have been even more tormented than it was. Things in the kitchen kept going wrong, and Jerry finally took it upon himself to come in to check on me. For a moment I wondered if this male was actually entering the kitchen—terra incognita for most men, and in Jewish households for most anybody but "Mama"—to help. I sincerely hoped so, for I was becoming aware that I needed all the help I could get.

Jerry went to work. He pulled the steak from the oven— after having been there for an hour or so at 200 degrees, it was now a sullen gray—and poured Midge's orangey steak sauce over it. He extracted the potatoes from the still-melting grease and put them under the broiler. He threw out the avocado. "Hard as a coconut," he said, which I understood meant that that avocado was about as hard as a thing could get.

There was nothing he could do about the tea. In the South everybody knows that tea that has been allowed to get cold cannot be sweetened properly, so I had known enough to add sugar immediately at the boil, thereby fixing what in Union City we called "sweet tea"; but I had not taken the tea leaves out. When I poured the tea into glasses, the color was not the spirited one of memory but a pensive purple, and Clayton offered that he hadn't seen anything like that "fascinatin' fluidity" since his folks had had a gully washer in the back forty.

Capping the climax (to Midge it was "clapping" the climax) was the pie. The trouble was that when I had made the pie dough, I had dismissed the recipe line that read, "Don't overwork" as I didn't know at what point "overwork" set in. So I had pounded it, thrashed it, and pummeled it, and in so doing had produced a slab of concrete. Jerry saved me yet again by scooping out the apples. "Call it 'accidental applesauce,' " he said, "and eat up."

Jack tried to be supportive. "Great steak," he said, though any taste came solely from the steak sauce. Afterward, he lifted up his glass, which contained not my tea but beer, and asked the others to join in. So I did, after all, receive my toast.

In the letter to my mother, I said, "My dinner was swell."

"Swell" was a word that I find in virtually every letter I wrote or received, and it described big items and little ones. (Wasn't it "swell" that the British had sent a thousand planes over Cologne? Wasn't it "swell" about the Battle of Midway? [This about a momentous win and a real turning point in the Pacific War.] Wasn't *Pride of the Yankees* just "swell"?) Something better than "swell" warranted "killer-diller," which did double duty as adjective and noun. (The Doolittle raid was a "killer-diller"; Robert Taylor had "killer-diller" looks.) In the case of my dinner, however, I felt I had gone far enough—too far—with "swell."

After that dinner Jerry and I got very close. We talked about a lot of things, some of which involved cooking, some of which didn't. He considered me his confidante, and he talked to me about everything. He told me he had no luck with girls—"I not only can't get to first base," he said, "I can't even get up to bat."

He said he had grown up the oldest child in a poor family and that all of his siblings had dropped out of school to go to work. He had not dropped out of school. During the day he'd gone to school and at night he'd worked. "I wanted to set an example for the other kids," he said to me. "I couldn't let them think that all there was to life was how you were born." I learned a lot from Jerry and came to some very serious insights through him, one of which brought about in me a truly seismic change.

When we cooked together, it was with some puzzlement on my part, for Jerry's cuisine of choice was not Hawaiian but Mexican. I considered this: if Jerry was Hawaiian, why was I learning to make *ropa vieja* and flan rather than things with pineapple and coconut? Where was the poi I had heard about in that song "Little Grass Shack"?

It was a couple of weekends before I learned the reality. It was when I asked Jerry about the hula code, about what "you Hawaiians" were trying to convey with all that "swaying and swooshing." At this point Jerry admitted that he had not been "hatched" in Hawaii. He'd been born in Mexico, he told me, and the only thing Hawaiian about him was that green Hawaiian shirt. "When I bought that thing," he said to me, "it gave me the idea to solve a lot of problems by just being Hawaiian." And hula dances? "No hulas in my family," Jerry told me. He laughed. "But if you want to learn the *jarabe tapatio*, I'm your guy."

This was a puzzler. Why the charade? Why had Jerry been trying to pass as something he wasn't? It was unlike Jerry to pose. Even Jack would have said that Jerry was guileless, easy to read, open. I had been presented with something to consider seriously. Was there something wrong with being a Mexican? I didn't know. The fact was, if you grew up as I had, you knew something of Mexico's history and geography, but what you actually knew about Mexicans was precious little, mainly images of Leo Carrillo and Delores del Rio on-screen and Mexican dancers who did the Mexican hat dance. And these things seemed not only unobjectionable but downright enchanting.

Jerry was quick to inform me that this was not a view uniformly shared by those who lived in the American West. "To them," Jerry said, "I'm just the guy with the mustache sleeping in the street with my sombrero over my face and my poncho slung over my shoulder." In the West, he said, Mexicans were looked on as inferior beings, shiftless and lazy. These were adjectives I was very familiar with, ones I had often used myself, though never in connection with Mexicans. Jerry didn't have to spell it out, for I knew what he was telling me: Mexicans were the western version of "niggers."

It all fit. According to Jerry, there were "Mexican jobs"—positions that nobody else wanted, mostly as unskilled laborers, though there were also Mexican gardeners and nannies, employed because they came cheap. Jerry talked about signs, and they rang a very familiar bell with me, only here they said, NO DOGS OR MEXICANS ALLOWED. If I had thought I was well schooled in American prejudices—against blacks, against Jews, even the southern one against RomanCatholics—out of nowhere came a new one. And it had me asking myself, If Jerry chose to be "Hawaiian," who could blame him?

My mother had thought it was time for me to be grown-up

when I was preparing for my wedding, and I want to believe that I put myself on the road toward maturity in this moment with Jerry. For the first time in my life I faced the fact that the sentiment I had tossed off so cavalierly, the one I'd told myself exhibited proper social attitudes and at the same time showed off my good manners—"Don't be ugly to darkies, but keep them in their place"—was in fact the very model of genteel racism. Was this what Jack had had in mind when he had called me "Miss Scarlett" on that hayride night? Had I now, finally, come to Scarlett's "tomorrow"?

Yes, I thought I had. But I had to go through some steps to get where I knew I wanted to go—which was from woolly-headed—or, to be more accurate, cotton-headed—to a head that was clear for thinking. I was having an epiphany, and I thought back to our Union City mentor, Miss Brookie Simmons, who, when she had had a particularly impressive one, would say, "And the scales fell from my eyes." For what it was worth, the scales had fallen from my eyes, and I knew I could no longer be a participant in the game of prejudice and bigotry.

So now I would say, "Do not speak or act in a way that is degrading or damaging to your fellow human beings." Of course it was too pretentious to speak out loud.

But I did say it to Jack. That night, in bed, I repeated to him the whole of my new thinking. "So?" I asked him. "What do you think?"

Jack looked at me long and hard and said, "I think it's time for a celebration."

I agreed that it was a time for a celebration, and Sunday

afternoon we went to the Green Spot and we sat at a table and Jack held his beer up high and toasted me, and this time the toast was not a pretense, as after my first dinner; it was for real. We clinked glasses and we kissed, we kissed and we clinked. When Midge came over to see what all the fuss was about, Jack said, "We're celebrating a conversion." And when Midge looked puzzled, he said, "Stella's decided she doesn't want to be Miss Scarlett anymore."

I thought I should write of my epiphany to my sister Ruth, and she wrote back that when she had been in New York she had "worked hard" to free herself of southern prejudices— "not that there are none up there," she added. "Anyway, welcome to the club."

Jerry's skills as a cook had come through his father, who worked in a small Los Angeles Mexican restaurant, where Jerry had helped out from the time he was a little kid. But was Jerry going to be a restaurant man himself? No, he was going to be an aeronautical engineer.

Every Sunday we made a practice of having a few of the cadets to the house, and I would fix dinner for them, always the dishes Jerry had taught me—guacamole to go with the ubiquitous beer, and then *ropa vieja*—really the only things I could do.

After dinner, we would sit around and talk about various topics, but it was hard to stay on anything but the war. German troops were making their presence felt in central Europe. Their presence was especially onerous in Czechoslovakia, for in that country, in a little village called Lidice, there had been a stunning act of reprisal: in answer to the assassination of the deputy

Gestapo chief Reinhard Heydrich, the Germans had gone about executing all village males and then had set fire to the town. As for the German presence in Africa, the news was equally dispiriting, especially the word that Field Marshal Rommel had captured the Libyan city of Tobruk.

After we had had enough of this kind of talk, Jerry would take out the guitar he kept at the Folsoms' and don his Hawaiian shirt. We would sit around and sing, even Jack, who had no genes at all for carrying a tune by himself but could sing along with others; and whenever Midge had time off and Wes was home, they would join us.

Jerry knew all the current songs—bitter ones like "Paper Doll" and witless ones like "Pistol-Packin' Mama"—but what he knew best were the Mexican ones. He had a favorite singer, Lydia Mendoza, and he sang her songs over and over, especially "Mal Hombre" and "Sola." He kept coming back to them, each time singing with a deeper melancholy. This was a brand-new kind of singing to me, and it seemed to me that neither Frank Sinatra nor any of the rest could top it.

Wes sang along with Jerry. Having often long-hauled to Texas, where Lydia Mendoza—"La Mendoza," Jerry said she was called—had achieved living sainthood, Wes knew her songs very well and sang them in Spanish, just as he had heard them. He could also sing harmony, something I could not do and something he did without thinking, without effort, as all natural-born harmonists do. Wes and Jerry sang most of Lydia Mendoza's songbook, and when their voices came together on "Nunca," I felt that if bliss had a sound, this was it.

• • •

I ALWAYS SAID good night to the boys a bit sadly, but I was never too sad, for I knew that I would see them again— sometimes Martin and Edgar and Alton, but always our core group of Jack, Jerry, and Clayton—the following weekend. What I did not know, could not know, was that one Sunday night when I said good night, there would be for our little group no weekend to follow.

It was on a typical Wednesday afternoon at the Scuttlebutt when it happened, when Lamar came in and delivered one of his bits of news—this time a terrible bit. It was of an accident—"an awful one," he said. And when I ran as usual to Midge with my heart in my mouth and saw an unsmiling Midge, there was a moment of real terror. Jack? Something about Jack? My knees went weak. But it was not about Jack, for Midge immediately called out, "Jack's okay." Still, I knew from her look that it was something desperate. And it was. It was Jerry.

I had never known death in an intimate way. My grandparents and an uncle had died, but my grandparents and my uncle had been figures in my life, not intimates. In Union City when I was six, a neighbor child had died, but after a couple of weeks of avoiding her house and her family—as if the place where she had died was haunted by her spirit and as if having such bad luck had made the family pariahs—I resumed my normal life because I was six, and at six there is no such thing as having an intimate friend.

But Jerry and I had exchanged confidences, had talked over our place in the world, had teased, laughed, commiserated, sung songs together, danced the *jarabe tapatio*. I had lost a true friend. I had lost Jerry Bulla. Jerry Bulla was a casualty of war. It had started already, and we were not yet even in the real thing.

Midge and I held on to each other. "Not Jerry, not Jerry," I said over and over, and Midge said, "The poor kid, the poor little kid." The engines on Jerry's plane had quit, and the plane didn't have enough altitude for parachutes. Jerry's pilot and his instructor had gone down with him. Midge had known all three. I had known only Jerry. They had all just died out there in the desert.

In another month there was graduation. Along with their second lieutenant's bars, the men were to get their wings, and I had thought earlier that since no one was going to be there for Jerry, I would pin on his wings after I had pinned on Jack's. At the ceremonies at the air base, the commander pinned Jack's second lieutenant's gold bars on his jacket, and I pinned on his wings. Jerry did not need me to do it for him.

There was no joy for Jack and me at the Arrowhead Lake Springs Hotel graduation party. What was supposed to have been a festive event in posh surroundings—with me in my new green satin dress—was for us a sorrowful duty. Jack gathered the other cadets around and made a ceremony of taking the wings that would have gone to Jerry and putting them in an envelope to be sent to Jerry's family, and though everybody said a word or two about Jerry, it didn't help much. So Jack and I decided to quit the party early and go to our room. In the morning we got up early and played tennis on strange-looking courts that sat on flattened hilltops, but there was no fun in it.

Later, when we got back to the Folsoms, I asked Midge what

to do with Jerry's guitar and shirt, and she said to send them to his family. No, I thought, I'm going to give the guitar to Wes, to learn to play during those long nights on the road. That's what Jerry would have liked. And that Hawaiian shirt I was going to keep for myself.

While we grieved over Jerry, our mood was only reinforced by the war news. In August, Canadian commando troops lost over three thousand men in a failed attempt to raid the coastal French city of Dieppe, and the Battle—the siege—of Stalingrad had begun.

CHAPTER 7

As we made plans to leave Victorville, there were things for Jack and me to feel upbeat about. Jack had finished his training, was now an officer, and, as far as he was concerned, was now ready to launch into military adventures. First, however, he was being sent to Salt Lake City for future assignment. What his being an officer meant to us in a practical way was that we could now afford to go into debt.

The debt involved a car. The Victorville bowling alley manager had been drafted and was selling his car, so Jack bought it. When you bought a car in those days, you bought a used one, for new cars were no longer being manufactured. (This presented no hardship for the automobile manufacturers, however, for they were now turning out vast numbers of military vehicles—jeeps, tanks, and so forth.) Our car was a 1940 Silver Streak Pontiac, which Jack, harking back to his Shakespeare, called "a glistering phaeton." It was a two-door black coupé with a sure enough silver streak down its entire length and so streamlined that the backseat passengers rode with bowed heads. Jack gave the bowling alley manager a hundred and fifty dollars and a promise to send him a check for the other hundred and fifty. Since the West was still getting all the gasoline it wanted, off we would go to Salt Lake City in the Silver Streak.

Jack also needed to buy Army Air Corps officers' uniforms. These were, of course, regulation: khaki shirts and pants for everyday wear, and a couple of sets for dress. Dress uniforms consisted of hat, pants, shirt, and jacket, the latter curiously called a "blouse." They were wool and they cost a lot, and though there was something of a clothing allowance, it didn't cover it all. This meant more debt, but this debt was paid for by deductions taken from Jack's paychecks.

The dress uniforms came in two colors, "pinks" and "greens." The pinks were not actually pink but a light beige-gray, and the greens were just plain olive drab. Of course, no matter what the guys wore—enlisted men or officers—one item was always present, something that went around their necks, and that was their dogtags. Jack's were incised with his officer's number (0727680), his blood type, my name and address as his next of kin, and that *H*.

The hat, always "green," was brimmed and structured by means of a metal rib. The rib caused problems for officers who flew. When earphones were placed over the hat, the rib bent and the hat thereby was forced to drape. Some officers removed the retaining rib altogether and wore the hat in a perpetual slouch. The slouching hat was actually the mark of the flying officer—pilot, bombardier, or navigator—and the casual attitude it symbolized was called "raunchy." Enlisted men applied the word in admiration to officers who bent the rules, and it was true that the men who went up into the wild blue yonder bent the rules often and without apology.

As we were leaving the West Coast, there was news of some moment. It was something we had been awaiting—an attack on mainland America. A Japanese warplane had been launched from a submarine and had bombed Mount Emily, Oregon; incendiary bombs had also landed in Brookings, Oregon, and forest fires had been ignited. The incident had no meaning to the war, as it turned out, and was seen as merely a reprisal for the Doolittle raid on Japan, but we all began to believe that if there were to be any more direct hits, they would come in just that way—from Japanese attacks on the West Coast. And chances were good that in Salt Lake City, Jack would be assigned to some base in the West.

In Salt Lake City we stayed in a hotel and got out and walked Salt Lake's broad avenues as much as we could. The city was full of military men, and Jack, now an officer, was newly "taking a salute," not giving one, and I was interested to see how he dealt with this. He seemed to do okay—a little self-conscious at first maybe, but soon responding quite well. Perhaps there was something about "taking a salute" that appealed to every officer, hawkish or dovish, autocratic or democratic.

Staying at our hotel was another new officer couple—Paul and Phyllis Blumenthal—and when we went out in the car, they came with us. Paul and Phyllis were Jewish and were from

Nebraska. *Nebraska?* I received the information with some disbelief. Just as it was hard for northerners to believe that Jews lived in the South, it was hard for me to believe that Jews lived in Nebraska. My father had an aphorism he liked to repeat, that the only place you won't find Jews is in a Christian cemetery, and the Blumenthals seemed to bear this out. Even more interesting, at least to me, was that Paul's father was a dairy farmer who bred cows and sold milk to a creamery. And more surprising still, the farm had originally belonged to Paul's grandfather, who had come to Nebraska at the turn of the century.

Paul had been to college, but the farm was his passion. Phyllis joked that the Blumenthals had a "dairy dynasty" and that Paul loved those cows as much as he loved her. Paul laughed but agreed that he had every intention of going back to the farm after the war and, when the time came, of turning the farm over to his own kids. "The farm's part of the family," Paul said. "Even the cows are part of the family."

Many things about the Blumenthals were interesting. In Miami Beach, we had balked at going twenty blocks to a synagogue, while the Blumenthals had regularly attended a synagogue in Omaha despite the fact that they lived more than fifty miles from it. It surprised me that there were so many Jewish houses of worship in the Midwest and that they represented such a variety of Jewish thought—Orthodox, Conservative, Reform. It was a world, of course, that Jew-store families never knew. And I learned from Paul that there was at least one rabbi there who was so averse to rites and ceremonies that he would not even permit a Bar Mitzvah. (As my mother would say,

Whoever heard?) The rabbi was from Germany, the home of the Reform movement, but even though Paul had German lineage, his folks were not Reform but Orthodox, and insisted on ceremonies. "My parents think that if you don't have a Bar Mitzvah," Paul said, "you might as well be a *goy.*" In so isolated a place, the Blumenthals also managed to "keep kosher" by having a standing order with a kosher grocery store in Omaha, which they picked up on Friday mornings at the nearby bus station.

Paul Blumenthal was not too tall but was sturdily built. He looked like what he was—a descendant of a German-Jewish family, and as usual some outside influence was credited for his blondness. Paul was also very funny, though his funnyisms were not what I was accustomed to. I was accustomed to New York Jewish funnyisms characterized by wry insider comment, the kind of "hard joking" occasionally heard in the South when one Negro joked with another, the subtext of the joke being a hard truth. Paul, however, was light and sassy. When I first met him and asked him if he was a practicing Jew, he laughed and said, "No, I think I've got it down pat."

Phyllis was from a large Jewish family in Omaha. Like Paul, she was new to me. She was not a "Jew baby," as southern Jewish children called one another, and not a northeastern Jew. And like Paul she spoke in an accent neither southern (or its offshoot, Southern Jewish) nor New York (or its offshoot New York Jewish). Phyllis had other language surprises as well, one of which was that she called a green pepper a "mango." When I heard this, I could scarcely wait to dash off a note to my mother.

Phyllis, small, dark, and bright-eyed, was not at ease in the place she found herself. She was clearly longing to get back to Nebraska, where she could have a proper home, with a proper husband and a proper family. The army life of uncertain postings, transitory friendships, and catch-as-catch-can housing was not for her, though she was definitely trying hard.

After three days in Salt Lake City Jack received his orders, as did Paul. Just as we had expected, Jack and Paul were to report to an air base in the West—Davis-Monthan Field in Tucson, Arizona, a Second Air Force installation. The reason the different divisions of the Army Air Corps were called Air Forces was mysterious, and it was only in 1947 that the Air Corps would separate from the Army, after which it would be called the Air Force.

The day before we were to leave, we and the Blumenthals crowded into the Silver Streak and tooled around in a whirlwind tour of the sights. Since we were in Mormon country, we visited the Tabernacle and talked about the pros and cons of multiple wives—the boys teased and said, "What a paradise," while Phyllis and I said, "What a nightmare." It remained for the Great Salt Lake to be the hands-down highlight. It was a remarkable lake, one that so seamlessly merged with the sky it was hard to determine where the lake ended and the sky began. But what interested the guys was that it was situated on a barren white plain called the Bonneville Salt Flats, the site of famous automobile speed records. The boys gave us Salt Flats names and numbers—369 miles per hour, set by John Cobb in 1939, for example, which was faster than most current planes.

We remembered another, and more gory, story of the Flats, the one about the Donner party, which had traveled through the Flats seeking a shortcut to California, had lost time there, and had been trapped eventually in a Sierra Nevada winter, where those who survived had been forced to resort to cannibalism. We talked about this, and about how the tale might have been hard to believe when we'd read about it; but here on these primitive Utah salt flats, where it had been spawned, it seemed entirely plausible.

I thought it may have been the Flats—so bleak, so ghostly—that made me all at once sick to my stomach. Indeed I was so sick that as we were returning to the car I threw up. The next morning, I threw up again. Was it flu? Excitement? I didn't know it then, but of course it was neither. We were in a hurry to leave, and I didn't have time to think about it.

The Blumenthals were also going to Tucson, but they decided to go by train rather than in our car. (If they didn't want to ride with bowed heads all the way to Tucson, who could blame them?) So we left them and started driving toward Tucson. It was a trip we much looked forward to, since it would take us down the famous road of the canyons.

The trip, however, was not quite what we had hoped for: first of all, our overnights were not at romantic little inns but at "auto camps," which were so far from being bowers of roses that we wore our bedroom slippers in the shower. Furthermore, I didn't stop throwing up during the entire trip. As Jack said, whenever I wasn't throwing up, I threw up. I threw up so much that if we had stopped the car every time I wanted to let go, we would have arrived in Tucson after Jack had been declared AWOL. Trying to outwit this, we bought a cooking pot with a lid, and I held it close.

As to the glorious canyon sights, with my head mostly over the pot, I could not mount the effort to look out the window at the colors of the spires of Bryce and the cliffs of Zion, and I managed only to half-listen to Jack's descriptions. I should have known—even Jack should have known—why I was feeling so nauseated, but we didn't.

IN TUCSON WE roamed the streets before pulling up to what was called a "motor inn," an upscale version of the auto camp, and took a room. The owner was a Mrs. Rosen, so we knew right away she was Jewish. When we checked in, she took a long look at me and wanted to know if I had the flu. Since I didn't know, while Jack went the next day to report to Davis-Monthan, Mrs. Rosen took me to a doctor.

I was examined, I was questioned. And as I sat across the desk from a Tucson doctor, I learned I was pregnant. The baby was to be born in April. And while Mrs. Rosen smiled and said, Mazel tov, I pondered.

With our lives what they were, we had not planned on having a baby, and I tried to consider myself as a mother. I had never been called upon to "baby" somebody; I had only *been* babied. Wait a minute. Actually I had babied a couple of "somebodies"—a little boy who lived across the street from us in Union City and a little girl born to my mammy. I had sung to them and put them to sleep, I had taken them for walks in my doll carriage, and when they had stopped nursing, I had given them their bottles. I had cuddled them and kissed them. Well, I'd kissed the little boy, for my mammy wouldn't allow me to kiss her baby, perhaps thinking that my mother, as a white woman, would disapprove. At any rate, remembering my delight in being a pretend mother, I felt my maternal instincts were intact. Besides, my pregnancy was not a big worry, just a little something to think about. And the birth was seven months (a lifetime!) away, so there was no urgency.

Jack wanted a boy, no doubt about it, because . . . well, because why? To continue a sports dynasty? So the baby could have a shot at becoming president? It was not like Jack to fall in with what was currently considered the ideal—boy first, girl second—but it was definite that he wanted a boy. I could only conclude that going off to war with no certainty of a future, Jack wanted to know that should the worst happen, he would have a son standing in for him.

When Jack reported for duty at Davis-Monthan he learned he would be an instructor training crews for combat duty. I wanted to believe that Jack had been given this instructor's assignment because the Air Corps had recognized his brilliance, but Jack said no, it was clearly the result of his having put down on a form at sign-up that he had been a writing lab "instructor" at the University of Florida. "The word 'instructor' jumped out at them," Jack said. "They didn't read any further than that."

What it meant for practical purposes was that Jack would be stationed in Tucson for some time. This did not altogether suit him, for it meant he wouldn't be seeing action immediately (after all, combat was what he had been training so diligently for). And he warned me that being an instructor in no way guaranteed that in the near future he would not be sent out. "I could be out of here at anytime," he said to me. "A snap of the fingers, and I'm overseas."

Overseas! The word brought with it what we saw in news-reels: bombers flying in huge formations over enemy territory and being shot down, and anti-aircraft fire—*ack-ack*—targeting the crews as they parachuted to earth. Each time I saw such footage, I would think, This is where Jack will be, in the nose of one of those planes, figuring out the whens and wheres. And I saw flak bursting around him.

While we tried to find a more permanent place to live, we stayed with Mrs. Rosen. With my appetite now that of a post-hibernating bear, I spent a lot of time in Mrs. Rosen's kitchen. "I'm in there," I wrote to my sister Ruth, "like a fixed appliance." Mrs. Rosen fed me a lot of Lipton's chicken noodle soup, whose easy-to-prepare envelopes of dried fixings had come onto the market in the nick of time. Like my mother, Mrs. Rosen thought chicken soup took the place of doctors. Her word to me all day long was, "So you'll have some chicken soup and you'll feel better."

Mrs. Rosen was part of the small Tucson Jewish community. She went to services on Friday night, and when the first Friday night came around, did we want to go with her? Well, I did, but Jack didn't. Jack did not want to get involved too deeply in the Jewish community, he said, for it might expect something from us that we would be unable to deliver—a devotion to rites and ceremonies. We had a slight dustup about it, but when I said I was not about to disappoint Mrs. Rosen, Jack yielded.

We went with Mrs. Rosen to her Reform temple. I was a little surprised to find the Blumenthals there, since they were Orthodox. I thought that perhaps they were ready for a switch and, with the change of locale, could do it without fanfare. It was great to see them, and after services we joined them and the other congregants for a nosh at the one Tucson Jewish delicatessen.

Paul Blumenthal's assignment in Tucson was not like Jack's. He was a member of a crew being readied to be "shipped out," an expression I shrank from, bringing to mind, as it did, body bags and wooden coffins. In reality the expression merely meant leaving one facility for another, and in Paul's case it meant he was going overseas, at which time Phyllis would be going back to Nebraska.

LIKE VICTORVILLE, TUCSON was situated in a desert, though it was a desert metropolis, not a desert village. It had a valley virtually all to itself, and it spread out and out, sparkling like a diamond, because a dazzling sun shone upon it every day. Since it was a sand city, water was at a premium, but unlike Victorville, where nobody gave planting a whole lot of thought, Tucson made a fetish of growing green things. Every house, every business, every institution had, in addition to the usual gamut of cactus varietals, its bush here, its hedge there, its little patch of grass, all coddled and cosseted by Mexican laborers who, when it came to it, got down on their hands and knees and trimmed with the kind of scissors usually seen only in sewing baskets. Mexican laborers were indeed all over town, doing any job asked of them—and chiefly the ones that non-Mexicans did not want, just as Jerry Bulla had said.

In Tucson, however, when we weren't thinking about the war, we were thinking not so much about Mexican laborers as about the weather. Though I had experienced the desert climate of Victorville, I recognized that Tucson was on a whole other meteorological level, and when we arrived there in the late summer, the Tucson dryness and heat were full upon us. Routines changed because of the heat. At the base, mechanics could not work during the midday hours because the metal on the planes singed their hands.

The place we found was a small cottage in a court of six identical small cottages. (I would have wished for Paul and Phyllis to be in one, but their situation called for just a rented room. Whenever we went out dancing at the base, however, they always came with us.) The cottages were concrete block, white with blue trim, lined up around a sward of the obligatory grass. Exterior appearances notwithstanding (at first glance they seemed the size of a Tennessee outhouse), the cottages had several rooms—living room, dining room, bedroom, kitchen, and bathroom. Since our particular cottage was an end one, it was the one with the view, the view being "A" Mountain, a Tucson landmark. The cottages were located on Speedway, the main east-west Tucson artery, on which was also located, just a few blocks to the west of us, the University of Arizona. There's no denying that every time Jack and I passed the campus, we thought about college and how it was in our future, just delayed "for the duration." Still, now in my head I was saying it as "if all's well *after* the duration."

The cottages had an answer to Tucson's heat and dryness, one not exclusive to our cottages but one seen throughout the city, in automobiles as well as in houses. The answer was simply a wad of excelsior stuck in a window. The excelsior was in a box open on two sides, and into it water from a container continuously dripped, and behind it a fan blew. This primitive contraption enabled Tucsonians to go on with their lives, otherwise a pretty iffy proposition. Of all the things we liked about our cottage, it was the cooling device that we treasured.

As the heat bore down on us in Tucson, so did the signs of the war. Davis-Monthan servicemen milled in the Tucson streets, and since Davis-Monthan was a hub for planes flying around the country, visiting crewmen with an hour or two to kill milled as well. Reminders of a nation at war were constantly in the Tucson skies, and when we civilians looked up at a particularly large formation of planes glistening and soaring and thundering overhead, we broke into applause.

The newspapers and the radio were full of war news, and movie houses spun out newsreel after newsreel of whatever pictures they had been able to cobble together. Surprisingly, there was an even-handedness, and both successes and failures were shown. We inevitably responded to the good news—the British recapture of Tobruk, the Soviet counterattack at Stalingrad—with loud cheers, and to the bad news—the launching of the first German surface-to-surface missile, the scuttling by the French of their fleet at Toulon—with an uneasy silence.

Tucson undertook the usual drives for rubber, metals, and, at this date, for cans of fat like bacon grease or renderings from beef fat. As always, the collection spots were service stations, but Tucson added a wrinkle by sending out an open-bedded truck to roam the streets with a banner on its side proclaiming

POTS AND PANS FOR VICTORY. That truck was the final resting place for the pot and lid—scrubbed, boiled, and bleached —that had accompanied Jack and me on the trip down from Salt Lake City. "Use it up, make it do, wear it out" was the slogan we all lived by.

Our court of cottages was populated exclusively by military couples, the men, with one exception, either pilots or bombardiers. We got to know them all, and some of them became our best military friends, in particular Bill and Peg O'Connor, who lived just across from us. Bill was doing the same job as Jack—training crews for overseas assignment—and Peg was pregnant like me, so we had a lot in common.

The O'Connors were from Boston and were very Catholic. Peg O'Connor was the Irish Catholic lass of your imagination. If her name didn't convince you, you were ultimately persuaded by the fact that her skin was fair, her hair was red, and her speech was flecked with Irish intonations. She did everything required of her by her religion; prayed every time she felt a prayer might be useful, invoking "Jesus" and "God" and "Mary" often (sometimes putting them into service simultaneously, as in "Holy Mother of Jesus God"); did not eat meat on Fridays; went to mass every Sunday morning.

Peg had chosen the church she attended for specific reasons. She went not to one of the old, old churches full of history to which the Mexican and Indian (or, often, Mexican-Indian) populations flocked but to one that attracted only "real" Catholics. The Mexicans, especially the Mexican-Indians, according to Peg, had "funny" ways, dressed "funny" for church, and performed funny ceremonies. It was clear that in her view

Catholics of European extraction were what God had intended, and she very much missed her big Irish Boston cathedral, and especially her priest, whom she referred to simply as "Father." I think she could not make herself believe that a priest in a Tucson outpost could have the kind of inside track that "Father" did.

I had the impression that as a Catholic, Peg, felt close to us as Jews, perhaps because in Boston, since both Catholics and Jews were straight-ticket Democrats, Catholic politicians could count on the Jewish vote. Furthermore, Peg seemed beyond seeing us as "different," no doubt because her Boston neighborhood was populated by Irish, Portuguese, Italians, Jews, and whatnot. Few nationalities or religions startled her, except, of course, Catholicism as practiced by the Mexicans and Indians of Tucson.

Bill was what we called "cute." Peg called him her "darling Billy," which with her little brogue was "darlin' Billy." Bill made us laugh, and the girls loved him. One of the reasons was that he was slim and agile, which made him perfect for jitterbugging. And jitterbugging was something some husbands—Jack among them—stayed away from, protesting that it made them feel just plain silly.

Bill was also good company, the one who always had a new way to have fun, the one who'd come knocking on our door, open it a crack, and ask, "Can Jack come out and play?" "Play" was tossing a football around in the sward. Although they were the same age, Jack and Bill acted with one another like an older brother (Jack) and a younger one (Bill), and for the usual reasons. Jack liked Bill very much. Even if they didn't agree on everything, Jack said Bill had a "dependable" personality, meaning that once you knew him, you knew him. There were no surprises from Bill, but also no hidden depths. As Jack said, Bill was relaxing.

After playing ball for a while, the boys would sit in the courtyard imbibing a cocktail Bill had invented that he called the "Arizona Sunset," a gin-and-pink-grapefruit-juice concoction. Bill decreed that it had to be drunk facing west. "If you don't face the sunset," Bill said, "the gin gods put a curse on you." Bill created his drink in a silver cocktail shaker that he deeply treasured, its many dings and dents notwithstanding. The one household chore he took seriously was polishing his silver shaker.

As for religion, outside of going to mass on Sundays and employing the usual "Jesus," "Mary," and "Joseph" exclamations, he left most of it to Peg. Bill was sweet, eager to help, and the one I thought the most vulnerable. After Jack, I was most scared for Bill O'Connor.

A couple of doors away were James and Jimmie Lee Stallings, from Texas. In their town twenty miles from Dallas, James had been the high school quarterback—a "watch-pocket quarterback," as small quarterbacks were called after the small pocket at men's waistbands that held their watches; and Jimmie Lee had been a clerk in the town's "ten-cent store" ("tin-cint" she said), what Woolworth-type stores were called in the South.

It might have seemed that the temptation to call them "Jimmy and Jimmie" would be irresistible, but given James's personality, we never dared—we called him "Jim" maybe, but never the diminutive "Jimmy." The fact was, he *was* small in stature, but he made a great show of manliness, and he attempted to divert attention from his size with feistiness and swagger. Jimmie Lee told me that she had had an exceedingly big crush on him but had been so in awe of him that when he'd first asked her for a date, she'd said no, no, she couldn't go, she had to wash her hair. If James was small, Jimmie Lee was tiny, and so thin and pale as to be just about translucent.

Being Texans, James and Jimmie Lee were of course Wasps, and they attended First Baptist in town. Jimmie Lee said the only Jews she had known were the Bornstein family, who ran the shoe store and went to the Jewish temple in Dallas. Their son Leo, she said, never dated the town girls and finally married a girl he had met at one of the Jewish parties in Dallas, one whose family owned a dry goods store in another small Texas town, which I took to be a Jew store. "Leo Bornstein was so cute but he never looked at any of us," Jimmie Lee told me. "He just dated the girls he met in Dallas. Maybe he just liked big-city girls." Well, maybe.

As you might imagine, James was a pilot, for it would be hard to imagine that he would be other than the one in control, and it is altogether likely that he had maneuvered until he'd gotten what he wanted. His regret, he often stated, was that he wasn't a fighter pilot. "God, how I envy those guys," he would say. "They can just get up there and hotdog around," which of course pilots of big bombers could not do. It seemed to me a given that when the boys finally got overseas, James would be the one who flew more missions than anyone else, who fought to stay beyond his required time, and who would emerge much decorated.

Jack neither liked nor disliked James, for there was no way to make a judgment, he said, no way to "get in." Still, Jack very much admired James's skills as a pilot. "He's not just blowing smoke," Jack said. "He's very, very good."

The McTigues lived right next door to us, though they were actually not "the McTigues" at all but Lieutenant Harvey McTigue and Helen Bascombe. Helen worked on the base, and scuttlebutt had it that she was engaged to a lieutenant who had trained at Davis-Monthan and had shipped out some months earlier. "The McTigues" were not what you would have expected from "shack-ups," which is what folks who participated in this kind of arrangement were called. Far from being a suave "smoothie," Harvey McTigue was a hearty, burly young man, an ex–college football player from Oregon; and Helen, a rancher's daughter from near Phoenix, was neither overtly nor subtly seductive.

Perhaps not seeing herself as fitting into a company of wives, Helen kept pretty much to herself. But Harvey, as one who had played college football, was in demand by the boys, and when he came home, he was immediately called over to join the group that sat around the courtyard. "Hey, Harvey, they're cold and they flow," they would say, meaning the Arizona Sunsets, "so get your butt over here." Harvey was a man comfortable in his own big body, and his booming laugh constantly rang out. He was a mine of locker-room jokes (Jack said) and football stories—anecdotes about himself and his fellow linemen, or "pachyderms," as he called them, who were all in the service.

Harvey kept up with all of them, so he had current "pachyderm" stories as well. "My boy Swenson is over in Newport News with the Navy, and damn if he's not wrestling for some Navy team," he said, and added, "Me, I can't stand wrestling. Holding on to somebody's B.O. is not my idea of a good time." Harvey clearly enjoyed having a fine time with his buddies, and his buddies in the courtyard liked having a fine time with him. "You gotta like being with the guy," Jack said. "He enjoys himself so much, it's kind of contagious." Harvey was, like James, a pilot, and it was unthinkable that there would be a circumstance when this big bear of a football lineman would be at a loss.

In one of the two cottages that fronted Speedway were the Hoffenhauers. Mrs. Hoffenhauer was always careful to make clear that Hoffenhauer was a German name (and not Jewish, I took it) and careful to refer to her husband as "the Captain," despite the fact that being a captain in Tucson was not a "big deal" (a new phrase now coming into common currency), as Tucson was awash with majors and colonels, even generals. "In Germany," Mrs. Hoffenhauer would say, "the Captain's family was known as the *von* Hoffenhauers. There's some evidence that they were related to the kaiser."

Captain Hoffenhauer was a veteran of World War I, had been regular Army until he retired, and had been called back into service as a Post Exchange (PX) officer. Mrs. Hoffenhauer was overweight and talky, the Captain small and reserved. I guessed their age to be something around forty-five, so they seemed to me middle-aged. She was fond of what she called her "seniority" and said to us wives of lowly second lieutenants,

"You girls have so much to learn about the Army." And I guess we did. The Hoffenhauers used the base for just about all aspects of their lives, from shopping to Saturday night dancing to attending the nondenominational Protestant chapel.

In spite of the fact that we lived intimately—perhaps *because* we lived intimately—we had issues with each other. I, of course, had an abiding issue with Mrs. Hoffenhauer. How could I not when there was a neon sign on her forehead that flashed WE ARE NOT JEWISH? And Peg had an issue with "the McTigues," especially with Helen. "Father would know what to do," Peg would say. According to Peg there was a crucial problem, for living as she did, Helen had put her soul in danger. "Mark my words, she's going lickety-split to Hell," she predicted. Peg was also wretched over Helen's overseas boyfriend. "Jesus God," Peg pleaded to the above, "do something for the poor thing. He doesn't even know his girlfriend's living in sin." As time went on, I became aware of just how much Peg's religion—and its strictures—dominated her life.

At any rate, according to rumor, Helen finally did break it off with her overseas boyfriend. Peg said, "At least that," and joked that she was going to grant Helen "limited absolution." I knew that Helen must have sent her fiancé a "Dear John," and though it might clear the air for Helen (and other women in her predicament), in the process it surely broke a serviceman's heart, so I was never positive it was the way to go.

Peg and I talked about everything. The only thing we didn't talk about was the danger. We knew we felt the same about it—that we were living precarious lives with desolation perhaps waiting for us—so we left the subject alone. Still, we ran our lives very differently, and not just our religious lives. It seemed to me that in all matters Peg O'Connor simply saw herself in a normal situation for a young married Catholic couple, only she was playing it out in Tucson instead of Boston, and Bill was working for the Army instead of for the city of Boston. In Tucson, as she would have in Boston, Peg not only dutifully cleaved to her religion, she also made a top priority of housekeeping, grocery shopping, and cooking, which she performed with well-honed skills, having been, as the oldest of six children, her mother's chief assistant in all matters, including kitchen duty. Peg could even make gravy. (I felt about Peg's ability to make gravy as my mother did about Ruth's ability to make faced buttonholes.)

As for me, I never doubted that I was living my married life in unusual circumstances. Jack and I focused on the war and not on trying to live a typical marriage. Still, I had to keep house, and as yet I didn't have much of a handle on it, especially the cooking part. Then, very soon after our arrival in Tucson, to further complicate matters food rationing came along.

Peg and I went to the local Office of Price Administration (which everyone called just the OPA) to get our ration books — books of red stamps for butter, fats, cheese, canned milk, canned fish, and meat (except for chicken, which was not rationed), and stamps of other colors for canned and dried things. Each stamp had points, and each point counted toward an allowance. Peg tried to advise me, but I was very bad at staying within my allowance, and on one occasion I used up all my red stamps on a rib roast — sixty-nine cents, eight points a pound. At home, I put it in a pot, covered it with water, placed it on the stove, and let it boil. When I called Peg over to help me with the gravy, she felt moved to invoke a whole roster of holy figures. "Holy Mother of the Lord Jesus and Saint Peter, you've drowned the poor creature," she said. "I'll have to give it artificial respiration." Still, I learned something very useful: it is very hard to ruin a rib roast. No matter what you do to it and no matter what its appearance, when you cut it up, it tastes very good.

At the OPA office we also stood in line for books for sugar and coffee—a half pound each per week per person—which seemed quite generous unless you were planning to bake a cake a day or to drink way too much coffee. At the office they asked how much stuff we had on hand and then took away stamps commensurate with what we said. It was the honor system, and it was remarkable how people "wrecked their brains" (to quote Midge Folsom) to remember every little item on their kitchen shelves.

Even after we left Mrs. Rosen's, I—but not Jack—would join her for services, for I very much wanted to spend some time among Jewish people, even if these Jewish people of Tucson were very unlike my Jewish people of Miami Beach. The dissimilarity was a reflection perhaps of the polarized essences of the two cities. That both cities had much in the way of natural beauty could not be denied, but Miami Beach chose to enhance its beauty with state-of-the-moment edifices and Tucson chose to form itself from its own sand and clay.

I very much looked forward after services to the klatches at the delicatessen, especially after my nausea period passed, which was achieved with an assist from my sister Minna, who had written that when she was pregnant, she had discovered the virtues of saltines and fizzy water. Jack, though he shunned the services, always joined the delicatessen crowd. If any of the congregants were outraged by Jack's stance, there was no hint of it. My feeling was that it was nothing new to them, that they had no doubt observed it often among various members of their own families. At any rate, they welcomed Jack warmly when he turned up at the delicatessen, and Jack slipped happily into the role of general bedeviler while we all ate what passed for New York corned beef.

We talked a lot about the plight of the European Jews, though we still had very little to go on. Early in the year there had been a mention from a group of twenty-six Allied nations fighting the Axis powers, a group that called itself the Declaration by United Nations. In a report the group noted the German government's intention "to exterminate the Jewish people in Europe," though there seemed to be no follow-up to this. The only significant news in the latter part of the year was an item in the Tucson paper that reported a half-hour conference in the White House with Jewish leaders. It was a conference that turned out to be the only interview Roosevelt granted on the subject.

CHAPTER 8

Jack quickly got into his job at Davis-Monthan, where his duties were to train bombardiers for crews assigned to the four-engine B-24 bomber, called the Liberator. Crews for the other four-engine bomber, the B-17—the Flying Fortress— were trained elsewhere and were usually assigned to England. B-24s went to southern Europe, usually Italy. From there their bombing runs took them over, among other targets, the Ploesti oil fields. I was now getting to the point where I could recognize a few planes: the B-24 (with its twin rudders) and the B-17 (with its single one); their little brothers, the twin-engine, twin-rudder B-25 and the twin-engine single-rudder B-26. I could also recognize the cargo plane, the C-47, which surprised me by having—its size notwithstanding—only two engines.

Training at Davis-Monthan included day and night flying. When Jack had night flying, if I wanted to have the car, I took him out to the base in the Silver Streak. At around four in the morning, I would return and watch as the planes landed. The way they came in always took me by surprise. Their angle of descent was such that they appeared to be automobiles, headlights on, descending from a steep mountaintop.

As I waited, I waited scared. I knew that Jack's plane should come in, but I could never convince myself that it would. And as I sat, not able to doze, not able to do anything but watch for planes, I would think back to a lot of things—to necking in a dark car on a remote street in Miami Beach, or to waiting for an order of hamburgers and Coke to be delivered on a window tray at the Pig Trail Inn; or I would think of the fishermen who stood patiently night after night at the rail of the Miami Beach causeway staring into the dark, unreadable bay.

I too was a solitary watcher in the dark—though unlike the fishermen, I was restive, not patient—and I watched until the arriving plane was finally Jack's, and he would walk straight out of the plane and into the car, and we would go back to our little cottage. After I fixed breakfast, he would go to sleep, then get up around nine, have another breakfast, and go out to the base again for his on-field duties.

GAS RATIONING HAD finally overtaken the West, and we now plastered our windshields with the stickers that the East had known for some time. No special treatment was given to the men in service: they were given their A stickers (three gallons per week per car) just like everybody else.

The wives developed a system for shopping whereby each took her car out one day a week, with everybody in the court piling in. Though we were ever heedful of the message on the back of the sticker, which asked, "Is this trip necessary?" sometimes we had to make an extra trip, and when we did, we tinkled the Mexican bell that dangled in the courtyard to announce that a car was leaving the premises and whoever wanted to could come along.

I got to know Davis-Monthan very well. Our lives centered around the air base, though our social lives no longer included the Blumenthals. Paul had finished his training and had been shipped out, and Phyllis had gone back to Nebraska with a promise to write. The night before Paul left, we gave him a party in our little cottage, and Jack wrote him a poem that ended, "So good luck to Paul as he goes off to battle / To fight for the honor of Blumenthal cattle." We invited the congregation and laid in a supply of hard and soft drinks, and after everybody left we noticed that the soft drinks were finished but the hard drinks lingered on, thus confirming once more that Jews were not much on whiskey but big on ginger ale.

In the mornings I sometimes went to the tennis courts at the base, hoping to find some good tennis to watch, or I helped catalog books in the little base library. I joined other wives who served as hostesses at tea parties for servicemen, and we occasionally took the men out on tours of the city. Figuring they had seen enough of the bars in the Mexican ghetto, we took them to the rest and the best of Tucson, as Tucson was, after all, an old, old town with historical sights. So we led them to the majestic St. Augustine Cathedral and El Presidio Park and to La Casa Cordova and other last-century adobes. And when the boys had time, we wound up with lunch at the old, very old El Charro Restaurant.

Davis-Monthan had an officers' club, where we could eat and dance to the club orchestra. If, musically, we wanted to hear the real thing we went to the PX and listened to the juke-box—to Jo Stafford and Frank Sinatra, of course, but we also listened a lot to Ray Eberle. When Ray Eberle sang "A Nightingale Sang on Berkeley Square," he was suddenly as swoonable as Sinatra, and you could almost hear him say, Take that, Frankie boy.

At the PX we could find everything from clothes to food-stuffs at prices cheaper than the same stuff carried by local merchants (who held their tongues because it would be considered unpatriotic to speak out against the military). We could also find silk stockings after the commercial cupboard was bare, though even the PX ran out after a while and we took to wearing pretend stockings, which were bare legs with lines of crayon down the backs to imitate seams. We called them V-stockings—V for victory. V's were attached to a lot of things. We had gray-colored V-pennies, for example, made of an alloy, and we had V–window shades made out of paper. Lucky Strike "green" wasn't the only thing that had gone to war.

As Davis-Monthan had no accommodations for birthings, Peg and I went to the civilian town doctor who had diagnosed me. He was a cheerful man who did not offer much in the way of advice, and nothing at all about the perils of weight gain. In the end I think we managed our own pregnancies, and by instinct, which in my case was sometimes on track, sometimes not. It was on track when I gave up smoking, but definitely off when it came to weight, because I got very fat. Since my doctor never cautioned against it, I had to believe that he held that a well-padded mother produced a bouncing baby, and indeed when I went for a checkup with my extra ten, twenty, then forty-five pounds, he sat across the desk gazing at me as if at a prize heifer who was going to win him a ribbon at the county fair.

Jack thought my weight gain was cute and called me Mrs. Five by Five, taking his cue from a current song. I was half a foot over five feet tall, but that I might get to be five feet wide was a real possibility. What I wore during this rush to girth were two maternity jumpers—one dark blue, one black—with an assortment of blouses. To allow for burgeoning weight, the jumpers, their basic form a tent, had a progressive line of snaps. The idea was to keep moving the snaps until you had reached the last one, at which time the jumper would be fully extended. In my case, several more snaps would have been helpful.

I couldn't avoid calories; they lurked everywhere. There were ladies' luncheons at the base, which invariably featured chicken à la king (basically cream with a few chicken chunks and pimientos) and a nice plump pie for dessert. There were a lot of these ladies' luncheons, the war notwithstanding.

Peg and I attended them often, but not as much as the regular Army ladies, who attended them without fail. It was their opportunity to catch up on the scuttlebutt, which featured the location and status of all of the regular Army officers, where posted, when promoted, what honors. The ladies could name officers up and down the line, with their rank seemingly part

of their names: Colonel Pascal, Major Hoving, General Tobias
—never Tom, Bob, or Charlie. Though I listened carefully, I
never heard a Jewish name, and I had to conclude that Jews did
not join the regular Army. Jack said the reason was obvious.
"Why join an organization that's trying so hard to keep you
out?" he said.

If in our early days Jack had called me "ingenuous" for abiding by "face value," he couldn't call me that any longer, for at
these ladies luncheons, Peg and I were making a point of getting
inside the heads of these regular Army ladies. It was easy. All we
had to do was watch reactions. Information about postings, it
seemed to us, was received with a bit of a show of interest, but
that of promotions or honors was received quietly, and we
guessed that the women were spinning their wheels to figure out
whether the news was good or bad for their husbands.

It was at one of these luncheons that I learned that a commander of Allied forces for North Africa had been named, and
I heard for the first time of "General Eisenhower." At the announcement, Mrs. Hoffenhauer was ecstatic, and crowed loudly
over "the Captain's" name so closely resembling "Eisenhower,"
perhaps thinking this was a good sign. She was also quick to
announce that she had once met "Mamie." Oh, what a darling!
she said, as Peg and I rolled our eyes. So charming, so elegant!
Indeed, Mamie Eisenhower was so this and so that, it was hard
to believe that a creature of such superlatives could dwell
among us.

At these luncheons I soon recognized that all the Army wives
did it—showered encomium upon encomium on the wives of
their husbands' superiors, since the wives stood in for their

husbands. When the wife of the base commandant was in attendance, the compliments flew so thick and fast, you had to look twice to assure yourself that it wasn't Eleanor Roosevelt the women were talking to.

All encomiums were accepted by the superior officers' wives with equanimity, for favor-currying was what they excepted. They were confident that their gowns would be received with reverence, their jokes with laughter. After watching these performances, Peg and I were sincerely thankful that we had no control over our husbands' destinies, certainly none as regarded their Air Corps ranks. After one such luncheon Peg said, "If I had to laugh at that joke the commandant's wife told, my face would hate me."

Still, it must be said that promotions, being part and parcel of military life—regular Army or not—were also the soul of gossip, and Bill O'Connor and Jack were not above sipping their Arizona Sunsets and talking about some "desk jockey" getting a promotion by playing golf with the group commander or by letting the commander flirt—or worse—with his wife. Some simply flattered outrageously. All of this was called "brownnosing" and Jack said to Peg and me, "If you think the wives are dedicated to brownnosing, their husbands are masters." Some practitioners of the art, according to the boys, were subtle; others were obvious. Bill had a definite feeling about the adjutant. "God, he's always stuck up the colonel's rear end," he said. "He's like an extra cheek." A promotion didn't usually come in these ways to the men who flew—a promotion was supposed to be based loosely on a time schedule— but it was not unheard of.

Jack and I knew we were on borrowed time in Tucson. It was an anxiety always with me, and now that I was pregnant, there was the worry that Jack might not be around for the birth of our baby. But if we lucked out and the baby was born in Tucson, my mother said she would come to help out. In the meantime the mails were full of my mother's admonitions. She was not perturbed by my weight gain and indeed exhorted me to more, more, more. "Eat plenty, sweetheart," she wrote. "Don't forget you're eating for two." I wrote back, "Don't worry, Mama. I think I must be eating for three or four."

When 1943 came around, we were still in Tucson. Peg planned a birthday party for me and festooned the court in balloons and crepe paper. The party was set for after work, and at five o'clock the Arizona Sunsets were set to cooling in the refrigerators and the wives gathered outside to wait for the boys. My birthday party was also to be a celebration of Ruth's marriage. I had had a letter from her saying she had married her OCS boyfriend, was now Mrs. Philip Heckerling, and they were going to be stationed in Texas. "You'll like Phil," Ruth had written. "He's as nuts about big bands as you are."

In the court we waited. No boys. We waited some more. We began to worry a bit. Finally the Captain arrived, and what he had to tell us sent us running to our radios: the base had received a report that Japanese submarines had been spotted off the coast of Los Angeles, and all crews had been sent out.

This could not be, I thought. Jack on active duty? I flew into alarm. Wait! Wait! He was not overseas yet! We were in Tucson, Arizona, not London, not even Italy! Yet the radio was full of the news. Yes, Japanese submarines had been seen. And yes, bombers from Davis-Monthan had been sent out. But of an actual engagement the radio said nothing. When I called the base, I got no answer of any substantive kind, only that Lieutenant Suberman could not be reached.

I heard nothing more until Jack came home. The men had flown over the entire area, but when they flew out over the sea to "get those yellow bellies," as his commander had urged in his pep talk, there were no submarines to be seen. The crews were told afterward that the sighting of Japanese submarines had been somebody's mirage, an illusion, a rumor. "There might actually have been submarines," Jack explained to me, "but if there were, the brass ain't telling."

That night I hugged Jack extra close, for even if I didn't get to have a birthday party, that I was able to put my arms around him was my ultimate present. Jack, of course, had bought a real present for me—a Mexican silver charm bracelet from which dangled a hay wagon, a record, a pie, and a pretty good replica of the Silver Streak. I thought a submarine might also be appropriate, for that day's experience was a model for us, for the time when Jack would be in combat and I would be at home. Still, the bracelet as it was suited me just fine. What it told me was that for one who always claimed impeccable credentials as a hardheaded realist, Jack could on occasion pass for a pretty fair sentimentalist. And on this night when I hugged him extra close, he hugged me extra close as well, and then bent over and kissed my stomach.

AT THIS POINT in time the war news had been taking a turn for the better. A German field marshal had yielded to the

Soviets and surrendered his troops at Stalingrad; also, the Allies had won what the papers called the Battle of the Bismarck Sea. As far as the CBI theater was concerned, Japanese troops were in retreat across the Yangtze River.

Oddly, the good news produced in Jack some mixed feelings: on the one hand he was happy about the progress of the war; on the other, he felt that he himself, as he would say to me, was "training other guys to do my job." Add to this that he thought it was a war that had to be fought, a "good" war, and here he was still fighting it in Tucson, Arizona. I did not answer him when he said these things, for there was nothing I could say that would not be interpreted as self-serving.

As a matter of fact, the air war was curious. Our planes were all over Europe bombing a myriad of targets, but with the exception of the Doolittle raid, there was no bombing in the Pacific, no bombing of Japan. Before and after Pearl Harbor there had been fighter planes—there'd been a pickup squadron nicknamed the Flying Tigers, noted for ferocity in intercepting Japanese bombers, and after they disbanded, there were other fighter planes—but there were no bombers in Pacific action. As I understood it, the problem was that we had no bases from which our current bombers could reach Japan.

Still, with Jack in Tucson for a while, we had time to think of what was coming into our lives in more predictable ways, and we turned to the most predictable thing of all—our forthcoming baby. We had already decided to be as untraditional as possible and forgo the Jewish custom of choosing the name (or its American equivalent) of a relative who had passed away. We were open to anything.

And so it was that we got a name from a movie. The movie was *Casablanca*, the noble hero in it was the owner of Rick's American Café, and we had found our name: our baby, if it was a boy, would be Rick. We did, however, yield to custom for a middle name and chose Ian, a broad Americanization of Isaac, Jack's grandfather's name. So Rick Ian Suberman was out there waiting to be born. Or perhaps Gillian Honoré. Gillian Honoré? This exceedingly pretentious name came from the desire of two would-be sophisticates to pay homage to both the English and the French, who were, at that point in our lives, our intellectual role models. Why they were was rather hard for me to speak to, as I was still finding my way in intellectual matters, but I certainly admired the French for their food and their clothes, and I trusted Jack that the English had superior literary skills.

This was about as seriously as we thought about our forthcoming baby. Because we were not surrounded by family—especially grandmothers—we were on our own. More to the point, the usual dreams of prospective parents did not seem appropriate for us, for our future was still dominated by the demands of war. Having a baby was a sidelight, fun and games, and naming it after the owner of a movie saloonkeeper or because we thought of ourselves as Anglo- and Francophiles was part of the fun.

With the time of birth approaching, we did the things we wouldn't be able to do afterward. One of the things was a visit to Mexico. Mexico was only down the road, and you didn't have to have a passport, but it had a customs border, and that made it a foreign country and gave it a bit of excitement. You got into it through the border town of Nogales, which was divided into American Nogales and Mexican Nogales.

American Nogales was squalid and ugly, and I hoped for more beauty from the Mexican side, for I was remembering the songs of Lydia Mendoza, and I had also, like all Americans, been steeped in the romantic, idyllic James Fitzpatrick movie travelogues ("And now we say good-bye to the lovely, mysterious land of . . . "). Sadly, however, Mexican Nogales was a replica of American Nogales, and if La Mendoza was singing from a jukebox in one of the dozens of bars on the seedy Mexican streets, I never heard her.

We were finally into the target month of April, and things did not work out as planned: my mother did not come to be with me for the delivery, as she could not get a seat reservation on the train. My father wrote, "Could I let Mama go from Florida to Arizona sitting in the aisle on her suitcases?" Well, no, he could not. "Mama don't believe it," my father went on, "but I told her you could probably have the baby without her."

My delivery was in a Catholic hospital staffed by nuns. When I first learned that I would be in such a hospital, what sprang to mind were gentle movie nuns, and it seemed to me that a nun-staffed hospital was the ideal maternity venue. Unhappily, my thinking had to undergo almost immediate revision.

Rick's was not an easy birth, and my stay in the hospital was not easy either. The nuns were not the nuns of movies but of real life, and many of them were indifferent and, it seemed to me, disapproving. Whether this disapproval came from my being Jewish and not eligible to produce another Catholic, I can't know. But what I do know is that when I was having the kind of pain I couldn't believe I was having, none offered to hold my hand, and though it might have been true that I was reacting out of all proportion to reality (I did notice that the Indian and Mexican women in labor confined themselves to walking mutely up and down the halls), I was clearly in need of more than an impatient look. After the birth, when I asked about that brown streak down my belly (the line that had formed when the skin fell back into place, and which went away in weeks), I did not want a nun to look at it as if it was the mark of Cain and tell me that it was the price you paid for becoming a mother. I furthermore did not want to be told that I was "vain" when I asked if my weight would come off, which it did, quickly, perhaps to spite that particular nun. By the end of my stay, I was no longer thinking of nuns as angels.

Peg, whose Dennis Patrick was born just days after Rick and in the same hospital, took the nuns in stride. She had gone to a Catholic school, and having experienced—even been a victim of—their whims, she had nary an illusion about them.

The day after Rick's birth Jack came with flowers, a new charm for my bracelet—a wee boy baby—and a western leather jacket with fringes down the sleeves. Rick was delivered with forceps, so his soft head was initially misshapen, and I will say that the nun who brought him in to me was of a sweeter nature than the others, and she had the sensitivity to cover his head with a diaper. I could see his eyes, however, and they were as blue as the ocean in summer, and when I dared to peek under the diaper, I saw sunny hair. Jack had his son, and he was exceedingly satisfied with him. I had my baby, and he was beautiful and I was exceedingly satisfied as well.

Mrs. Rosen pronounced Rick "a perfect little man." A perfect *menscheleh* is what she actually said. And my perfect *menscheleh,* as long I had a say in the matter, was going to start his life with nothing in the marrow of his bones but healthy cells.

Jack and I had to think about—debate about—Rick's circumcision, though there was never any doubt that he was going to have one. Whether one was Jewish or not, circumcision was becoming de rigueur. When I thought about this, what passed through my mind was that since babies' *putzels* now looked pretty much the same, future Nazis were going to have a hard time spotting a male Jew, since they could no longer depend on simply ordering him to drop his pants.

I was surprised to discover that I wanted a *bris,* the circumcision ceremony, since in the past I had agreed with Jack that it was a bizarre custom—watching the *mohel* slice off the end of the *putzel* and then having a party afterward. But I was not in the mood to intellectualize and said that if I wanted a *bris* and a *mohel,* I should be allowed it. Jack, however, wanted a hospital and a real doctor, so we debated.

In the end the decision went both ways. Thanks to my having to be in the hospital for the then-customary ten days, there was enough time to allow for a circumcision, and without asking questions the doctor had simply taken Rick into the operating room and had done the job.

Still, on that same afternoon, several people from the synagogue sneaked in a bottle of wine, we drank a *l'chaim* ("to life") toast to our new son, and I called it a *bris*. It gave me a chance to use a word my father used a lot because it was a word that expressed pride: it gave me a chance to *kvell*.

Once at home, our lives went into instant reorganization. We were now not just we two but we three, and the "three" was important out of all proportion. Neither Jack nor I had ever known a baby intimately before, and we marveled at everything Rick did. He was clever, he was sweet, he was funny —especially funny when during diaper changes he hosed us down with a delicate spray.

As we all know, caring for babies is not all fun, and some of it is downright onerous. Notwithstanding the message of the leather jacket Jack had given me—that I was not to consider myself a prisoner of the house—there was a lot of work to be done, and chiefly by me. It was being said these days that the man in the military was "putting his life on the line," and I couldn't in good conscience ask for Jack to do more. What Jack did was telephone from the base a lot, and when he was home, he contributed tickling and cooing and the occasional diaper change.

I, as with all mothers, was where the buck stopped, especially when I was still nursing and Rick was having nighttime feedings. And when the doctor said that Rick wasn't getting all he needed from nursing, I sterilized bottles and made formula.

I worked almost around the clock. It was overwhelming, mind-boggling, especially for a new mother like me who didn't know anything. Happily Rick did, and I early on learned that Rick had been born sensible, that he didn't just get that way later. When I feverishly flipped the pages of the hospital-provided baby-raising book to discover if I would be arrested if I didn't wait four hours between feedings, Rick gave me good advice. He yelled, *I'm hungry! So why not just feed me?*

I learned some things on my own. I finally eschewed the Bathinette, which had to be filled with a bucket carried from the faucet, and plopped Rick in the kitchen sink. I gave up using the thermometer to test the water and used my elbow, that handy-dandy heat-measuring device mothers always have with them. I took advantage of the dry Tucson air: after I had hung out Rick's diapers, I went straight back and collected them.

I was making it as a mother. What I hadn't realized was that when your baby gets born, you get born as well. You get to be somebody new, or at least to be a newly reconstituted you. It may have been because there was no grandmother around to second-guess me, or it may have been because the father was mostly unavailable, but in my case I got to be a responsible me, a me that could take charge. And it seemed to suit me just fine. I was finally escaping my "youngest child" mind-set and beginning to believe in myself.

Though I had less time now for corresponding, I did write to Phyllis Blumenthal, who reported that Paul was in Italy and that she was pregnant. "Paul is thrilled," she wrote. "He wants a boy to keep the dairy dynasty going. But I think a girl would suit him too. After all, there's always time for more."

The O'Connors and the Subermans sometimes got out their baby carriages and walked around Tucson. We took in as much as we could, including any religious processions taking place in the Mexican neighborhoods—the "barrios"—and we burrowed around in the Mexican shops that carried religious trinkets—skeleton cutouts, miniature coffins, skulls made of sugar—in preparation for Dia de los Muertos, the Mexican Indian festival honoring and remembering the dead. It was, we learned from a parish priest, an event that joined Roman Catholic All Saints' and All Souls' Days rituals with two-thousand-year-old Mexican Indian traditions. Peg interpreted the trinkets in her own way. "Mother of God," she said, gingerly picking up a paper skeleton and pulling its string to make it jump, "these people are just *primitives*."

One day when she said this, all at once things began percolating in my head, and I remembered rituals and ceremonies I had observed through the years, had been puzzled by, but had never before questioned. *Primitives*, Peg had called these Mexican Indians, for their rituals and ceremonies.

What immediately leapt to mind was a Catholic practice of the kind Peg herself would participate in. I had seen it in action with the St. Pat's kids in Miami Beach when after a particular Sunday just before Lent the kids had come back from church clutching a bit of a palm frond from the previous year's Palm Sunday to take home to burn, the ash of which on the following Wednesday—Ash Wednesday—they displayed on their foreheads. I was told by my St. Pat's friends that this was a sign of penitence and a reminder of our mortality, but if I could not fully grasp its metaphorical significance, it didn't matter and I didn't think about it anymore. Now I considered it. Wasn't that splotch of ash stuck with a bit of oil on the forehead as eccentric a show of religious devotion as paper cutouts?

I was not going to let my own people—Jewish or Southern—off the hook either. In the Passover seders I had attended,

wasn't that practice of holding a chair empty for the arrival of
the prophet Elijah also eccentric? And could I forget how often
in Union City I had seen the Baptist preacher hold the nose of
a baptism seeker and dunk his head under the waters of the local lake?

As we started for home, Jack and Bill walked ahead of Peg
and me. Peg was talking about some of the things we had seen,
and I was still deep in my thoughts. "How can they call themselves Catholics?" Peg said, as we walked along, pushing the
baby carriages. "We never have anything like that in Boston."

Was I hearing a cue? In any case, I took it. I blurted out,
"Don't you?" I couldn't stop myself now, and I found myself
telling Peg what I had been thinking. And I said something
about prejudice. I think it helped that I could talk about prejudices from personal experience—both from the giving and
the receiving ends.

Peg looked at me. Then she laughed. "I guess I'll have to
think about it," she said.

I knew Peg, and I knew that she would.

I don't know whether my courage to speak up came as a
kind of homage to Jerry Bulla or from my having become a
newly confident mother. It didn't matter: I had actually done it.
And it would not be the last time. In later years I would often
find myself in situations where speaking up was obligatory.

There were certain caveats, however, and I devised a proto-
col. If I was among male buffoons—men who thought that a
woman speaking out created the same noise as a barking
dog or, worse, a yapping puppy, or if I was among those who
thought that because I was not a Wasp my views would not be

worth anything—I walked away or, when that was not feasible, I just kept quiet. In these cases I would be merely spinning my wheels, and having been in numerous cars stuck in the sands of Miami Beach, I had learned that spinning your wheels only digs you in deeper. But with people who would listen and on whom I could make some sort of impact, I felt a distinct obligation to say clearly how I felt—that bigoted remarks were not acceptable in civilized society.

Peg was not a buffoon, and she could hear me. And as I found out, Peg did think about it, though not on the spot, not even, to my knowledge, in the weeks and months ahead. It was only much later that I understood that she did. But when I finally learned about it, it was embedded in an event so anxiety filled that I could feel almost no triumph at all.

AT DAVIS-MONTHAN Jack had been hearing that a new bomber—the B-29, the Superfortress—was in the pipeline. Not only was the B-29 to be the largest, heaviest, and fastest of all the military bombers, it would also have the longest range. Furthermore, it would be the first military plane to be pressurized, so it could fly at altitudes of thirty thousand feet, which put it above *ack-ack*. What with the bomb load capacity, the pressurization, and the altitude capability, the Superfortress, now in production at the Boeing plant in Wichita, Kansas, would give the United States the ability to bomb Japan systematically. Jack said the Tucson men stood a very good chance of launching this new plane.

Jack's guess was right. The Tucson men were indeed chosen to launch these B-29s, and in August, when Rick was just past four months old, Jack received orders to report in three days to the 20th Bomber Command, in Great Bend, Kansas, and wait there until Wichita said that the B-29s were ready to be picked up. All the men in the court except the Captain had received the same orders.

Almost lost in the excitement was that Jack had been promoted to first lieutenant and had come home one night wearing a silver bar instead of a gold one. I wondered if the Army didn't have it backward again, for wasn't gold more treasured than silver? At any rate, the days of Tucson had come to an end.

Just before we left, there was to be a truly sorrowful moment. At our last delicatessen klatch, someone brought out a letter he thought we all would want to hear. The way he said it, together with the look on his face, told us immediately that it was bad news. And bad news it was. The letter was from Paul Blumenthal's father. He was writing, Mr. Blumenthal said, because the synagogue people had been close to Paul, and he knew that they would want to know about Paul, the awful news that Paul had been shot down over the Ploesti oil fields. "Paul's gone," Mr. Blumenthal wrote at the end of his letter, "but I hope he knows somehow that the farm will always be ours. Paul's son will have it." We didn't want to think of the possibility of Paul's not having a son. It was unthinkable that he would not.

CHAPTER 9

Just before we left for Kansas, there was big news on the world scene: the Allies had invaded Sicily. It was a clear indication that Italy was about to fall, and my father wrote, "Mussolini must be kicking himself that he joined up with that *momser*. What a *schlemiel*. The Italians never did want to get into bed with Hitler," he added. "Now let's see what they'll do." My father was expressing what everybody was thinking—that Italy would get out of its alliance with Germany as soon as possible. It turned out that everybody was right: in October of that year, having imprisoned Mussolini, Italy declared war on Germany.

Getting ready to go to Kansas, our little family had two problems: we had to get gasoline for the trip and we had to find a way to take milk bottles along. The former was solved when the OPA issued the men Supplemental Mileage Ration books, the latter when a couple of the guys on the base (carpenters in civilian life who no doubt longed for jobs of a more custom nature than nailing barracks stairs) made us an icebox. It was a simple affair, a divided metal box with a lining—one side for ice, one side for bottles—and a hose and pail for the dripping water.

I left Tucson with all kinds of feelings: I was sorry to be saying good-bye to the town where Rick had been born and I was sorry to have to exchange a nice little house for who knows what; I was sorry to leave nice people like Mrs. Rosen and the others of the Jewish community. Still, a lot of nice people were going with us. Over and above all my feelings, however, was the awareness that Great Bend put us one step closer to Jack's being overseas. My feelings notwithstanding, with the icebox and all the bottles and ice it could hold, a couple of suitcases, and a thermos of coffee—for we had a full twenty-four hours of travel ahead of us—we piled into the Silver Streak and set out.

We had to make many stops along the way, chiefly to warm bottles. We stopped at some exceedingly odd places to do it. Once when nothing else was in sight, we spotted a cabin in the woods, and the recluse who lived there warmed the bottle over the only heat available, the chimney of his oil lamp. But we finally made it, and we checked into a roadside cabin outside (way outside) of Great Bend. The next day Jack would look for an apartment. We had tossed the "Do I or don't I say I'm Jewish?" question around before deciding that Jack should neither advertise it nor deny it. He would try to confound the issue by giving his name as John Suberman, for though it's true that

John is generally considered the formal name for Jack, no Jewish Jack was ever John—Jacob perhaps, but never John. We had no idea if without the ruse Jack would have gotten the apartment, but at any rate, with a baby and wife to house, Jack was not about to let a little white lie get in the way. "If it's bad, it's for the greater good," he said.

Whenever we met up with other Jews serving in the military, these kinds of problems poured out. One guy, whose name was Rosenberg, said he had been turned away on the grounds that "you let one Jew in and pretty soon you've got the whole tribe. You understand." What Lieutenant Rosenberg understood was that Jews were not welcome in the house of this lady, who, having only the one apartment to rent, must have thought Jews would gather like cats on her back fence. I could now get in on these stories—thank you, Mrs. Gillis—and I had great success with Mrs. Gillis and her "lump."

I also brought to the table the story of one Bernie Kaplan. At one of the tea parties at Davis-Monthan, a Jewish serviceman named Bernie Kaplan had sought me out. Bernie was a guy with a lot on his mind, but uppermost was the harassment he was having to endure in his barracks. Being called "Jew boy" was apparently the least of it, being made a figure of fun the most. I listened to his stories—about the bucket put over his head because he had forgotten his "yammukey," about his letters thrown in the trash can because they "couldn't be for Kaplan since they don't have crazy writing." It didn't take much in the "brains department" (to once again quote Midge) to understand that in the military a Jewish boy with a heavy New York accent was a natural target for slurs and jokes.

I hadn't advised this sad boy to complain to the brass, for the epithet "crybaby" sprang to mind. What I did was introduce him to Mrs. Rosen's synagogue, and the congregation, as I had hoped, made a fuss over him and invited him to their homes and called him their hero. Still, it would have been understandable—and acceptable—if in this particular situation, Bernie Kaplan had simply put his Jewishness on hold.

It was something of a coincidence that at the same time we were hunting for housing in Great Bend, Ruth was writing that Phil had been transferred to San Antonio and they had been house hunting there. She said that they had not advertised their Jewishness either. "Phil's blond and blue-eyed," she wrote, "so we're keeping it our little secret." Phil Heckerling's silence on the subject apparently went as far back as his OCS days, when he and his roommate, a non-Jew named Gimperling, were known as Gimp and Heck. I suppose that this was interesting enough on its own merits without an investigation into who was Jewish and who wasn't.

Ruth wrote that in San Antonio they had found a converted garage to which a lean-to had been added to serve as a kitchen. Another feature of their new residence was a tin roof, on which rain and hail—Texas apparently had a lot of hail—sounded like a heavy barrage of machine-gun fire. "The war's on my roof," Ruth wrote. "It's the Germans against Phil and me. How did they find out we're Jewish?"

Very few Jewish servicemen advertised their Jewishness, and avoiding the issue was a tactic widely used when instinct told them protective cover was needed, for anti-Semitism had not abated in any substantial way, and there were even some who said that if it weren't for the Jews, we wouldn't be in this war at all. These people blamed the German Jews, who, being "grasping and conspiratorial," had brought the current horrors upon themselves. They also blamed "Roosevelt's Jews," those American Jews who "surrounded" Roosevelt and "manipulated" him. When it was pointed out that we'd gotten into the war only after Japan had attacked us, these people scoffed and said that Japan was taking its orders from Germany. You think the Japs could think this up on their own? they said.

The place Jack found for us in Great Bend was in the basement of a house gerrymandered into "rooms" by curtains. It was creative thinking all the way, for the owners had made an apartment out of nothing, and in the bathroom you could sit on the toilet and take a shower at the same time. The place was basic at best, but a daybed buttressed with pillows served nicely as a bed for Rick, and we had most of the elements needed for living. All things considered, we were okay.

Then Peg and Bill, unable to find a place of their own, moved in with us. So the owners put in two more beds, one more dividing curtain—never mind that there was nothing soundproof about it—and raised the rent. It was the norm: it didn't matter that the owners were well-to-do folks with a huge wheat farm and oil wells outside of town, they were going to get in on the game of gouging the military just like everybody else. My axiom of "If it weren't for the war, the war would suit me right down to the ground" did not apply in these cases.

Since Jack and Bill were home much less than they had been in Tucson, Peg and I were glad to have each other. When the men were home, we could always count on a visit from James and Jimmie Lee Stallings, the Texas couple we had known in Tucson. James seemed happy with the B-29 assignment, possibly because if he couldn't be flying fighters, the next best thing was piloting a plane with a lot of cachet. Harvey McTigue, our football-player Tucson storyteller, came over as well, though he was in Great Bend without Helen. There was no suggestion that they had broken up, just that she had stayed behind.

Whenever the men were off duty and together, they were the same old group: the men still asked for Harvey's football stories, and Harvey still told them. Harvey had a good time flirting with our landlords' German maid, Trudy, six feet tall and sixty-something. He would make a show of picking up her hand and kissing it, saying, "Trudy, my Trudy, remember you're going to wait for me." And she would say, "That's hunky-dory by me."

Bill still made his Arizona Sunsets, and he still insisted that they be drunk facing west, the murky basement notwithstanding. "I think the gin gods are testing us," he would say. "Let's show them we're up to the challenge."

As it turned out, B-29s were not available as yet for training, so the boys trained in B-26s and B-17s, which had some similar flying characteristics. Final training was to be at the air base at Salina, from where they would go to Wichita to pick up their B-29s.

So we saw a lot of Kansas. Before we were finished with it six months later, we had lived in Great Bend, Abilene, and Salina. And when I left, I took with me a lot of Kansas stories.

I had two initial shocks: one was that in Kansas domestic servants were neither black nor Mexican but just plain white;

the other was that I was living among Republicans. In the places I had lived it was taken for granted that everyone was a Democrat. In my Tennessee town, although the law said there had to be a Republican primary, no votes were ever cast. And in Miami Beach, even the parents of my rich Miami Beach Jewish friends were Democrats. My rich non-Jewish friends may have had Republican parents for all I knew, but if they did—and they probably did—they didn't mention it to us Jewish kids.

Here in Kansas people were unapologetically Republican. Well, why was I surprised? Hadn't Kansas been one of only ten states to vote Republican in 1940, when Roosevelt ran against Wendell Wilkie? The Kansas newspapers grumbled about Roosevelt, though with the war fully on, the decibel level was pretty low.

In other ways, however, Kansas was much like the South. Kansans ate home-grown vegetables and got their chicken and eggs from the backyard. There were some menu differences: Kansas was a beef state, and until the war—or so I heard—steaks had been an everyday meal; whereas in the South steak was a rarity (except for "country-fried steak," which is not what normally passes as a steak but a piece of round steak soaked in buttermilk and then dredged in flour and browned in lard). Kansas food was minimally enhanced, just salt and pepper, so blandness reigned. When there was a rumor that a steak restaurant in Salina—restaurants were still occasionally getting steaks—was heightening the flavor of their steaks with garlic, the military people were delighted, but the locals were appalled.

In Great Bend our landlords were Mr. and Mrs. Womble and their teenaged daughter, Anita. They never questioned me as to why Jack was called Jack instead of John, and they never asked me if I was Jewish. Perhaps they had known so few Jews— maybe none—that the question didn't occur to them, or per- haps our close friendship with the O'Connors threw them off.

The German maid Trudy—Kansas seemed to have a lot of people of German extraction—had developed such a liking for Harvey that it spilled over to his friends, and she came down often to talk to Peg and me. Her favorite word was "shtoopit," and she used it freely. To her credit Trudy always opened her conversations with an expression of outrage at Hitler. Though she hinted that before the war other Germans of her acquain- tance had admired Hitler, she never failed to call him "that *Stück* of *Scheisse*," which, if I had it right, translated as "that piece of shit."

Anita Womble was as talkative as Trudy and had a remark- able tale. Her life had undergone changes since the war, espe- cially her dating life. With the influx of servicemen, Anita now went out on dates every night, and just as routinely on the first Saturday morning of every month, her mother took her to Wi- chita to see the doctor.

Anita explained, with no discernible reluctance, that the doctor was checking her "good girl" status. This was accom- plished by examining her hymen to determine whether it was still intact. Anita expressed no outrage at her mother—or the doctor—over this invasion of her . . . well, her hymen. She said that all the girls went to Wichita to get checked, and then, she said, they went shopping.

Talks with Trudy and Anita were practically the only amusements Peg and I had, apart from walking the babies and grocery shopping. Grocery shopping was a little like a treasure hunt. A lot of foodstuffs were scarce, and if word got around that a shipment of a rare item—canned peaches or tuna fish, maybe —had been seen being unloaded, you waited in line for as long as it took to get the one-to-a-customer item. Some products, however, were never seen. Butter was one of these. Still, there was plenty of margarine. Margarine came in a white block and was accompanied by a little packet of yellow coloring that you were supposed to incorporate to make the margarine look like butter. The hitch was that the mixing required more muscle than most of us had, and we wound up with a hunk of something that looked like lard with bright yellow streaks. Dairy farmers lobbied to keep margarine white, to ensure that after the war, when butter became available again, housewives would flee the onerous mixing and return gratefully to the real thing.

We did, however, have an offer of amusement when one afternoon Mrs. Womble came downstairs and asked if we wanted to join her friends for some cards. We didn't keep up much with Mrs. Womble, though we did know that she played cards with her friends every afternoon in one of their houses. What we didn't know was *what* they played.

Denny and Rick were napping, and Mrs. Womble's invitation promised a diversion, so we said sure, we'd love to join Mrs. Womble and her friends. We went up the stairs, which opened into the commodious Womble house, and into the dining room. There we found eight or nine townswomen sitting around the table. We didn't know any of them. And if we had known any, we wouldn't have recognized them in their present attire.

One or two of the women were in no attire at all. A few sat in bra and/or panties. Others, fully dressed, sat with piles of clothes on the floor beside them. It seemed the ladies had been playing strip poker, and some were losing and some were winning.

Mrs. Womble told us how the game was played. They followed all the rules of poker and, she added, "We play for keeps." It was also allowable, Peg and I learned, for housecoats to be borrowed. Mrs. Womble laughed and said, "Otherwise, there was that one time when I might have gone home in nothing but my pearls."

Peg turned to me and asked if I didn't hear one of the babies crying, after which she and I grabbed each other's hands and fled back down the stairs. Back in the basement, we laughed "fit to bust," as we would have said in Tennessee and asked each other if we had actually seen proper Kansas ladies taking one another's clothes off. We agreed that we had. But why? Those women had plenty of clothes, and what they didn't have, they could buy. Money was no problem, for their husbands were, like Mr. Womble, in the lucrative wheat and oil businesses. So why? To ogle each other? To compare? Peg said that in the quick look she had gotten, she hadn't seen anything special. "Just the same old sags and bags," she said. "Mother of God, I wouldn't want to sit around a table and look at *that.*"

When we told the boys, they laughed and said the women just didn't have enough to do. Peg and I had to agree there was not much to do in this little midwestern town—just the usual movie and bowling and ice cream at the drugstore. And when we thought about it, it was Trudy who did all the cooking, the cleaning, and the grocery shopping. The only thing Mrs. Womble did was get all dressed up and go to church on Sunday with Mr. Womble and Anita. But enliven your day with strip poker?

Here was a conundrum: in what way did a devotion to strip poker jibe with the women's powerful interest in virginity? "Ach, it is just so *shtoopit!*" Peg said.

The boys were training hard, and if it was painful for me to be without Jack, it was worse for him, for he was without the other two of the triumvirate. Rick was at an infant's most adorable age, crawling around, trying to walk, smiling a very bright smile. I knew Jack missed him very much, and when he was home, they indulged in their favorite activity—napping together on the sofa, Rick on Jack's chest.

The end of Great Bend came quickly, and trying to get a bit closer to Salina, we moved to Abilene. Bill made the transfer with Jack, but Peg, thinking she might be pregnant again— the flimsy curtains between "rooms" discouraged but did not deter—went home to Boston. When I questioned myself as to whether I should go home as well—pregnant or not, and I was not—the answer was that no matter how little I saw of Jack these days, it was better than not seeing him at all; nor could I deny him whatever few moments he had with Rick. So when Peg and I said good-bye to each other, she went to Boston and I stayed in Kansas. We promised to write often, and we did.

If Norman Rockwell had worked in the Midwest, he would have chosen Abilene as his setting. The town's charms leaped out at you, even if our Abilene residence was not one of them. Our residence was in the backyard of a house, in what had been the maid's quarters on top of what had been a garage. There was a kitchen, but it had no sink, so when water was needed—for cooking, for dishwashing—I carried it in from the bathroom. The garage itself was now lived in by the owners of the house, two maiden sisters, who had rented out their house and had repaired to the garage after partitioning it into livable space.

The ladies—Miss Lucille and Miss Polly—went to church regularly every Sunday morning, but otherwise were home. They often asked me down when Rick was napping, and of course our talk was mostly about the war. We were, like all Americans, daily attuned to the latest developments in the German invasion of the Soviet Union and were anxiously waiting out the sieges of Leningrad and Kiev. So the news that the Russians had retaken Kiev was a happy something to talk about. In the Pacific there was also positive news: according to reports, the Marines had invaded Tarawa and Makin and had landed on Bougainville Island. Good, the ladies and I said, things are heating up against Japan.

Of greater interest to me perhaps than to the ladies was the news that Congress had recommended that Roosevelt put into action a plan to save the surviving Jewish people of Europe "from extinction at the hands of Nazi Germany." It was called the Rescue Resolution, and my father had written, "Resolutions is one thing. Getting it done is a big something else."

The ladies also liked talking about the town, about how Abilene had historically been the end of the Chisholm Trail, and about how "Ike," as they called General Eisenhower, had been raised in Abilene even if he had been born in Texas. Like the members of the Womble household, they too liked to gossip, and the stories they told—the ones about sexual exploits especially—were not always what you would expect from little old ladies. The stories didn't shock them—they told them with perfect equanimity—but they certainly shocked me, though I do not claim that I was among the world's most worldly.

You would have thought that one particular tale would never pass their lips, but pass them it did. As we sat in their little parlor drinking tea from porcelain cups and partaking of plum cake, they proceeded to tell me about a local group—a "club," they said. I soon realized they were talking about a sex club. And what a sex club it was. It seems the male pillars of the community had established this organization—"just over the restaurant," Miss Polly said, and the ladies flicked their heads in the restaurant's direction—under whose auspices they had sex with young boys. The women looked at each other, took a sip of tea, and smiled. "Men can be very naughty, you know," Miss Lucille said.

By now Jack's crew had been formed, so when he got his orders he knew the eleven men with whom he would be flying. The crew included the commissioned officers—pilot, copilot, bombardier, navigator, flight engineer, special radio operator—and the noncommissioned officers—right gunner, left gunner, tail gunner, another radio operator, and the top, or senior, gunner. There was also an alternating crew assigned to each plane. Jack's pilot, Lieutenant Colonel Henry Sullivan, was the squadron commander, so in effect Jack's was the lead squadron crew.

Jack's parents got to know his crew better than I did, for in a coincidence they actually had dinner together. Miami was the destination for one of the crew's training missions, and when Jack called his mother from the nearby Boca Raton air base, where they had landed, she made plans for the men to come to dinner. The invitation included only the officers, because as democratic in "real life" as Jack was, as democratic as the rest of the officers might have been, in the services, enlisted men and officers did not dine together.

This was a star event for Jack's mother for it concerned her soldier son, his comrades, and food. I had written to her that by now even the Kansas restaurants were bereft of steaks, so she resolved that steaks her dinner would be. Deciding on steaks was one thing; getting them was quite another. Still, Frieda and her friends knew how to deal with the black market, so Frieda simply went to her butcher, passed him an extra twenty-dollar bill, and lo!, eight two-inch-thick steaks were wrapped up and handed over, no red stamps asked for, no red stamps given. Black market or not, the men ate the steaks with gusto—"fat and all," Jack's mother reported happily.

Jack didn't say so, but surely he felt that going to Miami was a lucky break, for with the time growing short it was a way for him to say good-bye to his parents. And indeed soon after that mission we would move to Salina, the last stop before Jack would pick up his plane.

By now it was January—1944—and Kansas was cold. Still, the war news offered a bit of warmth: the Soviets had broken the siege of Leningrad, and U.S. troops had attacked the Kwajalein atoll in the Pacific, which meant that the war with Japan was seriously starting to develop. My wish, of course, was that in the event the B-29s were sent to the Pacific, the war with Japan would develop so fast and so successfully that it would be over and Jack would never have to go.

And so, on a freezing morning, I left Rick with the two ladies in Abilene and set out to find a place for us in Salina. It was sixteen degrees below zero, and I kept thinking of the weather in Miami Beach, which I had always taken so much for granted. Where was that never-never land? It was so long ago and so far away, it seemed never to have existed.

In Salina I found a little cottage. Never mind that it was in a neighborhood of chipped steps and peeling paint; it looked comforting to live in, for it had a fireplace, and I saw Jack and me snuggling before it on the cold Kansas nights. This did happen, but not very often, for Jack was away and away and away. So I snuggled with Rick, hugging him closer and closer as the nights went on, for I knew what was waiting for us.

At the Boeing Wichita plant, everything was on an emergency schedule. Jack and his crew went over occasionally to see how things were progressing, and Jack reported that the workers—men and women—seemed to sense they were in on something really big and labored without complaining, no matter the inconvenience. The too few hangars for such large planes, for example, meant that work had to done outside and in freezing weather, so the workers just bundled up and got to it. Kansans (and others) had responded in huge numbers to the Boeing call for workers, and almost immediately Wichita housing ran out; we heard that movie houses were staying open all night to provide the workers a place to sleep.

Since the plan was to train in the actual B-29 they would be taking overseas, in time Jack and the rest of his crew went to the Boeing plant to pick up their plane. It was an auspicious moment made even more auspicious by the fact that Jack's crew—and the alternating crew of course—got a plane named the *General H. H. Arnold Special.* It was so named in honor of the man who had got the B-29 into production, and there was a plaque inside the cabin that said so.

Whenever we talked about it, about Jack's leaving and my going back to Miami, we knew what we would be facing. Jack, going away, had the easy part: he would get his orders, pack some uniforms, and go. Because of Rick, my leaving required some planning. At first we thought that Rick and I would travel by train, but trains being what they were—jam-packed and erratic—and sleeping cars only a memory, we knew I could be stranded for days at a time. So we decided that Rick and I would go home in the Silver Streak. Jimmie Lee Stallings was going home as well, and James had decided that it would be unwise for her to drive their feisty little Chevy rumble-seated roaster, so Jimmie Lee would travel with me as far as Dallas.

So I waited for the day when Jack would tell me that he had received his orders to ship out, knowing that this time there would be no reprieve. That day came, and when it did, Jack didn't have to say a word: there was about him such an air of excitement—even exhilaration—that it was impossible not to know. My heart was already racing when Jack told me they had gotten their orders. I could only ask, When? Tomorrow, Jack said.

He didn't know where they were being sent, only that they were not to pack warm-weather clothes, and of course I wondered if this meant the European theater. Jack did not have to caution me to keep this information to myself—even though it was the merest scrap—for he knew that I knew the rule. Indeed by this time we were all schooled in keeping our mouths shut about anything that could be remotely construed as having military significance. We were well acquainted with the posters that cautioned LOOSE LIPS SINK SHIPS and the one with the legend SOMEONE TALKED below a picture of a house with a gold star showing in the window. It was not the issue of secrecy that made my heart race; it was the fact that Jack was on his way.

The next morning a guy from the base came by in a jeep, and Jack threw into it his B-4 bag, that soft-sided canvas suitcase with zippers and a handle that all the officers had. Before he got in the jeep, we said our good-byes. If earlier I had felt excitement coming from Jack, I now felt something else, something that resembled disquiet. Surely it must have been there, for a man does not go without some degree of apprehension into a place where danger and death lurk. So I did not cry, for I did not want Jack to think I was anticipating grief. And I did not want Rick to see me cry. I didn't want him to be scared; I was scared enough for both of us.

Just before Jack climbed into the jeep, he reached in his pocket and slipped something into my hand. It was a tiny silver charm of a B-29, and I thought then, as I would often think later, that this plane was both my hope and my despair.

CHAPTER 10

Within two days Jimmie Lee and I had gotten our Supplemental Mileage Ration books, and we were ready to leave. I hadn't written home that I was coming; I didn't want anybody to try to come to help us. It seemed good enough that I had the car, and that I had Jimmie Lee until Dallas.

I had sent a bunch of stuff home—clothes, my box of letters, some of Rick's toys—confident that I would get to Miami Beach before they would. The rest of it we brought with us: Rick's icebox was in the trunk, where it took up most of the space, and the car proper was packed to the ceiling. Whoever was driving had to do her best to keep afloat amid the mass, for there was always a box of something stuck under her right arm and something between her and the door, and several things next to her feet on the floor. As an extra person in the car, Jimmie Lee was ideal: she would share the driving, she was little and thin, and she was terrified of being in the way.

We drove highways, country roads, back roads, paved and unpaved roads. We had a lot to do besides driving: we had to scout around for the rare service station, which we hoped would have an adjoining café where we could find something to eat, and we had to take care of Rick's needs. Jimmie Lee was a second mother—and sometimes a first. "When James gets home," she told me, "we're going to have us a baby right off."

The car radio was a big help. We sang along with it and used it to keep ourselves both awake and informed. According to the radio reports, things on the war front in Europe were going well. The news Jimmie Lee and I wanted most to hear, however, was about B-29s. Now that they had left Kansas, we thought there might be some word about them, but there was no mention.

We kept the conversation going and laughed at some things, definitely at the roadside café–filling station sign that read, EAT HERE AND GET GAS. We stopped often at roadside cafés, where Rick, no doubt sensing that it was no time to be fussy, learned to be an eater at home in the world and consumed anything that was put before him—bits of pork simmered in milk, potatoes mashed with turnip greens, lemon meringue pie.

Jimmie Lee and I talked wife talk, and house talk, and family talk, nothing important, just a telling of ordinary things. Because I had lived in the South, much of what Jimmie Lee told me was no surprise. This didn't work the other way, for I felt sure Jimmie Lee would be *profoundly* surprised if I told her my way of life. I understood when she said that her family cooked on a coal stove and that they had a water pump in their kitchen. I understood when she laughed and said, "We're tryin' to break Mama of chewin' and spittin'. It just looks so bad in front of the children." But could she have understood my Miami Beach, especially if I explained it in the context of being Jewish? She would have been polite, saying, "I know what you mean," but she would not have known at all.

We didn't discuss politics. I knew what her views would be, having learned at the knee of my father—whose devotion to politics was second only to his devotion to business—that southerners were part of the coalition that kept the Democratic Party competitive, the balancing act that held together northern liberals and southern conservatives. So it followed that since Jimmie Lee was from the South, she was a Democrat, and being from the rural South, she was a racist.

I didn't challenge her, for holding to the status quo was what kept her world turning, and if I had tried to persuade her otherwise, she would have held to her—and her family's and James's—views. In the end, the kind of talk we indulged in, depthless and unstressful, seemed a sensible way to pass the time.

Before we got to Texas, we had two nights on the road. The first night we stayed in an auto camp, where we wore our clothes to bed (to keep something between us and the doubtful sheets) and gave ourselves spit baths. The next night we couldn't find an auto camp, which brought no regrets, so we slept in the car and in the morning looked for a service station with a bathroom where we could perform our ablutions and wash Rick's diapers. It was Jimmie Lee's idea to trap them in the car windows and let them dry in the wind sweeping by. "It'll keep them nice and sweet," she said. As we drove, the many inconveniences were made up for by the southern warmth that flowed into our Kansas-chilled bones as we went down through Oklahoma toward Texas.

In a small town twenty miles outside of Dallas, Jimmie Lee left us. For a lot of reasons, it was hard to see her go, and not just because she had helped with the driving. She had been good company. Rick was too, but he didn't offer much in the way of sharing the driving or reading the map.

Now Rick and I, just the two of us, drove east. Jack had marked my route on the map, so I knew I was to go through the southern parts of Louisiana, Mississippi, and Alabama, and then into Florida's panhandle. I figured it would take another two nights on the road. It was a very long trip, but it was not daunting, for there were things in my head much more fearsome than an automobile trip. Still, I would be without Jimmie Lee.

Rick and I had a lot of adventures. Nearing Lafayette, Louisiana, we had a flat tire, which, since nobody was around until a man came by just as I was tightening the last lug nut, I managed to change myself. The worst of it was that a flat tire meant that I would now have no spare. According to a wartime regulation, if you already had a fifth tire, you were allowed to keep it, but if that one went, the law said you couldn't buy another.

So I started down the road with a thousand what-ifs in my head. I stopped at a filling station–café and a man came out and said, *"Bonjour"* and then *"Comment ça va?"* I was in the

Cajun part of Louisiana, I found out, and the man was welcoming me. After deciding my French was all stutter and stammer, I relocated to English, told the man all about my husband going overseas and how I was driving to Florida and needed a tire, and he gave me one. In perfect English (of course) he told me that if he wanted to give a tire to somebody, nobody was going to tell him not to, and no, he said, he didn't expect pay. "Pay for doing something for the wife of one of our boys?" he asked. *"Mais non, mais non,* a thousand *mais nons."* He invited me to come into the café for a hamburger with "awnyawns," which, I found out, was a hamburger with onions, and he fixed Rick a creamed soup studded with bits of crayfish. Grateful and full of sautéed "awnyawns," I did get out a *merci beaucoup* and an *au revoir.*

With the extra tire, I went back to trying to get to Miami Beach, even if I first had to finish with Louisiana and get through Mississippi and Alabama. We drove steadily, and in some hours I looked at my map and the word "Florida" was winking at me. Come, it said. I'm trying, I answered. And then I was there.

I was in Florida, and I was driving the west coast outside of Fort Walton Beach, on a particularly desolate stretch around Silver Beach where nothing was to be seen but fishermen's shacks. Jack and I had driven over once from Tallahassee, and a beautiful beach it had been, very different from Miami Beach. Instead of coarse tan-yellow sand, the sand here was soft and white.

I was shocked out of my nice little dream by a man holding up his hands for me to stop. A fisherman, I presumed, of about sixty, though it had been my observation that fishermen invariably looked older than they were. The man leaned his head into the window, asked me to come with him, and nodded toward a house some distance from the road. When I asked why, he said something strange. It was about my hands. "You got smaller hands than me, little lady," he said. "Maybe small enough to go in and get it." Go in and get it? It seemed he had been trying to help his wife deliver a baby, and the baby, coming out feet first, had "got stuck." He told me he had delivered his other three children, but, he said, "This time I just can't get the hang of it." So I pulled the car to the side of the road and, with Rick in my arms, walked to the house. Still, I had already made up my mind that I was not going to "go in and get it."

Greeting us at the door of a screenless house were three towheaded children aged about two to five. They gathered quickly around Rick, speaking to him in a strange language that I finally identified as English spoken not in words but in syllables. I put Rick on the floor, and the children dashed about gathering things for him to play with—a dried starfish, an extra-large conch shell, some bottles that had no doubt washed up on shore.

This was no time for wondering at their speech or why on earth somebody didn't think to put in screens in a part of Florida notorious for its mosquitoes, for in the corner of the one-room house a youngish woman lay on a bed, wiping at her blond hair with a handkerchief. "Oh, Lord," I heard her say, "I've really had it this time." On the little table nearby I glimpsed a box with a small stack of diapers and baby shirts. When I went to her, I saw between her legs a baby all the way out except for its head. It was so blue and, when I touched it, so cold that it could have been pitched out of the skies during an ice storm. When I put my hand on the baby's neck, I could feel no pulse.

I knew not to go any further, for I was remembering something from my crash course at Jackson Memorial Hospital about not introducing infection. All I could do was cover up the baby with a towel. And when I turned to the man and asked him why he had not called for a doctor, he gave no answer, only reached into his pockets and pulled them inside out. I had often seen this as a comic bit of business in the movies, but this was not the movies and there was nothing comic about it. The man was telling me a dire thing: that he had no money —not for a doctor, not for a telephone, not for screens. If the man had been black, this would have been an old story, for it was a familiar one in the South—the tale of poor black families who lived their lives always dependent on the largesse of whites. But that white Americans could be living in such circumstances was brand-new to me. It was another moment when "the scales fell from my eyes."

I left some money with the fisherman, though I knew it would not do much for his life's problems, and went to a filling station that had a telephone and called the Fort Walton hospital. Yes, they said, they knew about this "deadbeat," and they would come out and "collect" the baby.

It was hard to forget that mosquito-filled house and the towheaded children who in their isolation spoke so curiously. It was 1944, and though help was coming through government programs and such, sadly it took its own sweet time about it.

In Tallahassee I pulled up to the house of the Satiskys—the people Jack had stayed with when I went to school there—and they welcomed me. In earlier times, they would have been shocked at my driving with a baby from Salina, Kansas, to Miami Beach, Florida, but they were not shocked now. As Mrs. Satisky said, "Everybody's somewhere and then they're somewhere else."

I started out very early the next morning. I was determined to make Miami Beach without another overnight stop, though it was not going to be easy on this convoluted route. About an hour after dark, when Rick fell asleep, I decided that I would just drive through the night, however long it took.

Driving through the night was an exercise in being alone. Few cars were on the road, and as the night wore on, I saw fewer and fewer house lights. It was okay. Rick was sleeping comfortably, I had my radio, and I had my spare tire. It was only when I passed a filling station and saw that it was closed that I realized I had a problem. Where, when I needed it, was I going to find gasoline? My tank was half empty, and I would have to keep my eyes open.

I never once turned off the radio. It was my companion, my entertainment, my caffeine. I tried not to listen to too many newscasts—and at night there were fewer than in the daytime —for by now the B-29s had no doubt gotten to wherever they were going, and if some of them had not made it, well, I didn't want to hear about it. But every once in a while I would glance at the charm bracelet on my wrist and rub its little B-29.

Through the night I listened to music, to Harry James and

Helen Forrest, to Ella Mae Morse and all the rest. Frankie Carle played, just for me, "I'm a Little on the Lonely Side," and a group called the Song Spinners sang "Comin' In on a Wing and a Prayer," about a plane returning home with one engine gone and the crew's only hope being their trust in the Lord. It made me think that at such a moment Jack would think a prayer a very weak reed indeed on which to depend.

At night there were a lot of clear-channel stations, so I heard stuff from Illinois, from Pennsylvania, and other far-off points, and then I happened to catch a Georgia station, and suddenly to my ears came the sermonizing of a Baptist preacher. That he was on at one o'clock in the morning was pretty interesting, but without a doubt the most interesting part was what he was saying about Jews.

As soon as I heard the word "Jew" coming from a rural southern voice, I anticipated the worst, and I thought the worst was upon me when he said that he knew how folks felt about Jews, that he knew "for a fact" that some folks hated Jews. I listened carefully. Was the man going to do the usual—rail against the Jews as murderers of "our Lord" and call for what was commanded in the Bible, an eternal curse upon them? Or, I wondered with some optimism, might he, as a preacher, be about to lead his flock into tolerance?

In the end, it was neither. Or was it both? As I began to listen hard, I realized he was talking about Jews as God's chosen people and was preaching an obligation to love them. And then he was saying, "I know you folks think you got reason to hate Jews, but I'm here to tell you that you gotta find a way to love 'em.'" He thundered a bit more: "I warn you now. God Himself wants you to, and you dassent disobey God. If you do, there ain't nothin' but the fires of Hell a-waitin' for you."

As I drove, I wondered how I should feel about this. In his own way the man was preaching tolerance. Did it matter that he was coming to it by the back door?

While I was mulling this one over, I saw that the gas gauge was definitely leaning toward empty. Well, I thought, if we run out of gas, we had slept in the car before and we could do it again. Still, finding gas seemed a better solution, for if we had to sleep in the car, I would have to get back on the road tomorrow with a wide-awake Rick and a sleepy me.

Now in Indian River country, I scanned the surroundings. I saw orange groves in full fruit to the left and right of me but no filling stations. In fact, not much of anything. Not anything for what seemed a very long time. Then my headlights caught a private pump behind a little house at the edge of a grove.

Without doubt these folks were asleep, but I was desperate, so I decided to knock at the door and throw myself on their mercy. In a few seconds, a black man answered. I told him my story, and when I had finished, he ventured out in his night clothes to give me enough of "the boss's" gas to get me home. He wouldn't take money, and he wouldn't take my stamps. "Just glad to do my part," he told me. It was time to say yet again what I had been saying lately a lot (though not always): If it weren't for the war, the war would suit me right down to the ground. I held out my hand and the man took it. It was an auspicious moment for me—the first time in my life I had shaken hands with a Negro man. It may have been auspicious for him as well, for I was sure there were not many occasions—maybe none—when he had been offered a white person's hand.

I got back on the road and was in front of my house at three o'clock in the morning. Rick had woken up, but now I had my mother's arms to put him into, and after the shouting and the talking, I finally fell into bed. And the next day bright and early there was a call for me, and the caller said, "Guess who."

It was Jack, and he was calling from Salina, Kansas.

So while I had been on the road alternately listening to and avoiding newscasts, Jack and his crew had had a delay. The reasons were many, but the bottom line was that there still were not enough B-29s. Things had kept going wrong and the planes had had to undergo modification after modification, most of which involved weight demands. The ferocious-looking twenty-millimeter cannon, which stuck out of the plane's tail and which the crew was so smitten with, had been replaced by twin fifty-caliber machine guns; the comfortable bombardier's seat had been removed and the bombardier now had to sit on backless steps; the rail car that had run through the tunnel connecting the front and back cabins was gone, so crawling was now required. So much were they at the mercy of weight, the planes went unpainted.

There were also delays because crews still had to be assembled. And then Colonel Sullivan—known, of course, as "Sully"—wanted to see the rest of the squadron leave before his plane did.

When Jack finally left Salina, I had been home for almost a

month. Since Jack had been living in the officers' quarters on the base and was on a daily alert, there was no thought of my rejoining him. And so the letters had started again.

JACK WENT OVERSEAS on April 14, and his first letter to me came on May 6. It told of the trip over, how they had flown (as a feint) in a northerly direction to suggest they were going to Europe when they were really heading for India and the CBI theater. India? India seemed an unlikely destination, for in talk of war there was little talk of India. Later letters would explain.

After a stop in Presque Isle, Maine, they flew to Gander Lake, Newfoundland, and from there nonstop across the Atlantic (Nonstop! Like Lindbergh!) to Marrakech, Morocco, where they had their first glimpse, as Jack wrote in a literary spirit, of the "Dark Continent." They were in Marrakech for a couple of days, living in tents and eating in mess halls served by Italian prisoners, one of whom introduced himself to Jack as Mario Malatesta. In his letter Jack asked, "Do you think his last name translates as 'bad balls'?" Mario had asked if Jack knew people in Boston and when Jack had told him he knew a few, Mario had said, "So maybe you know my cousin Vito?"

At Marrakech the men weren't allowed off the base, and they were pretty restless, especially since the base was, as Jack described it, "the planet's septic tank." Jack and some of the others passed the time playing cards, but many went out to the fence enclosing the base to have exchanges with the girls hanging around outside. *"L'amour, l'amour,"* the girls would yell, *"l'amour pour une leepsteeck!"* Since the men could not get outside the fence and had at any rate no *leepsteecks,* in the end there was no *amour.*

When they left Marrakech they had their first really bad moment: the B-29s, which had been performing flawlessly, were suddenly suspect. The engines were having to push hard for the power necessary to get over the surrounding Atlas Mountains. One plane went down, with a full crew aboard, and Jack said that their own plane just made it. "The crew inhaled all the way," Jack wrote, "and we finally got her over."

It was very worrisome that such a vaunted plane should have this kind of failure, and it was only when they got to their next stop—Cairo—that they discovered the problem: at Marrakech, the planes had been supplied not with the kind of fuel they required—100 octane—but with 80 octane. If this was an oversight or a scam, they never found out, but as Jack wrote, it had been "a deadly mistake."

They later found out that low octane had not been the only reason for the power insufficiency. There was also a design defect, one that had put overlarge cowling around the engines, what were called the "cowl flaps." In practice, when the flaps were adjusted to allow the necessary air into the engines, they rose to the point where too much resistance was created, and this in turn called for extra power, and extra power meant overheating and possible fires.

Though the abundance of detail in Jack's letters may have seemed a lot for me to digest, I don't think Jack ever considered not telling me the pertinent information about anything, even when it was technical. The fact was, I was getting to know the B-29 fairly well, and I could pretty much understand what Jack told me. At any rate, the flaw was noted and after the planes arrived at their base in India, it was corrected with a shipment of redesigned cowl flaps.

I could only gather that the B-29 was not turning out to be the perfect plane. The reasons were many, chief among them that there had been insufficient testing before the planes were released for action. It seemed clear that the crews would be test-flying the plane even as they flew combat missions.

Still, in a minor correction, the tail cannon came back into play. Reluctant to give up the psychological advantage this intimidating weapon offered, the crews constructed dummy tin cannons and placed them on the tail for all to see.

Approaching Cairo they flew over the North African battlefields where Rommel had fought and finally lost. Jack reported looking down on wrecked tanks and trucks and "all the detritus of war." It was an eerie, depressing landscape, he said, this desolate stretch of sand that not too long ago had held so much life—and, of course, so much death. Still, as they flew over North Africa, below them in Egypt were the pyramids, and Jack wrote, "They're mysterious and comforting all at once. It's like they're saying, 'This too shall pass.'"

In Cairo for two days, they finally got clean accommodations and took their leisure in the officers' club, playing dice poker at the bar. Jack was discovering that if in college the boys had filled their off-time with Ping-Pong, Air Corps men, himself included, filled it with any game that accommodated betting.

At the Cairo club the favored drink was something called a Kangaroo, which I took to be a gin concoction similar to Bill

O'Connor's Arizona Sunset. Jack had run into Bill in Marrakech, and Bill had told him that Peg's second pregnancy had been confirmed, but I already knew that. As to James and Harvey, like Bill, they were in different groups, so Jack hadn't seen them.

Meanwhile, another plane had been lost. In Cairo, a B-29 had crashed on the field while landing, and Jack said that the plane had burned on the field for hours after the crew had gotten out.

From Cairo they flew to Karachi, in India, and from Karachi to their destination, Salua air base, in Karagpur, a city outside of Calcutta. As they attempted to land at Karachi, there were two more crashes, almost all on board killed. Dust storms were the culprit. Dust storms! I had not thought of dust storms.

At Karagpur the men lived in barracks with thatched roofs, which extended to create a kind of porch, the floor of which was the bare earth. "Very tropical," Jack wrote, as if he had found himself in a romantic jungle. Their drinking water was stored in a canvas water bag hanging on the porch—a "Lister" bag, as it was known—which Jack described as "essence of chlorine" so filled was it with antiseptics. Their showers were outside, by way of a pipe supplying nonpotable water. "I wouldn't pay money for this," Jack wrote, "but it sure beats scrambling around in the muck of Europe."

Well, it certainly did beat that, for the British made a terrific show of providing their new allies with whatever conveniences were available, and each room had a "bearer" who saw to the officers' needs; they did the officers' laundry, fetched their cigarettes, and shined their shoes. If the returned laundry was always a bit grimier than when it went out and induced an epidemic of prickly heat, if the shoes gleamed with what you knew was red spit (red because of the bearers' habit of chewing betel nuts), the bearers were amiable and agreeable. When not performing their duties they squatted outside the barracks, chatting and smoking cigarettes. "The cigarettes send up smoke so foul," Jack wrote, "that we bribe them to go squat under somebody else's window."

Much of the heavy labor at the base, typically done by males in the United States—construction, road building—was done by women of the untouchable class. "It's so hot right now," Jack wrote, "the women work with their breasts bared to catch whatever breeze might pass by." He also described another paradox: when urinating, the men squatted and the women stood, their long skirts protecting their modesty.

At Salua the planes were open to sabotage, so the crews guarded them at night, the crew members alternating, always accompanied by Indian Gurkhas—Nepalese Hindus known to possess an exceedingly warlike nature. Jack said it wasn't easy putting time in with a Gurkha. "They look just like Japanese," he wrote. "Besides which there's a lot of hostility among Indians to the ruling British—the 'Raj' as they're called around here. So you're always looking over your shoulder."

Jack's letters were filled with descriptions, bits of philosophical musings, and personal sentiments. And just as he did not spare me the technical information, neither did he spare me the bad news—the crashes and the near crashes, the blunders, the losses. From the beginning we both had felt that we were in this together, and Jack understood that I would want to know what he knew, that I would want to react to what he was having to react to. Still, I read his letters with some wariness, wanting to know yet not wanting to. Even when he wrote, "I carry you and Rick around, one in each pocket, and when I need to, I take you out," it came to me as bittersweet.

Jack's letters to me were written on notebook paper, and they took about ten days to arrive. The time lag was unnerving, but at least I knew that he had been safe ten days earlier. My letters to him went through APO addresses and I often wrote on V-mail, a blue letter-and-envelope stationery combination, devised by the U.S. Post Office to save space—though how long they took to arrive was, to say the least, variable.

Most military mail was censored—recipients often reported cut-out spaces where places and dates had been—but officers' mail was only self-censored. Jack paid no attention to self-censoring. In any case, censoring was thought to be more trouble than it was worth, and even the enlisted men's mail was censored only casually, usually by the chaplain or by someone who'd gotten saddled with the job. Indeed, after all the disinformation given out about the B-29s' destination, after the "no clothes for warm weather" instruction, after the planes feinting in a northerly direction, when they arrived in India, the first person to welcome them was Tokyo Rose—that infamous English-speaking Japanese lady whose job it was to demoralize the American troops. She greeted them with "Welcome to India, boys. Don't forget to take in the Taj Mahal. It could be the last beautiful thing you see before you die."

Though the European theater might have seemed the more natural place for Jack to want to fight the war, in one way he was glad to be in the Pacific. In Europe, if he had been shot down and captured when flying against the Germans, as a Jewish American he thought he might have been sent not to a camp for prisoners of war but to a concentration camp. In the Pacific, the Japanese didn't care if he was a Jew, a Baptist, or a Rosicrucian. He was simply an American. "I like not having the qualifier tacked on as it always is at home, " Jack wrote. "Even if they're out to kill me, they're out to kill me not as a Jew but as an American."

THE MIAMI BEACH I had been remembering in Kansas was the Miami Beach of my kid days. The Miami Beach that I had returned to was no longer that land of trivial pursuits but a profoundly changed wartime city, and I myself was in a brand-new guise, a mother and a wife whose husband was overseas. I didn't play tennis much anymore, and I didn't fool around on the beach. When I went to the beach, it was to keep watch over my son as he played, though playing on the beach did not mean filling your bucket with shells and beguiling sea life; it meant picking your way among bits of wood or metal floated in from ships sunk at sea or chasing sea birds splattered with these ships' oil. And on hotel roofs across the street, air wardens looked to the skies.

My parents were very glad to have me home, no doubt chiefly because they could become acquainted with their grandson, who was their second, my sister Minna's being their first. Minna, with her need to distance herself from the crowd (in Union City she had insisted on doing the Charleston when everybody else was doing the fox-trot, and she had refused to bind her breasts with bedsheets to achieve the favored boyish look), had named her baby boy not Larry, Edwin, or Martin, as were the current preferences among Jewish mothers, but Major, though the choice was perhaps simply a nod to the world's current military preoccupation. But who was I to be judgmental when I had named my baby after a character in a movie?

The store personnel had changed a little. One of our full-time soda jerks, Patty, who had been with us for several years, was still there. Patty was the daughter of a Miami Beach fireman, lived in Smith Cottages, and was gorgeous—blond, satiny smooth, and "stacked," as the boys said then, with a smile to equal that of the girl on the Coca-Cola poster. She was indeed so gorgeous that she had no need to exercise her brain at all, not even to flirt. She had once had a boyfriend, an heir to one of the Florida sugar kingdoms, and every afternoon he had tooled over the causeway from Palm Island in his blue Cord convertible coupé to pick her up when her shift was finished. Why Julio hadn't been drafted, why he was exempt, had been a mystery, though perhaps looking elegant in jodhpurs and riding boots as you rode a horse around sugarcane fields was considered vital to the war effort. At any rate, Julio no longer came around, having become engaged to a Palm Beach debutante, someone his parents no doubt thought more suitable for their own personal scion than a soda-fountain girl.

Stan, the soda jerk who had the rich divorced lady waiting for him every night in her Auburn, had finally been drafted. The reason he had been hitherto classified 4F was murky, as he had no apparent physical defects and was in fact a pretty strapping guy, but, as my mother would say, who knew? It was not surprising that Stan had had little trouble finding women. I guess the actual fact was that the women had found *him,* for in these days of the draft, young men were in short supply. But now he was gone, and to take his place my father had hired some more high school boys.

I wanted to find out about Laura, and I spoke with Mrs. Dunlap, who told me that Laura was in the middle of divorcing Bobby and was traveling around with Don. "Laura just has no taste in men," Mrs. Dunlap told me, no doubt meaning that Don's father was a mere assembly-line worker in Detroit.

I did not return to work in the store on any kind of formal basis, though I reserved the right to be called upon, and when I was summoned, I filled in anywhere. I always took Rick with me, and after I had plunked him in his playpen, I waited for the inevitable wailing that meant *You are holding me without my permission! This is cruel and unusual punishment!* after which some OCS boy would lift him out, put him on a table, and give him whatever he wanted.

In the early evenings my mother baby-sat while I went to the Servicemen's Pier, though not to dance but to teach. There were classes in a lot of subjects; I taught English, and only to the foreign soldiers. Some of the British officers maintained that I was doing no favors "to those poor chaps" by teaching them American English and not British English, which they said — not always jokingly — was the choice of the cultivated. Well, I would tell them, hoping to make a point, the British are certainly hearing plenty of uncultivated American English right now. "Furthermore," I would add, "I wouldn't be surprised if they're not loving every syllable."

Occasionally I went over to Jackson Memorial and filled in where I could. The Red Cross Blood Bank was now fully established, and I participated sometimes as a donor, sometimes as a helper. There were two lines for donors—one for whites and one for Negroes. A Red Cross rule said that Negro blood went to Negro soldiers and white blood to whites. One might have thought that blood was just plain red, but the Red Cross thought differently.

Some things didn't change. The race tracks were still open, and the horse players still showed up at the store, though their ranks had dwindled to a precious few. As for my father and his love of the horses, he had just about given up going to the track, but the bookie across the street still beckoned.

The diminishing number of horse players was more than compensated for by the OCS men. My mother wanted to believe that the men came in because they had heard of the delight of mango-topped sundaes, but the real reason was to "hubba hubba" at Patty. Also it was a convenient place to buy that one required dating accessory. There was a bit of a complication when I was on duty at the register, but the men themselves worked it out by simply walking behind the counter to where the condoms were kept, opening the drawer, taking a package, and paying me as they left—no question asked, no answer given.

My father's store was not the only Miami Beach enterprise doing especially well. The presence of the military meant that all were thriving. The hotels had really lucked out: because of the tremendous fees the owners had received from the military, they were saved from sure bankruptcy. "Not only that," my father would say, "whether they say so or not, most of them are making a bundle."

Still, it cannot be said that this new prosperity influenced attitudes toward the war, for to a man the Jewish entrepreneurs wanted the war to be over, longing as they did for their sons, their brothers, their sons-in-law, their favorite nephews—many of whom were in the thick of combat—to be home. And they longed for an end to the Jewish horrors.

I was home, and home was now a wartime community, but my particular home was also a strongly Jewish community, and there was everywhere talk of the plight of the European Jews—emotional talk, angry talk, talk full of frustration. There were stories upon stories. Newspapers seemed more inclined now to do some serious reporting on the subject.

Sometimes a story would send out extra-powerful shock waves. The Warsaw ghetto uprising, which had actually taken place the year before, was one of those. Many of us had not even known of the existence of the Warsaw ghetto, and now we were hearing of the violent eruption there. The story was horrendous. It was of the ghetto dwellers attacking the Germans with whatever weapons they could devise and of the killing field that had ensued. But one particular detail embedded in the main story shook Miami Beach to its core—the account of the secret ghetto transmitter whose messages ended with the words "Save us."

By now it was late 1944, and at the urging of Henry

Morgenthau, the Treasury secretary and a Jew, Roosevelt finally made a statement about "crimes against humanity" being perpetrated by the Nazis—and the Japanese. This seemed to many to be a weak protest, and too late. Even my father was disconcerted, and he said, "Where were those guys when they heard about 'Save us'? I ask you, Where?"

When we got news that chilled, news that warmed sometimes came right along with it. As it seemed to speak to my new perspective, a bit of good news was especially interesting to me: the Supreme Court had ruled that no American could be denied the right to vote because of color.

Rick turned one year old, we had a party, and I took pictures of him covered in chocolate cake and sent them to Jack. I always had mixed feelings about sending pictures. What might pictures of loved ones gathered at a birthday party or building a sand castle at the beach mean to a serviceman? That the war did not fully occupy us at home?

At this time my sister Ruth came home, pregnant; Phil had been sent to Hawaii, to Hickam Field, the air base that had been in the thick of the Pearl Harbor attack. With Ruth home, the families decided that Rick and I should live with Jack's parents in their new house in town. The Subermans' younger son, Irwin, was now in the service, and a bedroom (with private bath!) had been liberated. Rick had another plus—another doting grandmother. This one would run to the black market occasionally and come back bearing rarely seen lamb chops for him. She would trim them to within an inch of their lives and dangle them before him. "Look, sweetheart," she would say. "You'll eat them like lollipops!" Another plus to living with

Jack's folks was that his sister, Sheila, was of an age where she still thought baby-sitting was a privilege.

Irwin was the model for the vagaries of military assignment. He had trained as an airplane mechanic at one of the local technical schools and had been working at the Miami Airport. When the Army took over the airport and offered him a sergeant's rank to enlist and do the same job he was doing, he took them up on it. Then, as the Army was wont to do, it plucked him from a job he was skilled at and sent him to gunnery school in South Carolina.

Just before Irwin left, he and Ruby Boniske were married. Ruby had gone to Miami High School, in town, and though there was not a lot of social interaction between Miami Beach Senior and Miami High, the Jewish groups kept loose tabs on one another, and I knew Ruby as one of Miami High's Jewish beauties. At Miami Beach Senior, Ruby might very well have been Carnival Queen, but at Miami High the ratio of Jews to Gentiles was nowhere near what it was like at Miami Beach Senior, so beauty titles stayed pretty much within the Gentile ranks.

When Irwin left, Ruby dropped out of the University of Miami to work at the Goodyear rubber plant, which had "gone to war." Ruby was making her contribution as an office supervisor. It was the kind of job many women took on, and even if you didn't wear snoods and carry riveting guns, you were doing your part by releasing men for military service. Instead of manufacturing automobile tires, Goodyear was now making anything the military needed in the way of rubber products, which let Ruby in for a lot of teasing. The question was, invariably, "Rubber goods for the military? You're turning out *condoms?*"

With Irwin gone there was yet another set of letters. In one letter to Ruby from South Carolina, Irwin wrote, "Looks like we'll be in the Pacific. Tell Jack I'm coming, so not to worry." In another letter, he told of learning something interesting about his name. "With the current rage for Superman," he wrote, "everybody wants to make a joke about 'Suberman,' so they don't connect 'Suberman' with being Jewish. And in the Army, that's not a bad thing."

Frieda had a lot of friends, and they daily filled the porch, where they did an assortment of things on the more or less permanently installed card table, and when Rick was napping, I joined in. In the mornings, with the card table extended by yet another card table, we put together aid packages, which we hoped would go to the concentration camps, to the Jews interned there, though we had little confidence that they would, even though the Red Cross had promised to see to it. "Fat chance," the women said. Maybe to the camps, but to think that the internees would actually receive the boxes "is to believe that Hitler has a Jewish star over his bed," they said. "What are we doing?" they would cry out. "We may only be helping the *grubbes!*" The *grubbes,* the gross ones, were in this case the beefy German guards.

But we kept filling the boxes—with toothbrushes, whole salamis, Band-Aids, cookies and candy and cigarettes—hoping, as we packed things in, that some poor soul's life would be brightened for a moment, and not because of what was in the boxes but because he would know that somebody outside the barbed wire was thinking of him. If the boxes didn't get to the concentration camps, we hoped they might find their way to the hard-pressed Russian soldiers. Even those who were Russian born felt this way, no matter that before the war they had made a practice of spitting whenever the old country was mentioned.

In the afternoons the porch table reverted to a card table, for bridge or canasta, although more and more often, the women were turning to mah-jongg. With its preset hands and clicking tiles, mah-jongg seemed to satisfy the need for order in an uncertain world. The game could be played for money, and the winnings went to the United Jewish Appeal, which, with its vaunted clout, would get the contributions into the proper hands. Or so we hoped. "We can only trust," the women said, "but who knows in this cockamamie world?"

And then one day it was a disheartened group that gathered. A morning item in the *Herald* had told of a memorandum written in the British Foreign Office, and it had chilled us profoundly as ice. The memo writer had succeeded in changing our feelings about the British, for when we read what he had said, we knew instantly—and sadly—that the British had failed us. The Foreign Office memo writer had written, "In my opinion a disproportionate amount of time of the office is wasted on dealing with these wailing Jews."

Wailing? With the British facility for language, surely some other word was available to the memo writer. How about *abused,* how about *hopeless,* how about *abandoned?* And the office's time "is wasted"? How about "We are looking into ways to rescue these suffering people"?

When Ruth's baby was due, we went out to Coral Gables—
a section of Greater Miami—to the local Army hospital there,
which in its salad days had been the Biltmore Hotel. It was no
longer the Biltmore Hotel that I remembered, for that Biltmore
Hotel had been a magnificent pink edifice with a Giralda tower
housing a bell that rang, and though it was still magnificent
and pink and had the tower, no bell sounded anymore. I also
remembered the Biltmore Hotel as the setting for aquatic galas
and bathing-beauty contests and alligator wrestling and syn-
chronized swimming and the largest hotel swimming pool in
the United States, the pool where Johnny Weissmuller, Tarzan
himself, was the swimming instructor. And among other things
I remembered was that you couldn't get a room in the Biltmore
Hotel if you were Jewish.

Now the Biltmore Hotel was an Army hospital, and as an
Army hospital its floor-to-ceiling windows had been sealed
with concrete and its marble floors covered with government-
issue linoleum. As an Army hospital, it did not discriminate but
allowed Ruth in as the wife of a serviceman, and after what
seemed to me a minimum of time—though Ruth might argue
with me about that—Dale Anthony was born. So Rick had a
new cousin, and my parents had their third grandson.

As I was now living in town, when I went to the beach it was
a "visit," though I still put in time doing various war-effort
things. Ruth and I spent some time at my mother's old treadle
sewing machine, making use of any fabric—an old dress, a
torn curtain, or a length of yard goods that had been tucked
away since Union City. We turned out jumpers, which we had
learned from our pregnancy days were unbeatable for versa-

tility. When we had done a few, we took them to the Community Church, whose collection was destined for "displaced persons," war refugees who found themselves far from home.

We occasionally helped out at bond rallies, once at the Roney Plaza, where Al Jolson—since *The Jazz Singer* the ultimate star for all Jewish people—was the celebrity attraction. And, as if wound up by a crank, he did it all: got down on his knees and sang "Mammy," said "You ain't heard nothin' yet," told war stories, and made people cry. For selling bonds, there was nobody like Al Jolson.

One day when Ruth and I took our babies walking, we discovered that something had been added to the Miami Beach wartime lifestyle. On the streets were German prisoners of war. Many of them had been captured during the North African campaign, but wherever we'd gotten them, they were now working at public labor jobs on Miami Beach streets. Actually, they seemed to do little more than lean on their shovels, but they had learned a little English and catcalled "Hubba hubba" to every passing girl. When Ruth and I walked by, they called out, "Hiya, mamas."

It was ironic that these Germans were working outside hotels that still posted anti-Semitic signs, and we had to wonder if the German soldiers were saying to themselves, See? Everybody feels this way. Although there was certainly no love lost between Ruth and me and these German POWs, for many Miami Beach women the hostility was intense. They were deeply offended when the POWs spoke to them, especially when the men spoke in German, and on one occasion Ruth and I watched while a woman we knew to be a German refugee returned their

German-language shouts with German-language shouts and then walked over and slapped several of them. This was another thing to wonder about—the thought process that had brought German soldiers to Miami Beach.

And that was my life at home as I waited for letters.

CHAPTER 11

What was going on at home was of course a minor accompaniment to what was going on in the various theaters of war. Jack was in India, in the CBI. His first two months had been mostly about training missions and "flying the hump," and actual combat was still waiting. An advance base for bombing Japan—or "A-7," as it was known officially—had been established outside of Chengdu, in western China. The runways for the field were built—and were still being built when the B-29s got there—by hundreds of Chinese laborers in family groups of men, women, and children, who split and pounded rocks with hammers and chisels. Jack wrote that they worked in robes, sitting down, and when they saw a plane coming in "they ambled out of the way and then got back to it." It seemed to me the ultimate in incongruity—those state-of-the-art monster American planes landing on airstrips of hand-hewn rocks.

To support a mission over Japan, the crews flew with fuel and bombs from India to A-7 over three valleys, or "humps," created by the three rivers that came down from the Himalayas. The route of these "hump flights" brought Mount Everest and the other north peaks of the Himalayas into view, and the crews flew it so often that it soon became routine, except for the danger (since the "hump" was Japanese-held territory) from Japanese fighter planes. "Mount Everest is magnificent," Jack wrote. "It rises majestically, fully confident of its supremacy." Still, after several hump missions, Jack noted, "We're tired of getting ready. We've even gotten bored with Everest. We want to get going."

The day to "get going" finally arrived, and the crews gathered for their briefing. As they gathered, they were "quiet, anxious, and ready," Jack wrote. Still, it was a no-go. There had been a change of plans, and there was to be no flight to Japan after all. Still, they were going on a mission: to Bangkok, the capital of Thailand, now an occupied Japanese puppet state. They would be flying over the Indian Ocean in what was called a part-training, part-combat mission. On this first mission Jack was in the lead plane. Like all bombardiers, he sat in the nose of the plane and was to some extent the plane's eyes. Bombardiers were constantly on the lookout for enemy fighters, and should one come into view, they were also in control of a remote turret gun.

It was a discouraging first mission. Of the one hundred B-29s that made the flight, each carrying ten tons of explosives, ninety-eight made it safely off the ground, though twenty-one of those aborted shortly after takeoff. It was not a total washout, however, for the men, Jack wrote, had been able to learn firsthand about weather foul-ups and mechanical problems and searchlights and anti-aircraft fire, though, Jack said, "The stuff they tried to send up petered out before they got to us," meaning the enemy fire was well below the planes. They had all gotten back safely—a case of so far, so good.

In a letter to Jack around this time, I couldn't help writing, "Please, darling, please don't be a hero. Please remember that if you risk your life recklessly, you're risking Rick's and mine as well."

And in his answering letter, Jack said, "Being a hero doesn't mean putting your life up for grabs. Being a hero means doing your job."

While the crews waited for the word of a mission over Japan, they continued to fly the hump and continued to seek out other targets. One of them was at Mukden, in Manchuria, a railroad yard used as a connection for Japanese shipping. As a fur wholesaler, Jack's father had bought furs in Mukden, and Jack remembered that when his father had been in business he had thought Jack might go to Mukden to take over the branch there. "I have to tell you, Dad," Jack wrote, "if Mukden is what it looks like from the air, it's cold and dreary as a tomb. I don't see me putting in a lot of time out there."

When they were not flying, they found ways to distract themselves. Jack wrote that Bill O'Connor came by, "cocktail shaker in hand," and after they had drunk "more Arizona Sunsets than we needed," they went off base to have dinner in the nearby village, at a restaurant surrounded by milling dogs. The menu said steak, but they were not beefsteaks. The restaurant was run by Hindus, and since their religion says that cows, as reincarnations of deceased ancestors, are sacred, they did not serve beef. Jack wrote, "We ordered what they said was water buffalo but might have been one of those milling dogs, for all we knew."

I got a letter from Peg telling me that Bill had written about this evening with Jack, and he had said that they had eaten together in "a restaurant so seedy that having a meal there ought to qualify as combat duty."

Jack played a lot of poker. The makeup of the poker group was rather fluid, but there were core players: Jack and some guys named Sidney, Dexter, and Marshall, all of whom I got to know through Jack's letters. They played almost every night and definitely on the night before a mission. A one-thousand-rupee note, about twenty dollars, was the standard bet, and in a single night the men could win or lose a lot. I took Jack's playing in stride. Whatever he could find to distract himself seemed irreproachable. I figured—then—that winning or losing at poker meant almost nothing, and the men might just as well have been running a tab, since what one man won one night, he could lose the next, and vice versa.

Attrition took its toll on the group. If a guy was there one night and not the next, a mention was made, but then talk of it ceased. When one of the core group—Marshall—did not appear, Jack wrote that there were a lot of rumors about what had happened to his plane but nothing definite. "Don't know much about it," Jack told me. "We're just hoping for the best."

The men found other things to break up the cycle of monotony and tension. One was the occasional surreal venture into Calcutta. In Calcutta, and especially at the Royal Calcutta Golf Club, the British, as at Salua, plied the American officers with niceties. And the British niceties, Jack wrote, were very nice indeed. From Salua the men would pile into an already overcrowded train, go to a posh hotel in Calcutta, and then take a taxi out to the club. Of the club, Jack wrote, "Those guys on Miami Beach who think they've got it made with their bath clubs would get heartburn if they saw this place." Then he added, "The only luxury they don't have is you." When I read this, I thought how much better it would be to have the luxury of him here than me there.

The club, according to Jack, was acres and acres of lush greenery surrounding a palace of a clubhouse, with the grounds dotted with tennis courts, croquet lawns, and bowling greens. Inside were several bars and dining rooms staffed by whole batteries of servants. Five men served each table, and Jack described them as scurrying around barefoot in white pants and long white cotton shirts, on their heads round turbans of white gauze, a trail of which floated down their backs.

The club's golf course was famously dotted with ponds. As Jack explained it, the Americans were supplied with caddies, and before they went out, they were told that if they hit a ball into one of the ponds—and balls were not only expensive but hard to get—they were to "resist the urge" to tell the caddies not to go into the pond after it. "We don't want you Americans to spoil them," the members said.

The idea of not "spoiling" your servants was a concept I was quite familiar with, only when I'd first heard it I had been living in the southern United States, not in Calcutta, India, and it had been applied to "niggers," not to Indians. As I learned from Jack, the Raj were not averse to calling Indians by that same epithet (in other parts of India the natives were known to the British as "wogs"), even though the Indians were actually as Caucasian as the Raj were. And since by now I no longer believed that the British set the standard for compassion and fair play, I was not surprised to hear this. About the caddies and the ponds, Jack wrote to me, "In the villages that the British had destroyed to make the golf course, the ponds had been used as natural septic tanks, and the caddies are no doubt wading into dense crap."

Calcutta itself, Jack wrote, was "teeming, helter-skelter, and cacophonous," with thousands of people living in the streets. "They do everything in the streets that human beings do—eat, sleep, defecate, fornicate," Jack said. "And they also die."

I wrote to Jack every day and tried to make my letters as long as possible. I made an effort to include world news and editorial opinion along with reports of Rick's progress and the usual family news. I eschewed V-mail when I enclosed pictures and newspaper clippings. I often sent packages, which sometimes got to him, sometimes didn't. I sent things he couldn't get at the base PX, things I thought would travel, like salamis and well-wrapped rye breads, which he received. But he didn't receive the calamine lotion for his prickly heat, and I pictured it landing in the hands of some puzzled frostbitten serviceman in Alaska.

After a while, every letter I received from Jack asked me, "So where's that second front?"

I CERTAINLY DIDN'T know where the second front was, but talk of one was now dominating all conversation. It was no secret; we were well aware that a second front was in the works. And we knew what a second front was: it was an attack tailored for the European theater. The plan was for Allied troops to come at the German troops from another direction and force them to battle on two fronts. It was said that this new strategy would change the course of the war. All we could do was wait.

In early June, D-day, as the momentous event was called, finally happened. Again I got the news from someone waking me and shaking a newspaper at me. This time it was Jack's father, and the newspaper headline said that Allied forces had landed at Normandy. "It's the second front," Alex yelled at me. "The second front!" In a man so careful to minimize excitement, this was a tremendous show of it. And who could blame him? This was not the standard news item, not the report of just another battle. It was weighty, and so breathtaking in its promise that I felt sure that our enemies would be surrendering before you could say "Up with Ike."

It *was* weighty, and it *was* breathtaking. But as we read the newspapers the next day, and the next, it became clear that the cost in lives of the D-day assault had been enormous. And it did not end the war. It might have been the beginning of the end of the war in Europe—and even this is up for argument— but it definitely was not the beginning of the end of the war in the Pacific.

Jack's letter about the D-day invasion was jubilant and rueful at the same time. He wanted to celebrate because it had actually come off, but the cost in men's lives sat poorly with him, as it did with all of us. And there was the guilt. "I ought to have been there," Jack wrote me. "I should have been there fighting the Nazis."

This down feeling was compounded by the fact that the men in India were still marking time. Jack wrote, "Even if the Normandy invasion helps shorten the war in Europe, here in India we know the end is still a long way off. We're just hoping that a big-time operation comes soon."

Finally the big-time operation materialized, the target definitely Japan. The run was to be over Yawata, a large coastal city on the island of Kyushu, in which was located one of Japan's biggest steel mills. The specific target was the mill's ceramic ovens, which explained why in Karagpur the men had been studying a model steel factory with a forty-by-forty-foot ceramic oven at its heart and why they had been devising methods for bombing the oven from an altitude of up to twenty-five thousand feet. But an oven of sixteen hundred square feet from an altitude of twenty-five thousand feet? "They're asking for miracles," Jack wrote. "Do I believe in miracles? Only if plenty of hard work precedes." He described the plan of attack: they were to fly "to target" individually, at various altitudes up to the maximum twenty-five thousand feet, and after reaching their initial point (the point where formations are set up and turns made), they would enter the target area.

They had their first snafu, though one definitely trivial, just before the mission when it dawned on the men that the outfits they had been assigned to wear were unusable. These were handsome tailored affairs designed to enable the wearer, after landing, to be appropriately attired for any kind of gathering in any kind of club. (The way I looked at it, any combination of a combat mission and a fancy club defied reason anyway.) The outfits included pants and a jacket—the shortened one called the "Eisenhower jacket"—and shoes so finely crafted they could take the wearer dancing. The uniforms were also wired for heat, the wires to be plugged into a socket on the inside of the cabin. But wait a minute: as the men were getting dressed, they realized that if they wore the new uniforms and had to bail out at twenty-five thousand feet onto snow-covered peaks, there would be no outlets to plug into and the wearer would freeze on the way down or after landing, take your choice. So they returned to the bulky old flying gear.

Jack's letter told me many things about this first foray over Japan, but I actually learned more in a copy of the *Plane Talk,* the in-house newsletter of the Boeing plant in Wichita, to which Jack, as crew historian, had been sending items. His plane, the *General H. H. Arnold Special,* was the factory workers' darling, and they wanted to be told of every mission, every incident. Because the workers were his audience, Jack wrote in a different way for the *Plane Talk.* He wrote more dramatically, and it was all heroic stories, all optimism, all the time.

On this mission the *Arnold Special* was the last to go, and Jack described in *Plane Talk* watching the other B-29s "thundering off the runway and fighting their way into the sky with their heavy loads." As evidence of the eagerness for the mission, Jack included a story about their crew's top gunner, how he had been sick and his place already assigned to somebody else, and then at the last minute the guy had come out, struggled into his flying togs, and yelled that he was going and "Don't nobody try to stop me." When I read this in *Plane Talk,* it sounded as if Jack had decided to put enough drama in it for a movie, but as if reading my mind, Jack wrote in his next letter to me, "It may remind you of a movie starring Van Johnson, but that's just what the guy did."

On the mission, as they approached the Yellow Sea they saw some airplane lights, and the gunners manned their stations, figuring it might be a Japanese night fighter. Even though it disappeared, Jack said in the *Plane Talk* that it was "a grim reminder that we were now over enemy territory." And when, over the sea, they saw a lot of enemy shipping below, Jack wrote that though the ship lights "blinked enticingly," they decided to adhere to what their mission commander had told them at their briefing—that they were not after small stuff like shipping but "really big game."

They found the target area surrounded by searchlights sending up what Jack called "wigwams of light," at the peak of which a B-29 might be caught. "Every once in a while," Jack wrote in the newsletter, "a necklace of fire would climb up the wigwam and disappear into an airplane." The entire sky "was lit by the dull red glare of bomb explosions."

If on the earlier mission over Bangkok they had "cruised" for thirty-five minutes, on this first mission over Japan, the target run, as Jack described it, lasted for "an eternity" of about five minutes, with the plane turning this way and that. In a burst of metaphor, Jack wrote that the plane was like "a tormented monster." After the bombs "clicked off one by one," Jack confounded the metaphor a bit by describing how Colonel Sullivan, a former West Point football player, "twisted for home like a broken field runner, skirting between the search-

lights." He recorded one light moment when, on the return
home, Sinclair, one of the gunners, having reported a big fire in
the target area, was told to get some pictures; and then another
gunner took a look and wanted to know if they wanted pictures
of the moon, which is what the "fire" actually was, the smoke
and dust having turned the moon a fiery red. Jack wrote that
"Sinclair's 'fire'" broke the tension, and they started thinking
about the moment when they could "paint another black
bomb on the silver nose of the *General H. H. Arnold Special.*"
As I knew by now, after each mission, if it was a "hump" one,
a camel was painted on the plane; if a combat mission, a bomb
went on.

What Jack did not tell *Plane Talk,* but what he told me, was
that the first foray over Japan had fallen well short of expec-
tations. Over the target, problems showed almost at once. One
was as mysterious as it was unsolvable. They had encountered
an unknown force that acted violently upon computations. The
force was so puzzling that no answers were forthcoming. What
they had encountered—what they had *discovered*—was the
jet stream. And as we now know, that stream of wind moves at
a speed of two hundred miles per hour and upward, and with
no adjustments made for this hitherto uninvestigated phenom-
enon, it played havoc with calculations. At the extremely high
altitudes at which the planes were flying, accurate computations were hard enough to come by, but when the effect of the
jet stream was added, bombing the target became a frustrating puzzle. Jack wrote, "After all our studying and planning,
hitting our target turned out to be a joke. Forget the ovens. We
were lucky if we hit the plant, maybe even the city." And since

the city was on the coast, Jack added, "It's even possible that we missed Japan."

After the first mission, I didn't have to wait for Jack's letters —or the Wichita *Plane Talk*—to tell me what the B-29s were doing. Every mission was a front-page news story. The *Miami Herald* of August 21, 1944, carried this item:

SUPERFORTS IN 2 RAIDS ON JAPAN
Enemy's Industrial Areas Pounded by Big Bombers; Four
Lost in Dual Action
By the Associated Press

Two B-29 aerial lashings of Japan within a few hours, including the first daylight raid on the home islands since the April 18, 1942 attack led by Lieutenant Gen. James Doolittle, were announced Sunday by the 20th Air Force. Bombing results were good.

The big bombers first hit vital war industries in the area of Yawata, the steel center on Kyushu island.

Japanese fighter opposition was relatively strong. Four American planes were reported lost due to enemy action. Twelve Japanese fighters were claimed destroyed, the communique said, with 12 more probably destroyed and ten damaged. Anti-aircraft fire was moderate to intense, and accurate.

JAPS CLAIM 25
Japanese broadcasts said 77 of the Superfortresses launched the daylight assault at 5 p.m., Tokyo time, and that 20 B-29's returned seven hours later to hit the same region.

Tokyo radio claimed 25 bombers were shot down in the first raid, including three by "suicide fighters" that rammed the Yank planes. It listed among the targets—Yawata, iron and steel base; Moji, big shipping port and coal center, and Kokura and Fukuoka in northern Kyushu.

All told, the Superforts have carried out six raids against major Japanese targets, including the two-pronged attack Aug. 10 when separate groups struck simultaneously at the great port of Nagasaki on Kyushu and the big oil refinery center of Palembang, Sumatra, in the Dutch East Indies— some 3,000 miles apart.

A Berlin broadcast listed the western part of the island of Skikoku, northeast of Kyushu, as another target. One Berlin broadcast reported that "at least 10" of the big bombers were shot down and that some of the American airmen had been captured.

Of course what jumped out at me were the casualty assessments. I came to understand that reports of casualties were typically different, depending on which side was reporting them. The United States might report "heavy demolition" with "only" two planes shot down and crews being picked up from life rafts, whereas Japan would claim that low-hanging clouds had "prevented any serious damage" and that nine planes had been shot down. I scarcely noticed when the news accounts, as they often did, misidentified the 20th Bomber Command as the 20th Air Force. The real dilemma was, always, which estimate of the number of losses to believe. It was a guessing game that was very hard to play.

With each account in the paper my hands shook and my heart banged away, and I would think of Jack sitting up there —sometimes for a twenty-hour stretch—in the glass nose of his plane, his eyes always scanning the skies. It didn't help much when he wrote that he had been promoted and was now wearing his "railroad tracks"—his captain's bars.

After any news item came the long wait for the letter from Jack that would tell me he had gotten back safely from that particular mission. I was grateful that missions over Japan did not happen every day, for that meant that news items did not appear every day. Still, I knew that before a mission could be mounted, there were those two or three preliminary hump flights. Planes were often lost on hump flights, and only occasionally were the crews able to save themselves.

On the layovers at the air base near Chengdu, a USO troop would sometimes come through. Just before one mission the actor Pat O'Brien came into the briefing room and gave the men the "One for the Gipper" speech from his movie about the Notre Dame football coach Knute Rockne. "He had everybody in tears," Jack wrote. "Can you imagine that the men teared up at the thought of 'winning one for the Gipper'? God, getting all worked up over a football game and in a few minutes we were going to be dealing with plane failures and *ack-ack*."

Jack occasionally went into Chengdu. It was a very primitive place, I gathered, with a single telephone line "strung on poles in the city center," Jack wrote, "proudly on display." There were signs of a city: a hotel, a public bathhouse, and some restaurants—one of them a "snake" restaurant, where you'd pick out your dinner snake from the wriggling mass on display, and a waiter would skin him. "They peel them like a banana," Jack wrote. "You have to admire their skill."

Jack found other things to do in Chengdu. He had heard

there was a synagogue there, and he wrote me about going there with one of the Chinese air-base workers to act as interpreter. He described it as a congregation of about thirty people, apparently Jewish but looking Chinese. Most interesting of all, Jack wrote, was that when he had made known to the rabbi that he was Jewish, the rabbi had said, "Funny, you don't look Jewish." I thought it might be a joke, and though I didn't want it to be, Jack added a postscript that said, "Gotcha."

Still, the part about the synagogue wasn't a joke. There actually *was* a synagogue, and there were a few Jewish Chinese people in it. No doubt these congregants were the descendants of the Russian Jews who had immigrated to China generations before and had bred with the native population. It was the Diaspora in evidence in China.

Between missions over Japan, there continued to be hump missions and attacks on alternate targets. After one of the Bangkok missions, I got a very sad letter from Jack—sad for him to write, sad for me to read. He wrote, "We saw a plane ahead of us burst into flame, and we followed the flaming path for about eight minutes. It seemed to go into a gradual dive and then it crashed into the sea. We saw another flame detach itself from the burning plane. They went down around the Andaman Islands, between the 10th and 11th lines of latitude, in the Indian sea. We could only report its position and go on." Harvey McTigue had been in that plane, and he was gone. "One of the really good guys," Jack said.

I wrote to Helen Bascombe and told her how sorry I was. She wrote back and said, "I always thought Harvey would die in this damned war. He liked the war. He didn't like the killing, but he liked the camaraderie and the idea of being on a team. I know that when Harvey went down, what he was thinking was that he had failed the team. It's very hard for me to know that." And she added a postscript: "I guess I'll have the sad duty of notifying the pachyderms." Those famous pachyderms —Harvey's fellow linemen, whom he'd loved so much. I had not realized until that letter that Helen had been so thoughtful, so sensible, and I wished I had gotten to know her better.

I had liked Harvey as Jack did, as a really good guy. That men were dying all over the world I did not lose sight of, but it took me a while to put Harvey's death behind me, and of course I never truly did.

THE SOLID SUCCESS that the B-29 men in India had been longing for came with their first attack on Omura, another industrial harbor town. To avoid the jet stream, they were flying at lower altitudes, and this time their calculations were accurate. When they came back, it was with a feeling of achievement, for they had bombed the mills "to dust," as Jack wrote. "It was a worthy target," he said. "Omura was important to Japan's capacity to make war." It was a time for congratulations all around.

Well, not quite. I had asked Jack about James Stallings, who always seemed so eager for combat, and in a following letter he told me something I was very surprised to hear: James, the pilot we had all thought of as so gung ho, had yet to go on a mission. He was doing a lot of aborting and with different excuses: the gauges showed that the oil pressure was too low, the remote guns were not working, power was lacking. Toward the end of the letter, Jack had a caution: "Before you start thinking badly of James," he wrote, "just remember something. He's the pilot, and the plane and his men are his responsibility. Eleven men. That's enough to give you second thoughts, isn't it?"

As for the successes, they were still erratic. In a letter after the second attack on Omura—what the men called "Second Omura"—Jack wrote, "This one was a real waste of time, energy, money, and lives. It was a case where weather predictions were so misleading that the entire mission failed. Everybody was in the soup over the target, unable to fly in formation, and dropped bombs according to radar calculations, which were no doubt hopeless."

Second Omura was actually a mission of many horrors, one of them Jack's alone. Colonel Sullivan had been forced to fly above thick clouds, so they were flying completely blind, never once seeing land—not over China, not over the target—and they had to rely on radar technology, which was just coming in as a navigational tool. Then, on the way back, Jack was told that a bomb had not released from its shackles and had gotten hung up in the bomb bay, the compartment carrying the bombs and from which they were dropped. The bomb was armed, which meant that it would explode on impact. So what Jack had to do was go back to detach it, for if it hung on, when the plane landed it "would bomb itself to hell," as Jack wrote. "I definitely didn't want to go back there," he said, "but it was my job and I had to."

He went back to the bomb bay, the door of which was wide open with a bomb half-released. I tried to imagine it. The ledge around the bomb-bay opening was about six inches wide, and it was this that Jack had to use for footing while trying to release the bomb. It took him several minutes to get the bomb out. "I tried to keep myself from looking down," Jack wrote, "for down there was nothing but cloud, and under that was nothing but empty space." I pictured him bending over an open bomb bay for several minutes, wiggling, thrusting, pushing a five-hundred-pound bomb caught up he knew not how. Did he finally have to kick at it? With this thought, my heart went wild, for I saw Jack standing on one foot on that narrow space, the bomb dislodging, and Jack, suddenly unbalanced, going with it.

In the end the maneuver did dislodge the bomb, and of course Jack did not go with it, but as he returned to his seat, he said, he now had another worry. He knew they were over China, and his navigator, Bert Alley, had said a lake was below, but sightless as he was because of the clouds, Jack had not been able to track the bomb's destination. Jack wrote, "All I can do is hope it landed in Alley's lake, and not on a town."

The next mission was one undertaken by their alternate crew, and it was an interesting mission from many angles. The plane got caught in a vicious typhoon, and Wes Price, the alternate crew's pilot, radioed back that he was heading for Vladivostok. At first it seemed a good way out; everyone assumed that since the Soviet Union was our ally, the plane would be sent right back. Well, the Soviet Union was our ally against Germany, but it was neutral toward Japan, and not wanting to stir things up, the Soviets interned the plane and crew. "So good-bye to the *General H. H. Arnold Special*," Jack wrote. "And hello to one of these new things they've sent over.

Too bad. We had gotten used to that old geezer and knew all its quirks." What this meant to me, of course, was that they did not know all the quirks of the new plane.

But this final mission for the *Arnold Special* was more than an internment at Vladivostok. It was an event that went down in the annals of the B-29 and even in the annals of the war and the Cold War. As it turned out, the interning of the *Arnold Special* was quite a Soviet coup. With no bomber of their own comparable to the B-29, the Soviets had been doomed to play a role as a lesser power in the Cold War they knew was coming. But with the B-29 dropped into their laps, they found a way to compete as an equal, for now they could build a super-bomber of their own. So they set about tearing the *H. H. Arnold* apart, copying it rivet by rivet, and eventually they built their own fleet of B-29s. In the Soviet Union it was called not the Superfortress, of course, but the Tu-4. And it made the U.S.S.R. a confident Cold War adversary.

As TIME WENT ON, fewer and fewer of Jack's letter contained joyful bits—no "bombing to dust," no "formation held," no "great weather for the job"—and I would gather that missions were usually falling well short of success. Indeed, Jack's succeeding letters would reveal a soldier full of pessimism. He wrote that he now had the Air Medal with "some clusters," but it didn't seem to do much for his mood.

Of the many reasons for this mood, one stood out: the growing acknowledgment that the B-29s stationed in India could not do the job. There was one good reason for this: Chengdu meant a round-trip of three thousand miles, to and from Japan.

"The distance is daunting," Jack wrote. "We're just too far away for sustained attacks. We need bases closer to Japan. We need the islands. We need the Marianas, Iwo Jima, Saipan. These would put us close enough to Japan to permit consistent and heavy bombing." The Pacific Islands, however, were not yet securely in our hands.

Bad news followed: Jack wrote that during one mission several planes had been lost. I could sense by the way his letter started that he was preparing me for some very bad news. I thought to myself, Please don't let it be Bill. Please don't let me read that. But that's what Jack wrote and that's what I read. One of the planes that had gone down on the last mission had been Bill O'Connor's. My heart went flying up to Boston, to Peg. In his letter Jack said that a raft had been spotted, and there was a report that rescuers had been seen, but he didn't know if Bill had been in the raft. "At this point we don't know much," Jack wrote. "We don't know who the survivors are and if those rescuers were really rescuers or a contingent of Japanese."

I had to write to Peg, and if I hadn't known that she had comfort around her, that she had "Father," who meant so much to her, I would have written with less faith in her ability to stand up to this news. I wrote immediately, and after several days she wrote back and told me what she knew, which was not much more than I knew. She had simply gotten a telegram saying that Bill was missing in action.

Peg wrote that her church was praying for Bill, which was in all ways a "great comfort" to her. "So many candles have been lit," she wrote, "the church is always ablaze. All for my darling Billy." Her "darlin' Billy."

She had sent a donation to a nearby convent, Peg wrote, and had asked the sisters to "pray for Bill's safe return." There was more. "And by the way," she said in her letter, "I sent a donation to that little Mexican church in Tucson and asked them to appeal to their parishioners to send up a prayer." It was then that I understood that Peg had thought about my chiding remarks to her in Tucson, but at this moment there was no way I could feel triumphant.

Notwithstanding D-day, the war in Europe, no matter what all of us had anticipated, was in no way winding down. The Germans were in fact fighting with a renewed fierceness, their rage no doubt fueled by their having been duped about the when and where of the D-day landings. Indeed, sadistic incidents increased. Almost immediately after the landings, the entire population of the French town of Oradour-sur-Glane had been killed. The men had been shot, the women and children had been locked in a church, and then the church had been set afire.

And Germany was still not through with London. Six days after D-day, German V-1 remote-controlled rockets— treacherous little "doodlebugs" and "buzz bombs"—pelted the city even more heavily than usual. And, about this time, we got more frustrating news: an assassination attempt on Adolf Hitler by some German generals failed, and everybody said, How come they're so smart at killing people until it comes to Hitler?

There was, however, some good news, some very good

news. So good that we thought we might have reached a turning point in the Pacific war: U.S. Marines had taken Saipan, and as if addressing the concerns of the B-29 men in India, there were now airfields for B-29s in easy striking distance of Tokyo. There was good news in Europe as well: after four years of German occupation, Paris was liberated by Allied troops.

My letters to Jack were filled with these bits of good news and with domestic happenings. Roosevelt was elected to a fourth term, with Harry Truman (Harry who?) as vice president. And though I tried to keep away from any depressing news, I felt compelled to write that my incomparable Glenn Miller—Captain Glenn Miller of the U.S. Army Air Corps— had been killed in a crash over the English Channel.

I was living from letter to letter, from news account to news account. Jack's last letter had been written after a successful mission (finally!), and it was full of cheerful comment. "No matter if we're not doing what the B-29 is capable of," he wrote, "we're getting to their oil refineries and their industrial complexes. We've shown them what we can do." Still, after Harvey's death and Bill's missing-in-action status, I opened every letter with fear and trembling.

And then came the day when I felt danger so strongly I almost stopped living.

It happened on an ordinary day, when I was walking around downtown. I gave the merest glance into a store window, and something caught my eye—a news machine across which a news tape was running. It was what one headline said— "100% turnover in B-29s"—that made me struggle for breath.

There were no other details, and my imagination careened this way and that. There was nothing to help me understand, for that ten-day lag meant that no letter already in the mails was going to help.

Once at home, I wrote Jack a feverish letter asking what it all meant, what a "100% turnover" meant, and as I wrote, the little B-29 charm on my bracelet swung around wildly. I ran scenario after scenario through my head, each one inviting more terror: Jack might not be there to receive my letter, or before the letter even arrived at the APO, I could get a telegram.

I was paralyzed with fear. I could no longer do anything without forcing myself. Since I wasn't eating and scarcely spoke, Jack's parents looked at me as if they suspected that I was holding something back, so I told them. They didn't know what to make of it either. Did it mean all the B-29 crewmen were dead, or lost, or so wounded that they were in hospitals?

I had no energy for the newspapers or for the radio. I did read that the Germans had counterattacked at Bulge, in Belgium. But though I knew this was important, I couldn't give it any real attention.

The only helpful thing was that it was Christmastime. Sheila was out of school, and she sensed that I needed her to take over with Rick. If Rick had an inkling that things were abnormal, he showed no signs of it, for Sheila kept him busy. Jack's parents did as well as they could. They tried to do ordinary things, and Frieda put extra effort into attempting to make palatable dishes out of ersatz ingredients, but we knew we were all just going through the motions.

I had had a letter from Peg. Did I know anything more about Bill? Well, no, I didn't. I didn't know anything about anything.

I waited for I knew not what. I couldn't look forward to the coming of the mailman—we still had a male mailman, a fellow of about seventy—for though he might bring a letter from Jack explaining why "100%" didn't mean anything, he might also be returning my own letter with something unthinkable stamped on the envelope. In fact, I could hardly bear to look out at the street at all, for while I didn't want to see the mailman, I most definitely didn't want to see a bicyclist wheeling up to our house, since bicyclists meant telegrams, and telegrams meant, well, telegrams meant . . .

At the end of the month there was news of the greatest import to the war: the Allies had defeated the Germans at what was later called the Battle of the Bulge. The war seemed to be all over but for the shouting. I tried to rejoice at the happy news, but the happy news was for the war in Europe, and I was still waiting for news that was much more important to me. So I continued to wait. And it finally came.

My news did not come by letter, and it did not come by telegram. It came by telephone. And the telephone call was not from China, not even from India. It was from West Palm Beach. And making the call was Jack.

He was home.

Jack's father drove me up to West Palm. Alex and I talked at the top of our voices, laughing loudly and often. Yes, even quiet, reserved Alex. I squeezed my arms to my chest to keep my heart from jumping out. And in my head, I sang a song over and over. It was "It's Been a Long, Long Time," and it seemed a song written just for me.

And then we were at Morrison Field, and there waiting at the gate was a tall man in a rumpled uniform standing beside a B-4 bag and wearing an officer's hat so raunchy there was nothing to it but droop. Was that man—not a boy, but a man—standing next to the guardhouse really Jack? Yes, it was Jack, and he was real. And that real man was moving toward the car and I was opening the car door, and I was dashing out of it and into his arms.

From Alex there was an outburst of tears. It may have been unexpected, but if there was ever a moment for tears to be shed by a father, this was that moment.

We had coffee in the coffee shop of the hotel where we had honeymooned, and after an hour or so, Jack and I were exchanging looks that didn't include Alex, so Alex got up and left, to take the bus back to Miami. The moment he walked out the coffee shop's door, Jack and I were on our way to our room.

There was not a holding out of arms and a walking slowly toward each other, as a romantic war movie might have had it. There was a tight embrace and then a falling to the bed. Was it a second honeymoon, an imitation of the first? No, I'd have to say that what transpired in that bed was not what one would expect of a second honeymoon. In our need—so long awaited—to express love, and in the intensity of how we expressed it, I would not say it was a second anything.

Jack had two days in West Palm to do paperwork, and we

spent the first day in our room, ordering room service and staying in bed. It was past midnight before we decided we really should get up, and Jack said he had something to show me. If I thought it was going to be a charm for my bracelet, it was not. In his B-4 bag, in among a pile of dirty laundry, was something I hadn't anticipated—a bumpy, lumpy cocktail shaker. It was Bill's, of course. When Jack had heard about Bill, he had simply walked over to Bill's bunk and picked it up. The shaker was not just a piece of sweet nostalgia; it was also a reminder that Bill was still missing. And it was also a reminder that, though Jack might be home, the war was still on.

We talked a little, but we agreed that most things could wait. We didn't have to "rediscover" each other, for our letters had kept us not only in touch but intact. Still, one item that couldn't wait was the "100% turnover." It wasn't at all what I had feared, Jack said, for it was the planes that had had the total turnover, not the crews. The attrition rate apparently came from crashes but also from major malfunctions or other problems, to the extent that 100 percent of the original planes had been lost or taken out of service and replaced with newer ones.

As we started on the drive to Miami and pulled up to a pump for gas, Jack did a strange thing. He told the attendant to fill the tank just half full. Having lived for so long in a situation when being out of gas meant sure death, he had a real wish to run out of gas. "I'm just going to get out of the car on U.S. 1," he said, "and laugh my head off."

On the way (much to Jack's disappointment, we didn't run out of gas) Jack explained why he had been sent home. It was because the era of the India-based B-29s was winding down.

The Pacific islands had been secured, and all B-29s were now being sent there. Some of the pilots (Jack's copilot among them), whose familiarity with B-29s was vital, had been sent over to the islands with a new crew, but Jack had served his time and, like most of the others, had been sent home.

What he had come home in was an old B-29 that had been taken out of combat service and made into a tanker. It was piloted by a Major named Gus Askounis from one of the other squadrons, a man very attuned to his Greek heritage. As such, he was a handy guy to be with, for at every place they landed on the way back—Khartoum, for example—they were invited to a home-cooked meal. Apparently Gus simply went into a residential area that was known to be home to Greek refugees who had fled the Nazis by way of the Nile, stood in the middle of the street, and shouted out in Greek, "Any Greeks here?" If a head popped out of a window—and heads popped out by the dozens, according to Jack—Gus shouted, "So how about a nice Greek welcome for some Americans?" Jack said it worked every time.

They'd landed at Borinquen Field in Puerto Rico, the last stop before West Palm, and were a long time getting out. It was a question of not being able to make ourselves leave. With but one short hop left, with home seeming within hailing distance, they were afraid to press their luck. It was typical, Jack said. Whenever planes landed there, any problem considered disregardable while on missions seemed gigantic on the home leg. So Jack's crew did what all the other planes did—checked and rechecked so often and for so long that the air-base personnel finally had to force them to leave.

Rick was waiting. Well, when Jack came into the house, he was not actually waiting, but taking a nap, and Jack's mother took the moment to hold her "soldier boy" in her arms. The last time Jack had seen Rick, Rick had been an infant, crawling around and making nonsense sounds—though Jack and I swore that once he had said, "If you insist"—and now he was walking and talking. When Rick woke up, when he looked to see who was hovering over his crib, I wanted to think that he knew it was his father. And when he said, "Daddy home?" I wanted to believe that he remembered him, remembered sleeping on his chest in Kansas.

Yes, Daddy was home, and he had left his part in the war behind him, though after his ten-day pass, we would set out again. This time was different, however, because though the war in the Pacific was still going strong, there was little chance that Jack would be sent overseas again. Furthermore, the Pacific war was looking better and better: while Jack had been on his way home, Allied troops had invaded Luzon, in the Philippines, and General MacArthur had entered Manila.

The war in Europe was still on as well, though barely, for it seemed genuinely to be coming to a close. And when the Red Army entered Warsaw, it was clear it was just about over.

But it was not all hallelujah all the way, for with the taking of Poland, Russian troops had entered the death camp known as Auschwitz and in so doing had opened it up for all to see the full extent of the horrors. All at once we knew everything. And all at once the theaters had a flood of newsreel pictures and we saw with our own eyes what we had only imagined. When we saw the pictures, what words did we use? "Unbelievable"? "Sickening"? "Monstrous"? We used all of them, and more. Miami and Miami Beach Jews were awash in emotion, and perhaps more than a little guilty at not having done more, persisted more, demanded more. But who knew? we kept asking each other. We were all excoriation and helplessness.

I wrote to Peg that Jack had gotten home, trying to keep it as low-key as possible. Her note back said, "Give Jack a kiss, God love him. And pray for my Billy to come home safely." I don't think Peg could ever understand that there are people in this world who don't pray. Those people say "hope" instead, and Jack and I hoped fervently.

JACK WAS ASSIGNED to Maxwell Field. This time we could use all the facilities, just as Jack had promised when I had visited him in Montgomery when he was a cadet, when he had swept an arm over the prohibited magnificence that was Maxwell and said, "Just think—one day all this will be ours." Our housing, however, was by no means magnificent. Since both Maxwell and Gunter were bursting at the seams, the military seemed unable to help us, and housing was take-what-you-can-get. We finally landed a room in an old southern mansion in Cloverdale, the best part of town, but despite the fact that the elegant widowed lady who owned the house was not in residence, she forbade us to use anything but the room and bath she was getting a lot of money for, and never, never the kitchen, which was in fact locked. We had every belief that we were living in the maid's quarters.

The only real benefits we got from Maxwell were the ability

to eat in the club dining room and to use the commissary, except that the commissary was of little use to me, since I had no kitchen. We ate out all the time, mostly at a little drugstore down the street that served food. It also had a jukebox, and it was there that I first heard a new crooner on the scene —Johnny Desmond, who was singing with Glenn Miller's army orchestra, still operating even if Glenn was no longer around.

After Maxwell, Jack was assigned to Buckingham Field in Fort Myers, up the road on the west coast of Florida. We found a house on the beach, one of those houses built on stilts so the Gulf waters could pass under during an excessively high tide, and in spite of the bugs we prepared to enjoy ourselves. Fort Myers Beach was notorious for its slick little no-see-ums— biting bugs so tiny that not even screens could thwart them— and for homely old mosquitoes. For self-protection, I hung laundry not on a line in the backyard but on the screened porch.

We knew we should be thinking about the future, for the handwriting on the wall said that the war was ending. It was a very hard thing to do. We needed an interlude, and Fort Myers was perfect for that. We had good neighbors; all of the men were stationed at Buckingham, all of them back from a tour of duty, and all of them glad to be home. It was a congenial group. Our next-door neighbor was a Captain Marvel, and as Jack was now, like his brother Irwin, often known as Superman, the neighbors said they felt safer having two superheroes in their midst. The neighborhood also provided children for Rick to play with, so things were relaxed. Well, pretty relaxed.

JACK'S BUCKINGHAM FIELD job was a breeze. He was in charge of a gunnery training program for bombing crews, but no one took it seriously because we were no longer counting the days until the war was over, just the hours.

Still, not everything in Fort Myers was completely relaxing. There was, for example, that particular telephone call Jack received from Marshall, the poker-playing buddy in India who had gone missing. When Jack answered the phone, I heard him say, "Well done, Marshall. Great that you made it." I knew who Marshall was, and I too was glad that he had made it. But then I heard Jack say, "First thing in the morning," and I wondered. No need to wonder long: Marshall was now in an army hospital in St. Petersburg, and it turned out he had been in one of the three planes that had landed in Russia near Vladivostok and had finally been let out. He had gone by G.I. truck from Tashkent to Tehran and then to the States. A long trip, he told Jack, and he had been told he had had a nervous breakdown. His memory was failing, he said, though his memory had apparently not failed so badly that he didn't remember that when he'd landed he had had Jack's IOU in his pocket. Marshall told Jack on the phone, "I hope you're still an officer and a gentleman," and Jack didn't say, "Well, Marshall, you would have lost it to me the next night"; he just said yes, he was, and would send him the money in the morning.

It turned out that Jack's IOU was for fifteen hundred dollars, give or take a dollar or two, and Jack tried to joke about it—joke me out of it—by saying that the IOU was probably what had gotten Marshall through. Happy as I was that Marshall was safe and well, happy as I was that Jack was safe and well, I was not happy with that IOU. I was in fact not happy with Jack or with his entire card-playing family. But hadn't I once said that I could not quarrel with anything he did while overseas? Still, it was my opinion that fifteen hundred dollars flung about in a poker game before going off on a mission was vastly different from fifteen hundred dollars in the bank when you're back in the States and with your family. I forgave Jack only when he had the grace to look sheepish.

It was certainly true that things were going at a breakneck speed toward an ending of the war. In the Pacific the capture of Iwo Jima meant that the United States now possessed Japan's last line of radar defense against American air attacks. It was also the prelude to the invasion of Okinawa. And in Europe U.S. troops reached the Elbe River in Germany, halting there to meet the advancing Russian troops.

There was bad news, however, that almost overwhelmed the good, and it came suddenly. I was sitting on the porch listening to the radio and some announcer came on and said, "In Warm Springs, Georgia . . ." When I decided to listen, what I thought I heard was that President Roosevelt had died. Of course not, I thought. But then the announcer said it again. Well, I thought now, he's just one of those untrained, temporary V-announcers who can't read and gets things wrong. But of course he had not gotten it wrong.

I waited for Jack to come rushing in, and when he did, we held each other in disbelief. It was unthinkable that our leader, our protector, was gone from us. That lovely man with the cigarette holder and the grin—gone. We had said to each other that at his Yalta meeting with Stalin and Churchill he had been pale and wan, but surely . . . surely . . .

That night the neighbors got together at our house, and we mourned. Whether we were Republicans or Democrats, that night we grieved together. My father telephoned and said that when he'd heard the news his stomach "got in a knot as big as the moon and Mama's too." He wanted to know what Jack thought this meant to the war. Well, what did Roosevelt's death mean to the war?

It didn't mean much to the war. Now Harry Truman was president, and events rushed ahead as they had before Roosevelt's death. The Allies continued forward, and battles were won. It was not too long before we heard reports that American forces had captured Nuremberg and Russians forces had reached the suburbs of Berlin.

The ultimate European triumph lay just ahead. On April 30 Rick turned two, and as a sort of belated birthday present, one week later Germany surrendered unconditionally to General Eisenhower at Rheims in France, and to the Soviets in Berlin. President Truman declared the following day, May 8, to be V-E Day—Victory in Europe Day.

Victory over Japan was still to happen, but Okinawa was finally in the fold, and U.S. air attacks continued over Tokyo. The papers carried accounts of leaflets being dropped over Japan that threatened destruction from the air if the Japanese did not capitulate. The United States was asking for "unconditional surrender," a phrase that had taken hold in the country. What it meant was that after the Japanese had given up, the United States would be free to dictate all terms. Jack was skeptical. He said he understood enough about how the Japanese had fought the war that "surrender" was not in their vocabulary.

In the midst of the anticipated victory came the news that the U.S.S. *Indianapolis* had been sunk by torpedoes in the Indian Ocean. I thought it was going to be over, I kept saying to Jack, who kept answering that only a catastrophe would make the Japanese yield.

The next week the catastrophe happened, visited upon the Japanese by a B-29 called the *Enola Gay*. According to news reports, the *Enola Gay* had dropped an "atomic bomb" on the Japanese industrial city of Hiroshima. An atomic bomb? What was this "atomic bomb"? We had not even heard rumors. And yet here was this bomb, and according to the first estimate, it had in one fell swoop killed over a hundred thousand Japanese.

Controversy started immediately over the morality of visiting such destruction on unarmed civilians. Those who cried out in dissent, however, were overwhelmed by those who talked about how many of "our boys" had been saved. The use of the atom bomb meant just that to many—a boon, a miracle that could bring this awful war to a close. It was only in later years that we had reason to recall what Oppenheimer had said when he was the director of the atomic laboratories at Los Alamos and was watching the mushroom cloud ascending from the first atomic-bomb test. What he had said was that he had unleashed "the destroyer of worlds."

You would have thought that Hiroshima would be the convincer, but it wasn't. The Japanese still did not surrender, and three days later another atomic bomb was dropped, this time on Nagasaki. This time the toll was a hundred and fifty thousand, and this time the Japanese gave up.

EPILOGUE

President Truman declared August 14, 1945, to be V-J Day, Victory over Japan Day. Since we were in Fort Myers, we did not have a celebration to equal New York's, having no Times Square to gather in, no ships' whistles to rend the air, no soldiers and sailors to walk through the streets kissing all the girls. But we had our celebration nonetheless, even if it consisted basically of Captain Marvel standing in the street shooting his rifle into the air, and us all cheering and repairing afterward to our house for whatever celebration came to mind.

In three days we were out of Fort Myers and on the Tamiami Trail back to Miami, back to Jack's parents' house in town. It was definitely time to put some thought into our future, for a question was waiting to be answered: what do we do now?

The answer came in one of Jack's visits to one of the military headquarters where he had been signing discharge papers and doing the things required to get back into civilian life. Among all the rumors floating around was one about a government program to subsidize returning veterans who wanted to go to college. Actually, this was not a rumor; it was a fact. Jack had discovered the G.I. Bill.

So what I saw in our future was something first of all for Jack, and it of course included tweed jackets with leather patches, for I still had my dream of Jack's going back to college and ending up as a college professor. What I saw for me was not so clear. I would have no G.I. Bill, and if I was to go back to college—and I was—it would be when the time was more appropriate. For Jack the time was appropriate immediately.

Before we could enter the future, there was a lot of the past clinging to us. Who could forget so quickly, who could ever forget? So we reentered civilian life little by little. Many of our friends were already back; some were still on their way back. Ruth's husband, Phil, whom I would now finally meet, wrote that he was waiting for a ship that would take him to the mainland. He was in a good mood, like everybody else, and wrote to Ruth that he was "saying good-bye to the waving palms of Hawaii to say hello to the waving palms of Miami Beach." Jack's brother, Irwin, had been on his way to the Pacific but Ruby had gotten a letter saying he was coming home. "When the Japs heard I was coming," he wrote, "they called up MacArthur and told him to meet them in Tokyo Bay," Tokyo Bay being the place where the "unconditional surrender had been signed."

We spent the days talking on the phone, visiting, gathering information. Who was here? Who was coming? What have you heard about Herbie? Seymour? Danny? We had the joy of finding out that Larry was on his way home, and we had to absorb the blow of knowing that Morty was never coming back. When we got together, we traded stories, stories about where we'd been and who we'd met, some funny, some not so. I guess you could say that these first days after the war were periods of intense ups and equally intense downs. It was a very peculiar time.

With plenty of gasoline now available, we did such things as going over to Miami Beach several times a week, sometimes just to roam around so Jack could see the changes. Not everything had changed—some of the infamous hotel signs were, in fact, still up. Still, Jack saw a change, and the change was in me. "I see you rising up in righteous anger about those damned signs," he said to me. And it was true. In the years that I had traveled around the country, I had undergone many changes small and large, and Jack was right. Sometime soon I would rise up in righteous anger and join with those whose mission it was to make them disappear. And down the road that is exactly what we did.

Still, when we got rid of the signs, other items would take their place on the list of injustices. The list has always been in something of a state of flux, with some items deleted, some items grayed out, some items reformatted in bold, and, sadly, in the fullness of time many items added.

What I had yet to come to terms with was my Jewishness. Not having had time to think seriously about it, I was still in a state of indecision. So I waited for a call I could answer, and it was some years in coming. But come it did, even if it took Albert Einstein to make it happen. It came in an answer he gave to a question about his Jewishness. What he said was that the "pursuit of knowledge for its own sake, an almost fanatical love of justice, and the desire for personal independence— these are the features of the Jewish tradition which make me thank my stars that I belong to it." This at last was a call I could answer, and I answered it with great pleasure. And if Jack wanted to demur and say that there were plenty of people who followed in just that tradition, not just Jews, I would say to him that this is a tradition of a *people,* and I am satisfied with it.

WHEN WE WOULD go from Jack's house in town to visit Miami Beach, we usually took Rick with us to see his Kaufman grandparents. Ruth's husband, Phil, was home—as Ruth had said, I did like him and not just because he shared my love of big bands, but for a lot of other reasons as well. Phil was also set to take advantage of the G.I. Bill, and he and Jack talked about possible career paths, though at the end of the evening when we went for a nosh at Wolfie's—which both Jack and Phil said was as good as any delicatessen in New York—they always ended up talking about their wartime experiences. It was typical. Whenever we were with those who had served, before long the men thought back to when they were in uniform, and the stories poured out. Some of them were unfinished, the fate of a comrade or a mission unknown.

Jack and I had an unfinished story—Bill O'Connor—and Bill was never far from our thoughts. We had heard nothing, not from Peg, not from any source. Still, on a night we had left Rick at home with Jack's folks and come home late from the movies, we finally had closure. As we approached the house that night, our unfinished story was waiting for us.

On the porch with Jack's parents and getting to his feet was Bill O'Connor.

The sight of him frightened me, for I could not have expected this. If Peg had known Bill was alive, she would have written me. Was this man really Bill, this pale, thin man? He may have looked very different, but the man Jack and I were screaming at, the man we were hugging hard, was truly Bill O'Connor. After we had settled down and Jack's parents had gone to bed, I asked why on earth Peg hadn't told us. Bill said she was following his instructions. He had called her from India, and knowing that he was coming back through West Palm Beach, he had cautioned her not to let us know.

Bill had not only lost a lot of weight, he looked much older. When he told his story, we understood why he was so changed, for the experience he was coming off of had been a harrowing one. He had been on a journey of months that had taken him through some of the most dangerous parts of China. It began when he was downed and was plucked from the sea by Chinese guerillas. He spent a month with them, making his way through Japanese-held territory in an attempt to get to an American base. This meant being taken on convoluted journeys, always at night, always on back roads, although mostly on no roads at all. As he was being shuttled from hiding place to hiding place, he was spirited through wild terrain, hidden in the backs of carts, and sent down rivers on barges. Bill figured he had lost about thirty pounds, and for an average-size man like Bill, it was a very marked loss. Bill said that he owed his life to those Chinese, those "little guys." He looked at us thoughtfully. "I shouldn't have said 'little guys,'" he said. "They were giants."

While we sat talking with this weary, somber man, we could recognize little of the jaunty Bill we had known, and we had to wonder if that person was still in him. He was. For when Jack brought out the bumpy, lumpy cocktail shaker and handed it over, Bill gave out a shocked "I'll be damned!" and took it lovingly in his hands. At one again with his silver treasure, and with all the Tucson and Great Bend memories no doubt pouring in, Bill was once more smiling and spirited, once again Peg's "darlin' Billy." As he ran his hands over the shaker, Bill laughed and said, "I kept telling you guys that if you stay in good with the gin gods, they'll get you through." Jack and I laughed back and said, well, he had told us *something* like that.

Bill was back with us, and he and Jack and I sat on the porch into the night. We sat remembering old friends, and old times, even if our "old times" were war times. The night went on, the evening air sweet and soft, Jack's parents gone to bed, Rick sound asleep, Jack and I easy and comfortable with a refound old friend. We talked on and on, my Glenn Miller records playing in the background, and we drank Arizona Sunsets facing west, talking all the while, until Jack looked over his shoulder and said he thought he saw the sun. And when I looked, the sun was in fact coming up, and I thought about how the sun would be rising on Miami Beach and how it looked when it came up out of the sea. And I thought that someday soon I would take Rick over there just as the sun was rising and show it to him.